Housing: Who Decides?

Also by Peter King

HOUSING, INDIVIDUALS AND THE STATE: The Morality of Government Intervention

THE LIMITS OF HOUSING POLICY: A Philosophical Investigation

Also by Michael Oxley

HOUSING POLICY AND RENTED HOUSING IN EUROPE (*with Jacqueline Smith*)

Housing: Who Decides?

Peter King
Senior Lecturer in Housing Studies
Centre for Comparative Housing Research
De Montfort University
Leicester

Michael Oxley
Professor of Housing
Nottingham Trent University

First published in Great Britain 2000 by
MACMILLAN PRESS LTD
Houndmills, Basingstoke, Hampshire RG21 6XS and London
Companies and representatives throughout the world

A catalogue record for this book is available from the British Library.

ISBN 0–333–76007–7

First published in the United States of America 2000 by
ST. MARTIN'S PRESS, LLC,
Scholarly and Reference Division,
175 Fifth Avenue, New York, N.Y. 10010

ISBN 0–312–23533–X

Library of Congress Cataloging-in-Publication Data
King, Peter, 1960–
Housing : who decides? / Peter King, Michael Oxley.
p. cm.
"First published in Great Britain 2000 by Macmillan Press"—T.p. verso.
Includes bibliographical references and index.
ISBN 0–312–23533–X
1. Housing policy—Great Britain. I. Oxley, Michael. II. Title.

HD7333.A3 K57 2000
363.5'0941—dc21

00–031125

This book is printed on paper suitable for recycling and made from fully managed and sustained forest sources.

10 9 8 7 6 5 4 3 2 1
09 08 07 06 05 04 03 02 01 00

Printed and bound in Great Britain by
Antony Rowe Ltd, Chippenham, Wiltshire

Contents

Acknowledgements

We have several people to thank for their help, advice and assistance in the writing of this book. Firstly, we need to thank current and former colleagues at the Centre for Comparative Housing Research. Tim Brown read parts of the manuscript and gave his usual forthright opinions (many of which were actually accepted). Andrew Golland read all the manuscript (parts of it several times) and prompted us into clarifying and amending our arguments to make them (more) understandable and accessible.

We have been saved from many embarrassing errors by the incisive and diligent work of Natasha Oxley who checked and corrected the manuscript. Any errors and omissions that remain are, of course, entirely our own fault.

Finally, we should acknowledge, that we are, just about, still friends!

PETER KING
MICHAEL OXLEY

1
Housing: Who Decides?

Peter King and Michael Oxley

1.1 Contradictions in housing policy

Housing policy, it seems to us, is in a state of flux. We appear to be within a period of considerable change which, potentially at least, might lead to a fundamental transformation in housing policy. Some commentators, such as Malpass (1999), go so far as to question whether we can still actually talk of there being such a thing as housing policy at all. Housing policy, according to Malpass, has been subsumed into economic policy, with housing being merely one lever to change economic behaviour and control the macroeconomy. Other commentators, such as Whelan (1998), suggest that the problem is too much government policy on housing and not enough individual choice and market decision making. What is in common though between these two poles is that there is no settled understanding of what purpose housing policy has. Is the role of housing policy to facilitate individual choice and decision making, or does it exist to meet some broader social objectives such as redistribution or equality? Should the state be doing more to ensure access to good quality housing for all its citizens, or is the problem that government has created unpopular and increasingly unlettable housing, which is then managed by unresponsive and bureaucratic housing organisations who put their own interests over and above those of their tenants?

Thus when one looks at housing policy in outline one sees an apparent contradiction. Governments over the last 20 years have consistently cut the level of subsidy going directly to housing providers, yet throughout this time has equally consistently increased the level of control it exercises over them. This means that as the stock of social housing declines government appears to be spending more effort on controlling the sector than when it encouraged the growth of council housing through long-term capital subsidies.

However, instead of reducing funding to social housing, government has merely transferred its commitment to housing allowances (Wilcox, 1997). This might, in principle, enhance choice and opportunity, but in practice housing benefit has served as a transfer to landlords, in that they have been able to raise rent levels. The open-ended nature of British housing allowances – whereby payments are linked to rent levels – has allowed landlords to increase rents with relative impunity. Thus governments in the 1980s and 1990s have increased central control over a declining sector, while at the same time shifting the balance of government subsidy into an area over which it does not exert such a level of control. It is true that since 1995 governments have indeed tried to restrict the growth of housing benefit, but reforms so far enacted have not had the effect of reducing eligibility for the majority. Controls imposed on allowances have instead been at the administrative level.

What is apparent in all of this is a lack of stability. This, we believe, comes about because housing policy is trying to do two contradictory things, and thus in a sense both Malpass and Whelan are right. Government is attempting to control housing providers and consumers to achieve its broader aims – housing policy is indeed subsumed into wider policies. Yet government has increasingly recognised that certain types of activity are counterproductive. Therefore local reference rents were introduced to moderate rents in the private rented sector. This aim was apparently to be achieved by changing the behaviour of landlords and tenants (Bevan *et al.*, 1995). The Blair government has also made it clear that welfare benefits should aim as far as possible to help individuals into work – 'The Government's aim is to rebuild the welfare state around work' (DSS, 1998, p. 23).

The contradiction[1] in this policy development is that, on the one hand, there is a presumption that it is only government who can decide on housing policy. It is where housing policy is seen as being either too important, or beyond the competence of local institutions and individuals, and therefore it is up to government to arrive at decisions on behalf of society.

But, on the other hand, government is trying to release individuals from dependency and make them more responsible for their own lives and well-being. Here there is a presumption that individuals are competent and capable of making decisions and taking the consequences. The state should encourage work, but this means that individuals can more readily care for themselves, leaving government to concern itself with those unable to work through no fault of their own.

There are then two attitudes, or presumptions, toward decision making which are operating side by side, but which are contradictory, in that it is difficult to see how greater centralisation and the subsuming of local interests into a national agenda is likely to create independence and responsibility. But these two attitudes are both substantial and worthy of active consideration. A belief in the primacy of the centre is embedded and the government is indeed held responsible and accountable for its stewardship of the economy and its management of key goods and services such as health care and education. Thus it is accepted that the government has a role in the satisfactory provision of services available locally. But there is also a considerable expectation that individuals should be responsible for themselves, as is shown by perceptions towards taxation (where it is believed, accurately or not, that a party cannot be elected on a ticket of increasing taxation, even if it wishes to spend the receipts on areas which the majority approve of and benefit from). Much of the attractiveness of Thatcherism to the electorate was based on this perception of independence, even if going alongside this was the actuality of strong central government (Gamble, 1988; Letwin, 1992). One might also suggest that the attractiveness of new Labour and Tony Blair owes more to their adoption of much of the Thatcherite agenda than to them being distinct from it.

We would suggest, therefore, that there is a key dichotomy apparent here; namely, that between social (or collective) and individual decision making. Both are seen to be important, but they tend to militate against each other. Our discussion raises the question of whether, in relation to housing issues, they can co-exist together without one becoming dominant and excluding the other.

Furthermore we believe that this issue of decision making goes to the very heart of public policy. The relative ability of individuals to make choices, and thus the implied role for the state, is central to the provision of welfare services, to the role of the market and to notions of justice, fairness and equality. Thus, while we concentrate on housing issues, this book can be seen as part of a wider debate on the nature of welfare and the role of state and market in the provision of welfare goods. Therefore what we explore in this book is the nature of decision making, primarily related to housing, but with broader implications for welfare provision as a whole.

One key element in this exploration of decision making is the notion of individual competence. If individuals are to make decisions on their welfare they must be competent and be capable of making rational decisions about their interests and how to achieve them. The limits of where that competence ends is, of course, essential for the determination of public policy. Are individuals competent to take decisions that maximise their welfare, or is this capability limited to only certain goods and services? If competence is limited, how do we decide where and should we assume that that limitation is the same for everyone? These are some of the questions which underpin the arguments in this book. We consider them to be of supreme importance for housing policy, where the public and private spheres so readily overlap. The issue of competence, its extent and its limits, will thus be at the centre of this debate.

1.2 A debate

Most housing texts, quite properly, adopt a particular position and develop this. Of course, part of this development is to explore alternative perspectives and criticisms which threaten the integrity of the adopted position. However, regardless of the perspicacity of the author, these texts inevitably consider alternative perspectives and criticisms with a view to demolishing them. One does not offer a consideration of these arguments in order to persuade the reader, but rather to show their weakness relative to the author's chosen position. With the best will in the world, then, the author will dwell on those points which favour his or her view; on the perceived weaknesses in their opponent's argument, but not the strengths; and on the gaps and omissions and not on its inner integrity.

There is nothing particularly unusual to housing texts in this process of selectivity. Nor are we suggesting that there are not some extremely well written and closely argued texts on housing, which while coming from a committed perspective, offer crucial insights. What we do see as missing, however, is an opportunity for the reader to engage with contrasting opinions on the same issue in a balanced manner, allowing him or her to see a range of views and perspectives *without* these being filtered by their opponents.

So instead of proceeding in the typical manner of presentation for academic discourse, we have constructed this discussion of competence and decision making in housing as a debate. This is partly because we fundamentally disagree with each other, but also because we believe that, by giving both sides of this issue full measure and then presenting counter-arguments, we are able to show the nature of this issue in all its complexity. Having spent many long hours debating and discussing these issues between ourselves we are aware of the intractability of these issues and of the unlikelihood of complete capitulation by one party to the other. Accordingly we have decided to each present our committed positions on decision making in housing and then to engage in a critical debate.

Academic housing texts usually fail to enunciate principles according to which action should be judged *and* to express a point of view on what needs to done. But the distinguishing feature of this debate is that we explore both founding principles and specific concrete policies. We both begin from differing principles and alternative points of view and we prescribe actions which follow from these contrasting perspectives. What we have done in this debate is to argue for our own positions as hard as we can and to contend with the opposing view. The key difference between this approach and other housing texts is that we have had to stand on ground not entirely of our choosing. Neither of us could take those points more amenable to our own arguments and ignore the rest, because the reader is able to read the full argument for themselves.

There are some other comments which we need to make about this debate. Firstly, as will be readily apparent, we do not have a common disciplinary background. King is a political philosopher, while Oxley is an economist. This may be seen by some as a disadvantage in that we might be using distinctive concepts or terminology and thus not be able to properly engage with each other. We feel that this problem does not appear and, moreover, we see benefits in this cross-disciplinary approach. By looking at the same issues through different prisms we are able to comment and criticise each other's position in a way that might be denied debaters from the same discipline. But perhaps more importantly, housing discourse itself does not depend merely on one discipline. As Kemeny (1992) has suggested, housing is a field of discourse and research and not a discipline in itself. Those undertaking housing research might be economists, geographers, sociologists, philosophers, anthropologists, psychologists and political scientists. All these disciplines bring their own insights, but they only see part of the whole picture. It is through cross-disciplinary dialogue that we further our understanding of housing, but also become aware of our limitations. We believe, therefore, that this debate is enhanced by a cross-disciplinary dialogue.

We do not, however, claim to be in anyway representative of our disciplines. Philosophers and economists, of course, have within their ranks people with widely differing views on the issues we have discussed. Our disciplines do, however, determine the way in which we think and the way in which we analyse particular problems. King is concerned with the competence of individuals (and the perception of their competence held by government and 'experts'), the extent of individual choice and the legitimacy of the actions of the state. Oxley is concerned with the production and allocation of housing, the effective demand for 'decent housing', the connections between markets and the state and the ramifications of the concept of market failure as they relate to the supply and consumption of housing.

Secondly, we need to make some comments about these positions which we argue for here. A debate between two people is unlikely to be comprehensive and we quickly realised that we neither could nor should deal with every possible position. We have also resisted the temptation of taking the most extreme positions possible in order to maximise the distance between us. Thus what follows is not a debate between two absolute extremes, but rather a debate which fits generally within the confines of what might be called liberal democracy.

What is missing then is any real attention to collectivist arguments from either the Marxist or Fabian traditions. This may be considered a serious omission by some, but we consider no apology necessary. A debate can be valuable even if it does not consider all the possible perspectives and comprehensiveness does not necessarily ensure an interesting and valuable result. We have instead chosen to debate those positions we are committed to in the hope that this will lead to a more convincing argument.

But there is a more substantive reason for rejecting collectivist positions and this is principally that, despite the weight of academic opinion, they are becoming increasingly irrelevant in the policy debate. Marxism may still hold considerable sway in certain parts of the academy,[2] and indeed there are no shortage of Marxist or neo-Marxist books and articles written on housing. However, the policy context in which housing discourse sits offers no tenable prospect for the Marxist position being given even cursory consideration. This may be a cause of regret to some (although not to us), but this regret cannot be allowed to deflect one from the conclusion that the policy debate in Britain, the USA and elsewhere is based around what can be termed liberal democratic principles. Collectivist perspectives have thus been pushed to the fringes of policy debate. The role of the market may be questioned, but only in terms of function and extent and not its continued legitimacy.

The debate now is not over whether capitalism can or should survive, but over the role of certain institutions within the capitalist state. It is commonplace to state that the centre or fulcrum of political debate has been shifted to the right, but this doesn't appear to have occurred to some in the academic community who cling to outdated ideologies. We, therefore, justify our debate as being one that is based around this new political centre. It is a debate over the extent and limits of the market and the consequent role for government. It thus connects directly with debates over the extent and means of subsidising housing; of the ways in which government action and markets enhance or limit choices; and, of whether the state is an enabler or disabler of individuals. We both accept a role for government, although we by no means agree on the extent of state involvement, its legitimacy or even on a methodology for analysing the relationship of the state to markets. While King sees government as at best a necessary evil, which in its current configuration disenfranchises individuals, creates dependency and reduces the effectiveness of individual decision making in markets, Oxley sees government as a liberating vehicle which is inextricably linked with markets to the extent that to talk of a dichotomy between the market and the state is misleading.

This debate is therefore between a libertarian and a liberal. We are aware that these are broad terms which mean different things to different people, and indeed have had different connotations in the past. Some libertarians choose to refer to themselves as classical liberals (Barry, 1996; Conway, 1995) seeking to reclaim the term 'liberal' from what might be called Rawlsian (Rawls, 1971), welfare or new liberals.[3] Also, the views which Oxley expresses might be considered by some to be social democratic.[4] However, we believe that the usage of this terminology is justified and fits within the terms of the debate discussed above. Thus King seeks to limit the role of government to that consistent with the maintenance of individual rights and Oxley seeks a much greater role for government as the regulator and indeed guarantor of market activity. Both of us accept current institutions and practices as we find them and argue that change can only occur from within the prevailing structures. Thus neither of us is a revolutionary, but then nor does either of us remotely accept the *status quo*.

The third and final point about our debate is to outline the process we have undertaken in the preparation of this book. So far as we can we have tried to follow the rules of debating in this project. Thus Oxley did not commence on his response until he had received King's opening statement and so on. In this way we endeavoured to ensure that there was a commonality in our aims and objectives and that we did not (entirely) misrepresent or caricature each others positions. We did not set out with a pre-determined and rigid structure or a catalogue of points that we were determined to make at all costs whatever arguments the other produced. There is thus an unfolding and developing dialogue with each reflecting and responding to the views of the other. None of the sections have been altered in the light of subsequent comments. Therefore what follows is a libertarian critique of contemporary housing policy and proposals for reforms by King. Oxley answers this in Chapter 3 and goes on to expound his welfare liberal approach. King responds in Chapter 4 seeking to show where the libertarian position is superior to that of the welfare liberal. In Chapter 5 Oxley comments on the criticisms raised by King, responding to the debate with a final statement of his position. Chapter 6 concludes the book with some fairly brief comments on the areas of commonality, but also on those points where disagreement is most pronounced. Neither party gives much ground, but we are both considerably more enlightened than when we began.

2
Individuals and Competence

Peter King

2.1 Needs and choices

According to Bengtsson (1995) the focus of housing research is, very generally, markets and politics. However, researchers and commentators tend to deal with these issues in either an 'objective' or positivistic manner which ignores the ideological and moral questions, or they are candidly personal about their own position. What isn't dealt with up front is the essentially normative aspect of markets and politics. These issues, which are about what *should* happen – about the ethics of government and market activity – are downgraded because they are deemed beyond scientific analysis, or are too closely related to one's personal value system and therefore not capable of generalisation. However, these normative issues are crucial to any understanding of housing policy.

Normative statements are those which seek to be *prescriptive*, in that they are concerned with what we ought or should do. In this sense they are the opposite of descriptive or scientific statements, which are concerned with what is. For example one can talk of both prescriptive and descriptive (scientific) laws. The former may be broken (as in the case of a constitution or penal code), but the latter cannot without its categorical refutation (to 'break' the law of gravity is to disprove it (Sparkes, 1991)). Normative statements are, therefore, those which relate to morality and social norms and concern the actions which individuals and groups ought to take if they are to be acting in a proper manner.

All political statements are inherently normative. We can state that all humans are equal regardless of sex, creed, ethnic origin, religion, and so on. This might be provable empirically, for instance by using IQ tests.

However, why would we seek to test such a statement? I would argue that it is simply because we already believe it. We believe it because we hold a particular normative position which implies all humans have certain qualities and are entitled to particular treatment as a result (this doesn't mean that we can agree on what the qualities and treatment ought to be).

Bengtsson suggests that housing researchers are reluctant to attend to normative issues for fear of being cast as either political or ideological. Yet, as he states, 'Markets and politics are in the centre of most normative discussions on housing policy. They are also the focus of housing research' (p. 123). No doubt this reluctance is due partly to the difficulty in discussing normative issues 'scientifically', which would then leave any research suspect. But Bengtsson disputes this and suggests it is possible to use scientific procedures based on the Rawlsian concept of 'reflective equilibrium' (p. 138), whereby one tests general theories against a range of substantive issues to assess their applicability. This will lead to an adjustment and eventual 'matching' of principles and the judgements formed from the substantive issues. In this empirical studies will inform the principles, whilst the principles might assist in the appreciation of the significance of the empirical data.

I would suggest that one way of discussing these normative issues is to build around the basic dichotomy between the competence of the individual as a decision maker and the role of the state as a regulator and provider of goods and services (King, 1998a, 1998b). I would argue that this can be done through a concentration on needs and choices in housing. Levine (1995) makes the distinction between needs, which are imperative states, and wants which are amenable to choices. Furthermore, according to this dichotomy, needs might be best met by government action, whilst wants can be left to markets.

It might appear that this distinction between wants and needs is a hard and fast one giving no opportunity for interpretation or argument. However, I would suggest that this is not the case and that the distinction between wants and needs is not concrete, but dependent on one's particular perspective. More specifically, the notion of need is not merely an empirical one, but dependent upon the normative conceptions of individual and social rights and obligations. Moreover, they are also conditioned by the current institutions of the state which create and maintain individual expectations (King, 1998b). Certain needs can be seen as being *instrumental* in that they depend upon the choices we have made (Griffin, 1986; King, 1998a). Certain things become necessary as a result of our past actions. These needs are distinct from *basic needs* which we all have by being human. It is these latter needs which we have regardless of our consciousness of them. However, this is not the case with instrumental needs which arise from deliberative acts we have already preformed. In this case the distinction between need and the dependent choices is not clear cut.

This distinction is particularly important in housing (King, 1998a). Because the need for housing is predictable – we know we will always need it – it is possible to suggest that choice, and therefore instrumental needs, dominate over the basic needs for shelter and security. The basic need is ever-present and thus it is overlaid with those subjective elements which the majority of us are able to exercise and which relate to amenity, location, price, style, and so on. It is hardly possible to fulfil instrumental needs and not to meet basic ones. What is important in this understanding of the role of housing is not merely the fulfilment of basic needs, but the provision of sufficient choice to match the subjective preferences of households. Housing is therefore best seen as an example of instrumental need, while health care has a stronger case for being seen as representative of basic need.[1]

The normativity of need has led some individualists (or anti-collectivists, as they are referred to by Percy-Smith, 1996) to suggest that there is no such entity as need. What are referred to as needs are in fact individual desires and preferences. In other words, they are more properly subjective wants which allow for no universal statements to be constructed about the general human condition. According to this view, anti-collectivists do not accept any objective notion of need as the basis for decisions about what society requires. Percy-Smith (1996) counters this by suggesting that need can form an empirical and objective basis for social policy, whilst admitting that there is a normative element to the formation of any concept of need. Likewise, Doyal and Gough (1991) see the concept of need as offering the potential for a universal statement on social provision. Both Doyal and Gough and Percy-Smith appear to rely on a definition of basic rather than instrumental need.

What is significant about this description of need is that it is seen as either a social entity or non existent. Collectivists, such as Doyal and Gough (1991) and Percy-Smith (1996), use need always as a social concept; as a means of defining the needs of a community. They then characterise anti-collectivists as rejecting the notion of need because they *individualise* the decision-making process. However, this dichotomy can be restated as a normative justification for a universalisation of a particular form of social organisation. Need is a necessary concept to justify the role of the state as the determinant focus of social policy.

Indeed Bengtsson (1995), in relating the issue of needs to housing, suggests that '(t)o be used in an argumentation for political intervention in the housing market, *needs* have to be defined as something different from the preferences at the bottom of the concept of *demand*' (p. 132, author's emphasis). Thus it is necessary for those adopting the collectivist position to *socialise* need and to reduce individual subjective perceptions to wants or demands.

The discussion which follows is an avowedly individualist approach to housing provision. I make no attempt to be comprehensive (although I hope I am fair and do not misrepresent). My aim is principally to expound a particular position and to criticise another. Much of this initial essay will consist of a detailed critique of the justifications for collectivised welfare. I am aware that much of the discussion is abstract and general. In particular, I make no concerted attempt to address concrete housing issues in this discussion. I shall seek to remedy this in the last two sections of the essay when I discuss the nature of housing subsidies and the possibility for reforming housing structures.

In these later sections the concentration is largely on the impact of housing subsidies, with little comment on other housing issues. This is partly due to where my interests lie, but mainly because of a belief that it is through the use of subsidies that wider changes can be attained. My point is that subsidies create incentives and change behaviour which impacts on other aspects of housing policy. Housing policy has its impact in no small measure because of the financial arrangements which support it. Governments seek to affect the behaviour of individuals and organisations by the manipulation of subsidies. Thus what I am essentially doing in this essay is presenting a critique of the contemporary ideology of welfare, and then going on to suggest how this position can be undermined by a reformation of housing subsidies.

But before starting on the critique of welfare ideology, I wish briefly to discuss my reasons for this long and abstract discussion. There are few attempts by housing researchers to return to first principles and ask fundamental questions about the nature of provision. It may be countered that this is a wasteful luxury, in that there are clearly problems which need solving now. However, the *real* problem, I would suggest, is that issues are only looked at in a piecemeal and non-holistic manner. There is seldom any attempt made to step back and gain a broader understanding of why and how problems have arisen. The result is frequently the continuance of poorly thought out policy, justified on the basis of an immediate imperative.

I would therefore argue that there is a strong case for looking at the roots of housing policy and where it fits into the broader spectrum of social and welfare policy. Housing is not immune to the effects of exogenous factors, nor does it operate in a political vacuum. I would argue that one cannot fully understand housing phenomena unless one is clear about the underpinning issues which have justified collectivised provision. This might mean concentrating on general issues rather than specific policy measures, but the resultant debate and the possible conclusions will be all the better for it.

My argument is that social housing provision has been justified by a number of abstract general principles, which are similar to those which have justified other elements of the welfare state.[2] We need to understand these principles, and to be aware of their strengths and weaknesses, if we are to more fully appreciate the possibility of reform and the future prospects for housing policy. I therefore would argue that the ensuing discussion, which is over two thirds of my initial contribution, can be justified in that it places housing policy firmly in the context of the mechanisms through which needs and choices do, can and should become operationalised by welfare policy.

Much of the ensuing discussion might appear negative, but I believe that a set of clear principles emerge and it might be best to state these at the outset. Firstly, as a political individualist, I believe that individual liberty should override all other concerns. Secondly I believe that there is no social or common interest as such, merely an aggregation of individual interests, which might tend to coalesce, but which will also contain incommensurable elements (Berlin, 1969; Gray, 1995a). Thirdly, I believe that individuals are competent and subjectively rational rights-bearing agents who are capable of determining their own interests and establishing a means of achieving them. Fourthly, it is my contention that a central government is neither practically nor morally competent to provide for individuals what they are more than able of providing for themselves. This means that certain forms of government action are not seen as legitimate. I shall return to these principles frequently in order to expound and justify them.

2.2 The role of welfare

I wish to proceed with my argument by looking at some of the conventional justifications for collective provision by the state. In doing so I seek to establish partly what I am arguing against, but also to help set the parameters of the debate. Hills (1997) suggests that there are at least five aims for the public provision of welfare services. Firstly, there is the relief of poverty and redistribution towards the long-term poor. Secondly, it can be seen as a form of insurance for all against long-term illness, unemployment, early retirement, family breakdown, and so on. Thirdly, the welfare state can redistribute income towards particular groups with greater needs, be they medical, familial or related to disability. Fourthly, it can act as a type of savings bank, smoothing out income levels over the life cycle. Fifthly, it can step in where the family fails, for example, divorce and lone parenthood.

These aims raise some interesting issues which are worth pursuing. What is noticeable is that Hills does not see the welfare state as being merely a safety net, but as offering security for all. Its aims are not just particularist, but are universal. This is a point made strongly by Field (1996) who argues for universality on the grounds of social cohesion. Field sees that universal benefits are inclusive in their operation because they enclose all sections of the community, regardless of class and income. He fears that a more targeted system of welfare would lead to disaffection amongst the more affluent tax payers, who perceive (rightly) that they are paying for the benefits of others while receiving nothing directly in return. But, as Hills points out, this universality means that the redistributive effect of the welfare state does not just depend on benefits paid out, but also on who pays in through the tax system. There is also the clear implication that the welfare state is not merely an exercise in altruism, but can be justified by appealing to the self-interest of tax payers who will receive a considerable proportion of their tax back in benefits (albeit mainly in kind rather than in cash payments).

Hills sees that these five aims overlap, and they are quite clearly complementary. Indeed I would go further to suggest that it is possible to reduce these five aims down to one, namely that of *redistribution*. Clearly this is so for aims one, three and five, where he suggests the welfare state exists to redistribute income between certain groups. But he claims it also operates to redistribute income from one part of the life cycle to another, in the form of education spending in early life and medical and pensions spending in later life, both funded out of earnings in the 'middle' period. Thus the welfare state redistributes income on the particularist ground of relieving poverty and need and on the universalist ground of ensuring security from risk.

Hills' discussion is clearly a useful one in that it seeks to suggest that the role of collectivised welfare goes beyond the notion of the safety net for those excluded from mainstream society. His aim is to lay the foundations for a debate, and in doing so to 'prove' that there is no 'demographic time bomb' which would necessitate drastic changes to the nature of the welfare state. Based on this foundation, he suggests that there are three options with regard to the future of the welfare state. These options are, first, the maintenance or improvement of provision, accepting a slow increase in the share of GDP spent on welfare, but keeping it within the bounds of the norm of spending in Europe; second, the reduction or limiting of welfare spending by linking benefits to prices instead of living standards (although Hills claims that this choice is not a sustainable one) and third, the maintenance of the relative value of certain items but with others reduced or cut altogether.

According to Hills, these three options represent the 'real choice' (p. 5). But this is only the case if one accepts the normative premises upon which Hills builds his argument. There is no attempt in Hills' work to question the role and purpose of collectivised welfare. Instead he is offering a justification for its continuance, if not in an enhanced form then in its current one. Hills offers reasons for maintaining what we are currently doing – this is what the welfare state does do (although without any suggestion as to whether it succeeds in its aims) – but he does not offer a justification of whether it should. His premise appears to be along the lines of 'if we can afford it we should do it'. As with Hills' earlier work on housing (Hills, 1991), he offers a sophisticated, yet pragmatic, case for what we now have, without dealing with whether we should have it or whether any alternatives would be better. In so far as Hills' discusses normative and moral arguments, he does so in terms of moving from current levels of provision and not from first principles.

One could suggest, of course, that pragmatism is a requirement in social policy. The basis of Hills' argument is that we have a certain level of provision at present and this cannot be merely wished away. Moreover, he contends that this level of provision is sustainable in terms of international comparisons and demographic trends. Thus the debate on the future of welfare is not one of the fundamentals of the role of the state and individuals, but about the extent of these roles in terms of what we now apparently expect. If the majority of citizens expect a certain level of welfare provision and are prepared to fund it then why debate whether they should be doing so? Instead, he appears to be saying, what is needed is a debate on the marginal impact of welfare spending, in the sense of whether welfare spending is to be allowed to increase by a further 5 per cent of GDP over the next 50 years (Hills, 1997, p. 14). Stated in these terms the notions of crisis and unsustainability are hard to credit. However, as with any argument using statistics, it is possible to state one's case so that its impact is minimised. Thus if one restates Hills' 5 per cent increase in GDP as meaning a shift in welfare spending from 25 per cent of GDP to 30 per cent we see that he is actually referring to a 20 per cent increase in welfare spending. Stated as such this appears to be a much more fundamental shift in spending.

However, is it really enough to base a debate on future provision merely on what we do now? Pragmatism is all very well, but it does tend towards too ready an acceptance of the *status quo*. Of course, it is not possible to wish away current provision and take a 'year zero' approach. But this does not mean that one should not base an argument on clear principles, even if that leads one to see the current levels of provision as illegitimate.

There is perhaps something of a post-Thatcherite reaction against an overtly ideological approach to social policy. The Blairite approach to policy appears more based upon steering a flexible way between ideological extremes (Blair, 1998; Giddens, 1998). They are attempting to provide a so called 'third way' between the individualism of the Thatcher years and the collectivism of Old Labour. What this amounts to in practice though is the creation of an ideology – the third way – out of the actions of government. It appears that political principles are to be forged as the outcomes of policy making instead of being the basis for deliberation on social policy.

But to suggest that this is presaging an era of non-ideological policy making would be wrong. The difference with the Thatcher period is not that there is no ideological basis to policy, but rather that the ideological underpinning is less obviously up front. It is less easy to state what the principles are. This might be because they are incoherent, as is the danger of trying to steer a course between the apparent opposites of collectivism and individualism. I would suggest though that there is now a more deliberate attempt to present policy making as a flexible and pragmatic process free from dogma. Hills' work on the future of welfare demonstrates this attempt at pragmatism, but also his work can be seen as demonstrative of a number of assumptions which characterise collectivist arguments.

There are three particular assumptions which I wish to consider here. These are, first, that all individual income can be restated as national income, and thus it is perfectly acceptable to talk of redistribution of national income as if no confiscation or enforcement is involved. Second, there is an assumption that poverty – and therefore the need to redistribute – occurs because of structural imbalances in the national, or international, economy which lead to inequalities. The third assumption follows on from this, and that is that inequality is necessarily undesirable and that it is the purpose of social policy and government action to rectify it. I would suggest that these three underpinning assumptions of welfare serve as the collectivists' justification for redistribution of income and property. They make redistribution seem *possible*, as all income is the nation's; *necessary*, as poverty is due to structural constraints beyond the control of individuals; and *desirable* to eradicate inequality. However, in doing so they make some far reaching assumptions about the competence of individuals to determine their own needs and set about fulfilling them. My aim is to explore these three assumptions in turn.

2.3 The nationalisation of income

A key collectivist assumption is that all income is to be managed by government who may accordingly determine what is done with it. This is seen most noticeably in the macro-economic notion of the national income which attempts to aggregate the incomes of individual households and firms into a purportedly meaningful whole. Government then is given the role of 'managing' this aggregate with the view of increasing it and attending to its distribution. Government's role is to manage consumption, distribution and production to ensure that certain key objectives such as economic efficiency, growth and equity are met. The emphasis placed on these objectives may differ according to the particular administration, but the motivating factor of government as regulator does not. In order to meet these objectives it is seen as both legitimate and necessary to redistribute income according to some set of priorities distinct from the distribution accorded by employment and property rights.

If certain individuals or groups are deemed to be receiving an insufficient share of the national income, then it is seen as legitimate public policy to channel to them an increasing share of this income. The reverse applies, implicitly or explicitly, that certain individuals and groups receive too large a share of the national income and thus should have a portion of it removed. It is perfectly possible to believe that the second proposition applies without accepting the first. Thus the opposition to so called 'fat cats' in the privatised utilities demonstrates a belief that some individuals receive too much, without it leading to a call to redistribute to the poorest. However, it is usual to see a connection between the two propositions in that it is held that some are too poor because others are too rich.

The corollary of this belief that all income is national income is that the distribution of income has no necessary relation to production. Barry (1986) suggests that the perceived relationship between production and distribution is a key split in political philosophy. Social democrats and social liberals, such as Rawls (1971), argue that the distribution of goods and services is distinct from their production. It is therefore acceptable to transfer these goods and services away from those who have produced them regardless of their consent. This perspective places the moral emphasis on the outcomes of distribution. An outcome is just because of the particular nature of the share out based on normative perceptions of equality and social justice.

However, classical liberals and libertarians see that the problem of distribution is solved by the process of production (Barry, 1986). Those who take the risks of production are entitled to its rewards and this outcome is fair, so long as ownership of the means of production has been legitimately gained. Thus there is no proper distinction between production and distribution. If an individual has the legitimate ownership of a good then that is fair and just. It is, therefore, ownership rather than distribution which determines whether an outcome is just. This means that any distribution which forcibly separates an owner from his/her property is an unjust one. According to this view, only voluntary acts by legitimate owners are just (Nozick, 1974).

Nozick referred to his position as the *entitlement theory of justice*. He suggested that a person is entitled to their holdings according to how they came about possessing them. If they have gained them legitimately then it is just that they have them, regardless of whether this leaves them with more or less than others. It is not the outcome itself that makes it just, but the process through which the outcomes occur. Legitimacy is gained through acquisition of holdings and not from their distribution.

Nozick bases his entitlement theory on a thorough-going political individualism in which he disputes the notion that there are societal interests for which the interests of individuals might be subsumed:

> there is no *social entity* with a good that undergoes some sacrifice for its own good. There are only individual people, different individual people, with their own individual lives. Using one of these people for the benefit of others, uses him and benefits the others. Nothing more. What happens is that something is done to him for the sake

> of others. Talk of an overall social good covers this up. (Intentionally?) To use a person in this way does not sufficiently respect and take account of the fact that he is a separate person, that his is the only life he has. *He* does not get some overbalancing good from his sacrifice, and no one is entitled to force this upon him – least of all a state or government that claims his allegiance (as other individuals do not) and that therefore scrupulously must be *neutral* between its citizens.
>
> (Nozick, 1974; pp. 32–3, author's emphasis)

An extension of this position is that there is no such entity as the national income, merely the disaggregation of individual incomes within a national boundary. It is not legitimate to redistribute this income according to some alternative notion of justice than that which has been arrived at by the process of production. Austrian economists since Hayek and Mises have argued that national economic aggregates are at worst fictions and at best merely metaphors (Hayek, 1988; Mises, 1981, 1996; Shand, 1990). As methodological individualists they have a profound distrust of holistic notions such as 'aggregate demand' and 'the economy'. These are convenient, but loose and indistinct notions aimed at conveying a holistic sense to social phenomena. However, these notions are entirely fallacious in that there is no single entity which can be called 'the economy'. Rather there are a myriad of disconnected individual actions which interrelate vertically and horizontally to form what appears to be a cohesive whole. This cohesion is, however, a *post factum* generalisation of the past activity of disparate individuals, firms and institutions. In this sense, economic and societal aggregates do not exist as separate entities in themselves. They are merely convenient (if misleading) metaphors for a complex of individual actions.

However, it is not the case that we can merely dispense with these metaphors. Infantino (1998) argues that collective concepts such as society and class are essential to the social sciences and to everyday life. Yet this should not be taken to imply that these entities actually exist. They are merely shorthand terms which help theoretical development and the discussion of practices, theories and concepts. It is inconvenient, if not impossible, to constantly refer to the economic decisions of millions of consumers and firms, yet this is what we mean when we talk of 'the economy'. What exists are the consumers and firms, the concept of 'the economy' is merely a convenient shorthand. The problem though is 'the reification of collective concepts' (Infantino, 1998, p. x). He sees this as the most frequent error in the social sciences, whereby these metaphors are seen as being entities in themselves. Therefore instead of talking of the actions of individuals, economists discuss the operation of the economy. According to Infantino, the question is not *whether* to use collective concepts, but *how* they are used.

This methodological individualist argument attacks the basis of the collectivist case for welfare provision, in that it questions what government actually represents, and also what it is that government is actually redistributing. Firstly, if it is illegitimate for government to control the income of individuals and firms without their consent, and if there is no such thing as national economic aggregates, on what basis does government action rest? How can government justify taxing the wealthier elements within a society to fund social housing for the poorer?

One argument could be that of implied consent. Governments are elected on the basis of manifesto commitments, and therefore if a government stands on a platform of increased taxation, then if elected it can be said to have a legitimacy. Yet, in most western democracies it is rare for one single party to win a majority of votes. The Labour party may have won the 1997 General Election with a majority of 170, but it achieved this with a majority of electors voting against them. The Labour party may be the largest single party, but this does not mean it has won the consent of all the people of Britain. In systems of proportional representation a majority government may be formed, but usually only, as in France, Germany and Italy, by several parties coming together to form a workable majority. The result of this, however, is a compromise in which those who, say, voted socialist might have to accept the policies of communists or environmentalists. Presumably, if socialist voters had wanted these policies they would have expressed their preference more explicitly.

Voters might not be voting for the same thing. They may vote for different parties within a coalition, or be attracted to one of a party's promises while being lukewarm towards the others. However, they are all presumed to consent to the same set of policies.

This idea of implied consent through elections also ignores the views of those who voted for the defeated parties. In Britain, in 1997, 57 per cent of the electorate voted for parties other than the Labour party. However, the election result is read as giving the 'people's' consent to the Labour manifesto. This is problematic as the very actions of a majority of voters were expressly to legitimise alternative sets of proposals. To argue that this view was the most popular (or rather least unpopular) does not detract from the view that it was not consented to by a majority.

Of course, it could be said that the majority of voters have consented by accepting the result and allowing the newly elected government to operate. There is seen to be a moral legitimacy in the process, rather than just the outcome, to the extent that any outcome is justified by the process. But then the same argument could be used to justify the recognised and constitutional governments in China and the USSR. The populace appeared to offer their consent by not overthrowing their leaders and by apparently accepting blatantly unfree elections. Inertia and a belief in the impossibility of change, however, do not offer particularly fertile ground for developing moral arguments.

Implied consent is an oxymoron. Consent can only be given and not assumed to have been given. Consent must be a deliberative act – an act of choice – rather than being something implied by the accidental arrangements of birth, location and circumstance.

The second problem which a refusal to separate distribution from production poses to collectivised welfare relates back to the issue of just what is being redistributed. Hills discusses the relative shares of welfare provision according to household income. However, what he is referring to is a combination of taxation, welfare services and benefit payments. Certain households are seen to receive more than they contribute, while others are left worse off. Hills implies that the moral efficacy of the system is in the outcome of this distribution. However, what is being redistributed is the income and property of certain households for the benefit of others. None of this income is owned as such by the state. It has been taken from certain groups who are deemed (although not necessarily by themselves) to be able to afford to lose it and given to others (and indeed often given back to the tax payers, who are presumably now seen in need of certain benefits or services in kind). The important point here is that the money does not belong to the state (or to the nation), but to private individuals and firms having been (one must presume) legitimately earned by them. The question thus changes from whether households have too much or too little, to whether they have gained their income properly or not and whether they have the ability to do with it as they see fit.[3]

If individuals have the legitimate right to their income and property, what counter right of the state exists which allows them to determine what proportion is to be redistributed and then to do so? One possible answer is to suggest that certain individuals have wealth and others are in poverty, not because of any merits or demerits which they might have, but because of structural problems within a society. Thus certain individuals are the blameless victims of circumstances which they cannot control, whilst others benefit from these conditions without deserving to. I look at this possible answer in the next section.

2.4 The structural causes of poverty

Murray (1984), in his discussion of social policy in America, suggests that it was the 'discovery' of *structural poverty* in the early 1960s which led directly to the development of government welfare provision. If individuals were not capable of weighing against the structural imbalances of the system, the answer was to change or redesign the system. As a result, government took up the role of ameliorating the effects of the structural imbalances in the American economy. However, this presupposition is not restricted to American thinking on social policy. This structural assumption also underpins the redistributionist ethic of British welfare policy. Indeed Hills' discussion on the future of welfare is based on the same assumption.

The effect of this assumption is that the victims of poverty are blameless for the position which they are in. Poverty is the result of the actions of the system and not of the victims' actions. It is seen as being embedded in the structure of a society and not curable merely by economic growth. Poverty is therefore seen as being built into the system and there is little which the individuals can do to lift themselves out of poverty. There is no such thing as the deserving or undeserving poor; there are merely blameless victims of forces beyond their control.

Indeed the very notion of applying judgements to the needs of individuals is deemed to be unacceptable. If poverty is caused by structural imbalances at the level of society, then individuals cannot be held responsible for their predicament. If they cannot earn a living, or have an income significantly below what is deemed satisfactory, this is seen not as the result of indolence or poor decision making, but because society has been biased against them. Thus welfare should not only be blame free, but also guilt free. It is not acceptable to suggest that an individual's situation has arisen as a result of their own actions or omissions.

Hills' discussion of welfare, and particularly when he discusses distribution issues, is rooted not in desert, but demographics. The assumption is that a certain distribution has arisen because of the particular *nature* of the British economy and society in general. The role of collectivised welfare is to deal with this structural imbalance which leaves these individuals worse off than others. Certain groups of individuals are seen as being incapable of changing their situation themselves because of structural barriers.

One could preface this argument by suggesting that some form of categorisation is necessary if one is to make some sense of the complex social inter-relationships which undoubtedly exist. If one is to eschew any attempt to categorise individuals into groups, then serious social science is impossible. Therefore, whilst one can see grouping households together for the purposes of analysis as being somewhat arbitrary and a simplification of reality, it is necessary if one is make any sense of economic and social data and to be able to use it in any constructive way.

Now much of this argument is undoubtedly true. Social scientists need to be able to draw meaningful conclusions for the more policy orientated to use and develop. Moreover, certain categories such as ethnicity, nationality and gender have an obvious usefulness. However, there is an important distinction between these categories and those used to discuss the extent of unequal distribution of income and state benefits and costs. Gender is obviously a category capable of self determination, as are others relating to sexuality and ethnicity. Economic categories though are externally determined according to the concerns of the analyst. One may consider oneself poor or wealthy, but one would not identify oneself with a particular arithmetical segment of the population as a result and nor would one necessarily be aware of the relative position one holds. One may take decisions on the basis of one's income, as one would according to one's sexuality or ethnicity, but not on the basis of one's membership of a particular decile based on that income. Membership of a particular decile does not assist or contribute to personal decision making. There is thus a false attribution of significance to arbitrary distinctions. It is therefore not the categorisation of individuals which is at fault, but rather the choice of significant categories and the uses to which they are then put.

The problem, however, is that policy is designed to operate at the level of the group, rather than the individual. Behind this is the presumption that individual households can be readily categorised into homogenous groups, allowing for a standardised response. It is supposed that all members of the group have similar needs which can be met programmatically. Thus Hills discusses the population as belonging within particular deciles ranging from the richest to the poorest. The relative position of these deciles, in terms of share of national income, or net receipts and costs from the welfare state, is considered and deemed significant. However, on what basis, other than arbitrary convenience, is this division into categories arranged? The only reason for determining their significance appears to be the very process of comparison itself which shows a considerable contrast in net benefit between the top and bottom decile. The division into categories can therefore be criticised as an exercise in self justification. The result though is that 'the bottom ten per cent' takes on an independent set of group characteristics with the effect of becoming an entity in itself. Thus there begins a process of reification whereby comparative data is used to compartmentalise individual households according to arbitrary criteria. A further effect of this approach is to centre only on outcomes, which themselves are separated from any sense of causality other than the relative position between particular groups (in this case the deciles). This allows for the conclusion that it is the distribution of incomes and benefits which is the most germane issue. Income distribution – and, of course, income acquisition – is depersonalised and nationalised and becomes a matter for structural realignment. The creation of wealth is taken as a given – presumably it is something which the 'nation' creates – and what is of concern is how wealth is distributed. The issue of how wealth was created, and therefore of how the relative position of individuals had initially come about, is not seen as important. All that is seemingly important is the outcomes of economic activity. These outcomes may be fair or unfair, in need of change or acceptable, not because of how they were arrived at, but as a result of their relative distribution. It is thus the *structure* of income distribution which determines its virtue or otherwise.

Murray's criticism of the structural perspective was precisely that it had the effect of removing any sense of blame or responsibility from individuals for the situation in which they find themselves. He argued that individuals were capable of materially affecting their position (see section 2.6, below), but that this ability to respond also had an impact on the very attempt to ameliorate poverty. Thus the attempt to alter the purported structural imbalances in the American economy merely created an incentive for those imbalances to grow. The very provision to prevent a particular social malaise merely encouraged its growth because there was now some economic virtue in being within a particular social position relative to others.

Murray felt that the increase in poverty recorded in the USA since the early 1960s was a direct response to the introduction of measures aimed at relieving poverty. Individuals rationally altered their behaviour to maximise their income and benefits from state-funded programmes.

Thus the provision of financial aid to lone parents had encouraged women to live separately from their partners and not to work because to do either of these things would lead to the loss in benefits.

As Hills argues, 'Murray's analysis has since been hotly disputed. In Britain concern has been expressed that teenage girls *deliberately* become pregnant to 'jump the housing queue' as lone parents' (1997, p. 26, my emphasis). Hills quotes a 1991 study by Bradshaw and Millar which purportedly found little evidence for young women becoming deliberately pregnant. On the basis of this, Hills dismisses Murray's notion that benefits alter behaviour. There are two points to consider here; firstly, whether Murray's views are being accurately described – and the word 'deliberate' is important here – and secondly, that there appears to be a paradox whereby structures are seen to constrain and limit behaviour, in terms of employment and consumption, yet changes in that structure caused by increased benefits are seen as not causing any change in behaviour.

Firstly, I see it as a gross oversimplificiation of Murray's argument to suggest that he sees it merely as a case of deliberate actions as a result of a particular benefit. He is not suggesting that there is a simple linkage between, in the British context, rehousing for homeless families and the decision of a teenager to get pregnant. It is indeed likely, as Bradshaw and Millar found, that 92 per cent of pregnancies were unplanned and that, therefore, the possibility of rehousing wasn't an issue (always assuming one can verify the truthfulness or otherwise of answers in a situation which the respondent might see as self-incriminating). However, Murray's point, as has been made by other writers such as Field (1996), is not that individuals act deliberately, but rather that the sanctions against irresponsible behaviour have been removed. The point is precisely that one does not have to plan because not only are there no longer social sanctions against certain types of behaviour, but also the consequences of those actions are now ameliorated by government action. It is thus the level of expectations and the conception of what is 'normal' within which rational decisions are taken which have altered. Thus certain acts are 'encouraged' because of the way in which state supports alter the consequences attached to those actions and make them free of personal responsibility. The decision making process itself is not changed, but the context in which it operates is. Changes in behaviour are therefore likely to occur over time and incrementally, rather than as a 'big bang'. Thus I believe Murray's argument to be a more nuanced one than has been suggested by certain of his critics. It also should make one wary of expecting rapid changes in behaviour on the removal of benefits. Any changes are likely to be over the long term, which will make it much more difficult politically to achieve any real change. Policy makers might in effect have to 'write off' a whole generation in the hope of influencing their children. I leave aside here this extremely complex issue, along with my concern over whether social engineering of any kind is justifiable.[4]

The second issue here relates to the logic of the structural explanation. It is argued that the actions of individuals are constrained by certain structural conditions within the economy such as the distribution of income. In this sense individual behaviour is constrained and therefore, one could reasonably suggest, changed as a result of structural conditions. Thus there are structural barriers which prevent individuals from rising out of poverty. Yet the very proponents of this argument seek to deny that changes in the structure, such as a redistribution of income in the form of welfare goods and benefits, have any effect on behaviour. This is, of course, a one-sided and untenable argument which sees negative consequences only in the constraints and not in the attempted solutions. One would assume that those commentators who suggest that state benefits have a neutral effect on individual behaviour would find the notion that the liberal capitalist state is neutral as naive. There is thus a problem with the logic of the structural explanation. Why is structure an important issue if changes to that structure have no effect on behaviour? One would have thought that it is precisely because of the centrality of structural constraints on actions and behaviour that structuralists seek to change the structure.

Whatever the manifest deficiencies of the structural explanation, it is a pervasive one. Its importance is as an explanation of what many consider the most pernicious social problem, namely social inequality. Indeed structural poverty can be seen as the dominant explanation for inequality. This issue of equality, and whether it is indeed a problem, is what I wish to consider next.

2.5 The undesirability of inequality

Income needs to be redistributed because of inequality. It is argued that the disparity between the wealthiest and the poorest is too great and thus the 'national income' needs to be reallocated amongst the population to create a fairer, more equal distribution. Some would argue that any disparity is unacceptable and needs correcting – the equality of outcome position – while perhaps a larger group would suggest a more equal distribution, without suggesting complete equality.

This latter, more discriminating, position in fact seeks to limit the extent of equality to specific issues. The call is not for complete equality in all spheres and in all situations. As Letwin (1983a) suggests, 'To make equality an ideal that is even remotely sensible, it must be narrowed'. He goes on, 'The most sensible limiting formula to have emerged is that people should be equal *only* in respect of certain goods which are both vital and general' (p. 3). Thus egalitarians limit their consideration only to certain items such as income, education, legal rights and political power. More whimsical desires and minority pursuits are not considered a suitable area to concentrate upon. This also means there would be no great clamour for income redistribution in certain circumstances, for instance, from the super rich to the merely rich. Indeed, as Sen (1992) has suggested, when one discusses equality it is always equality *of something*. Thus equality never involves purely abstract questions. The issue, for Sen, is therefore to establish *equality of what*? So when egalitarians discuss equality it is with some goods, service or issue in mind.

There is though an immediate problem even with this qualified form of equality; namely, on what basis it is assumed that equality should apply to the particular good and service. Presumably it is because individuals are already assumed to be equal. If individuals were not already deemed to be equal it would not be rational to distribute the goods or services equally. There is thus a degree of circularity in arguments for equality. As Letwin (1983a) has stated, 'equality is rationally defensible as a rule only when the persons in question are held to be equal, beforehand, in some predominant respect' (p. 8). Thus equality depends on the prior presumption of equality. It is a self-justifying rule.

So it is rare for egalitarians to argue for a complete equality of outcome, and there are good reasons for this. As Nozick (1974) has shown with his 'Walt Chamberlain' example, it is not possible to maintain full equality of income (or any other good) without continual interference in the preferences and choices of individuals. On what grounds could a government intervene to re-establish equality when a sizeable proportion of the population has voluntarily paid over a portion of its income to another for what they consider to be a worthwhile benefit?

But, while few would persist with complete equality, many would suggest there is a need for greater equality to ensure that the needs of all citizens are met. This is one of the aims of the welfare state as defined by Hills (1997). Similarly, Giddens (1998) has suggested that, 'The welfare state has two objectives: to create a more equal society, but also to protect individuals across the life cycle' (p. 10). Bobbio (1996) has suggested that the attitude towards equality is the defining distinction between left and right and the principal reason for persisting with this elemental political division. Equality is therefore seen as worth striving for.

But why should egalitarians seek to limit the level of equality, especially when we are discussing goods deemed vital and general? If equality is one, if not the main, aim of social policy, how can inequality be justified? Could it be that inequality is actually beneficial? It is possible to find arguments from the left which would suggest that this is the case. Some would suggest that economic efficiency necessitates a certain level of inequality to maintain incentives for endeavour and risk taking, or inequality might be tolerated to the point at which it maximises the position of the worst off (Rawls, 1971). It may also be tolerated because of the recognition that there is an inevitable trade-off between equality and freedom, both of which are seen as important (van Parijs, 1995).

The problem that remains though with all these arguments is that the level of inequality is immune to precise definition. What level of income inequality is compatible with economic efficiency? Economics is not such an exact science as to allow precise knowledge of the balance between maximising equality and efficiency, even if such notions could be defined sufficiently tightly themselves. In the Rawlsian scenario, how would we collect sufficient information across the community and ensure it was shared by the purportedly rational decision makers? In both these cases the satisfactory outcome could only be derived *post factum* and this would materially affect the propensity to co-operate. In the case of the trade-off between freedom and equality, at what point is this determined when individuals and groups might have differing views of their relative importance? How likely is it that left and right would agree on the relative merits of the two competing entities? It is likely that one view would have to be imposed upon the other with the effect that the freedom and the equality of one party is compromised to benefit the other. Thus in all these cases it is difficult to suggest what precise level of inequality is ever acceptable and how one would reach a conclusion upon this.

Moreover, if equality is the fundamental aim, why should it ever be compromised? How can egalitarians argue that a society containing some inequality is better than one with no inequality, *and still maintain a commitment to equality*? The clear implication is that there are other entities which might be as, or even more, desirable than equality. A generally high standard of living, even when there is considerable inequality, might be seen as superior to a lower standard of living distributed fairly. This might depend, of course, on whether the level of the poorest in the high standard society were better off than the commonly shared standard in the second example. However, it might also depend upon the numbers of those well above the poorest level in the richer society and thus upon whether a majority seek to preserve inequality as being in their own self-interest.

The practical restriction of equality operates at another level, which also serves to further compromise the principle. Narveson (1988) has offered the ingenious argument that the mainstream views on equality amount to little more than nationalism disguised as principle. If one believes that all people are equal and deserve to have their needs met, one should then extend redistribution to the entire global population. Thus one should not restrict the benefits from progressive taxation merely to the native population. One should seek to redistribute across national boundaries to the point where needs are met. Yet, whilst most egalitarians would adhere to an internationalist perspective in their concern for the poor, they are unlikely to suggest that the British 'national income' be 'internationalised' and made available to meet the needs of all humanity. However, if one is not prepared to undertake redistribution on this scale in what sense is one merely being an economic nationalist instead of an egalitarian? And merely to lobby for redistribution within other countries, or to insist upon a lower 'necessary' minimum in sub-Saharan Africa than in Europe or North America serves only to dress up the argument with a layer of inconsistent subjectivism (how can a necessary minimum be relative, and still objectively necessary?), without answering the nationalist charge. If one claims to have found an objective human need it must be universal and so must the prescription to meet it.

Regardless of the limitations placed on equality, the dominant consideration is still on the outcomes. Equality is seen as a distribution issue, albeit in most cases a moderated one. But it is possible to see equality as being about the proportionality of inputs. This is where we are concerned both with the manner in which goods and services are distributed *and made available* (Ward, 1983). Ward is concerned to show that there is frequently an inconsistency in those who argue that it is rational to distribute necessary goods and services on the basis of need or merit only (e.g. Williams, 1962). These arguments suggest that private wealth is not a rational means of determining who receives medical treatment or a first rate education (and presumably the same would apply to good quality housing).

But Ward suggests that when one considers outcomes as well as inputs, in terms of how the goods and services are made available, this is precisely what occurs. The wealthy who contribute more in tax to provide universal health care and education, which they or their children then enjoy, are being treated unequally for this service as they are paying proportionately more for it. Thus, according to Ward, there ought to be a correspondence between the level of payments made by citizens and the level of service they receive. If services are to be universal so should there be a common level of payment for the provision of these services. Any level of disproportionate payment would constitute inequality, as well as being irrational according to the argument that the only germane consideration is need or merit. If need or merit are the sole consideration why should certain individuals have to pay more for them?

Ward's argument has a direct resonance with the attempt to reform local government finance in Britain in the late 1980s. The introduction of the Community Charge as a flat rate payment for services provided by the local authority can be seen as a partial attempt to implement Ward's principle of proportionality (it was only partial in the sense that the charge levied varied according to locality, yet the standard of provision of many of these local services was determined by a common national standard. To be properly proportional would have entailed a common national charge or greater local control to vary services and allow the charge levied to meet actual local costs). The reaction to the implementation of the Community Charge, however, shows how deeply ingrained is the belief in progressive taxation and, consequently, the difficulties in gaining acceptance for equality based on inputs as well as outputs. This though should not detract from the case presented by Ward that arguments for equality based on outcomes offer only a one-sided perspective.

I would suggest that Ward's argument is increasingly important in the context of a highly constrained welfare state. If governments are intent on seeking to restrict the welfare state, either in terms of its rate of growth or absolutely, this is likely to impact increasingly on its universal nature. There will be a tendency to target resources more on the needy. But this will have the consequence of increasing proportionate inequality. The wealthier elements in the community will be expected to pay as before, but will not be receiving as much in return. This is why commentators such as Field (1996) have argued for the continuation of universalism as a principle for welfare provision as opposed to a further extension of means testing. Universal provision, where all receive welfare services, is needed to ensure social cohesion and a continued attachment to the welfare state on the part of the affluent. Field is not arguing for the kind of proportionality advocated by Ward, but he does suggest that there needs to be some link between inputs and outputs. The aim then for Field is the extension of universal forms of provision.

It is interesting, in the light of this point, to look at what has happened to social housing as a form of welfare provision which has never had a universal status. As a result direct expenditure to housing has declined in real terms whilst resources to universal services such as health care and education have increased. As Wilcox (1997) demonstrates, housing expenditure has declined from 3.47 per cent of government expenditure in 1990/91 to an estimated 2.05 per cent in 1998/99. Over the same period the share going on health has increased from 11.60 per cent to 13.02 per cent and on education from 4.88 per cent to 5.10 per cent. Social housing expenditure has thus been cut but, importantly, without any great national outcry. On the other hand, it is education and health care which are the principal priorities of the Blair government and this is manifested in their spending plans outlined in July 1998 (housing expenditure is merely linked to expected inflation). It is also likely that, alongside the performance of the economy, the government will be judged on the targets it has set for health and education. I would suggest that the primary reason for the disparity between housing and the other services is precisely because health and education are provided on a universal basis where there is at least some, albeit disproportionate, connection between inputs and outputs.

The marginalisation of social housing is further compounded by the means testing of housing supports. It is perfectly legitimate to counter the above argument on the trend in social housing spending with the point that the increase in personal subsidies in the form of housing benefit means that spending on housing has not really declined, but has merely been redistributed away from housing organisations to tenants. However, this ignores the effect of this change which, through the targeting of means tested benefits, creates a dependent minority isolated from the majority. There is no mechanism within this process to connect up those making the inputs and those receiving the outcome, because, at any point in time, there can be virtually no overlap between the two groups. Thus the further targeting of housing subsidies onto needy individuals serves to break any connection between inputs and outputs and to negate any sense of social cohesion. I would suggest that relinquishing any sense of proportionality in the provision of housing services has led to the marginalisation of housing as a welfare service and could perhaps demonstrate the consequences of reducing proportionality further.

This argument for proportionate equality also leads to a questioning of the means of allocating social housing. Arguments for proportionate equality would lead to criteria other than need being used to allocate social housing. It is interesting that in Britain the housing minister has intimated that need will no longer be the top priority for allocation, with a greater emphasis being placed on so called 'mixed communities' (*Inside Housing*, 5 February 1999, p. 1). Clearly the need to deal with the separation of the majority from the residualised minority of social housing tenants, which is a particular feature of British social housing, has now been recognised. The interest in Britain, on the part of both academics and practitioners, in Dutch models of housing allocations is also indicative of a growing perception of the need to deal with marginalisation and to reconnect social housing with the mainstream of British housing where, because of the size of the owner occupied sector, choice and popularity are significant elements in housing consumption.

There is a further consequence of seeing equality in terms of outcomes, and this relates to the practical effects of this perception. In order to pursue this notion of equality, government actually has to treat individuals and groups *differently*. The belief that individuals are equal in certain respects leads to the provision of specific services to certain persons and not to others. Thus, in the pursuit of equality, government actually has to discriminate between the relative needs of individuals within a community. Therefore, in a very real sense, government does not treat its citizens equally in that it is not neutral between the interests of certain groups.

This may appear to be a perverse suggestion to collectivists, in that government is accused of being biased towards those who have pressing needs, when this is precisely what it ought to be doing. This would perhaps be acceptable as a rejoinder were the state seen as a disinterested administrator of services and not as serving particular interests. However, for many collectivists, the state is a key element in furthering the interests of a particular class or a presumed 'establishment'. As I have discussed in section 2.4 above, much of the force of structural arguments, be they related to class, ethnicity or gender, is that they purport to show that the state is not neutral. It appears though that the state can become neutral when it comes to redressing past structural inequalities, even when it systematically discriminated before. I would suggest that it is rather perverse to see the state as neutral when it serves particular interests, but not others, and the entirely reasonable desire to assist those in poverty does not detract from this.

The question is, on what basis does government discriminate on behalf of certain individuals and groups in preference to others? Or, put another way, what grounds are there for treating some less equally than others? I presume that the most common argument for this differential treatment would be the belief in social justice, whereby the state is seen as having a responsibility for the well-being of all members of society. According to this view, it is a moral imperative for the state to intervene in market outcomes to ensure that individual needs are met. Furthermore the notion of social justice can be used to justify action against 'excessive' differentials of wealth and income. Of course, the notion of social justice relies on the presumption of the existence of holistic entities discussed in section 2.3 above. It relies on the existence of a national income and the premise that it is legitimate for government to distribute this income according to some sense of justice.

This view has been powerfully attacked by Hayek (1982) who argues that the notion of social justice is a fallacy which rests both on the mistaken reification of collective concepts and a misuse of the concept of justice. For Hayek, justice is a matter of the administration of law. A law is just, provided it is formulated according to general, abstract rules. Therefore one of the criteria for a just law is that it relates to all citizens under the jurisdiction of the particular rule of law. A law which discriminates by offering differential benefits is not therefore a just one. Hayek recognises that one of the outcomes of the application of these general and abstract principles is a considerable level of inequality. The actions of a market may lead to inequality and might be seen as unfair, in that those who work hardest or have the least might not benefit as much as the fortunate idler or the already rich. However, so long as actions have occurred within the law, they are not unjust.

Moreover, as the market is an impersonal process which delivers outcomes which are by definition unforeseen, the consequences cannot be seen as either moral or immoral. One cannot attach virtue or opprobrium to market outcomes because they were not the result of a deliberative conscious process (unlike government action which is). Critics of this view, such as Plant (1991), argue that the outcomes of markets can be foreseen – we know that there will be winners and losers. Therefore we cannot ignore the moral implications of markets. Plant is correct that outcomes can be foreseen in the sense that we know, in all probability, that there will be some inequality. It is not possible though to indicate which individuals will be treated unequally and whether this is unjust. It is only possible if one starts from the premise that inequality is wrong by definition. But this abstract dislike for inequality hardly takes the debate any further. Plant's argument rests on the assumption that if there is inequality the society or collective suffers and thus action is necessary regardless of the particular distribution. Plant only deals with Hayek's critique of social justice by ignoring his basic premises and persisting with the very fallacies which Hayek seeks to confound.

In place of the notion of equality I would seek to put the notion of neutrality at the centre of this debate. The very act of pursuing greater equality implies differential treatment by the state in order to pursue some end that has not been agreed by all parties on a voluntary basis (otherwise we could presume it would already be happening). However, if all citizens have the same rights then the state has an obligation to respect those rights equally. This means being strictly neutral between the interests of citizens, except where individuals are being coerced in some way by others.

Like the collectivist notion of equality this is very much an ideal which in practice would have to be qualified by other considerations such as efficiency and individual competence (for instance, at what age do we decide children are able to determine their own interests free from parental supervision?). I would argue (King, 1998a, 1998b) that generally individuals, at least with regard to their housing needs, are competent and thus it is possible, in principle, to achieve a high level of neutrality. I shall return to this issue again in section 2.6, below. However, the important point here is that, if neutrality is the key criterion for justice, inequality is not necessarily undesirable. Rather it is an inevitable consequence of social action which is neither necessarily moral or immoral. This does not mean that one should accept poverty and not seek its relief – we should actively seek to relieve it – but rather it calls into question how we set about dealing with the problem. My aim has been to show the deficiencies in arguments for greater equality, not that we should be selfish and disregard the needs of others. My view is rather that much of what passes for action based on social justice is arbitrary and serves to hinder the private interests of individuals without necessarily achieving any socially beneficial aims.

I have suggested that there are three crucial notions which underpin collectivist views on welfare. First, that income is national and therefore can be redistributed; second, that poverty has structural causes; and third, that inequality is undesirable. I have tried to show the limitations of these ideas. I now wish to take my argument a stage further by looking at just how competent the key players – individual households and the state – really are. The three assumptions behind collectivist views on welfare make some concrete assumptions about the competence of individuals (and consequently the abilities of the state) and how able they are to determine their own interests and make choices in order to achieve those interests. In the next three sections I wish to explore this issues.

2.6 Ignorance and competence

The merit good argument is frequently used to justify government intervention in housing markets. According to Bramley *et al.* (1995), 'The argument that a minimum standard of housing consumption for all types of household is a "merit good" that people should have access to, regardless of ability to pay, is one that most would probably subscribe to' (p. 218). This view is based on the importance which housing has in the lives of individuals and on the social consequences of poor housing. Good housing has an intrinsic merit, which creates a compelling argument for its provision to an adequate level. It is therefore incumbent on government to ensure that adequate provision is made. However, one can make equally compelling cases for other goods and services which are not seen as merit goods, and which therefore are not seen as needing to be provided directly by government. Staple foodstuffs are clearly an imperative, yet they are not provided directly. A market is still allowed to operate and subsidies are made to individuals to assist them in purchasing them. The assumed difference, which makes housing a merit good and bread not, is the issue of ignorance. It is presumed that we are all aware of the need for basic foodstuffs, yet we are not so aware of our housing need. As Oxley and Smith (1996) have suggested 'Good quality housing can be viewed as a merit good which will bring benefits to individuals over and above those which individuals perceive' (p. 11). The benefits of obtaining good quality housing are assumed to be beyond the perception of some and hence a market will tend to underprovide. Whether this ignorance is wilful or not, it will need to be overridden by central provision undertaken by those capable of perceiving the 'real' needs of individuals.

There are several problems with the merit good argument as it relates to housing (see King 1998b for a fuller discussion). The principal problem though is seen when one compares housing provision with that of other welfare goods and services also seen as merit goods, in particular health care and education. The argument that we are ignorant of our health care and education needs (although in the latter case the argument is weakened by the ability of responsible parents to choose on their children's behalf) is an understandable one. We know that we are ill, but not the cause nor how to treat it. We thus lack sufficient information to make an informed decision and therefore have to rely on experts. Likewise we might be ignorant of our potential unless it is tapped by formal education. There is then a strong case for stating that there would be an underprovision of these goods if left to a market, and accordingly both health care and education are provided by the state and enjoyed by the overwhelming majority of the population.

The situation with regard to housing though is somewhat different. The majority of housing is provided via a market in which it is assumed that individual households are competent and capable of determining their own needs. It appears that a majority of households are not ignorant of their housing needs and how to fulfil them. They are able to enter the housing market to fulfil their needs on the basis of personal choice. It is only a minority who are unable to afford the market price and thus for whom housing takes the form of a merit good. What this implies is that when academics and commentators refer to health care as a merit good they are referring to something intrinsic to the good itself. However, when referring to housing as a merit good, the criteria changes to the nature of households. Intervention in health care is necessary because of a knowledge deficit, which is assumed to be general, yet it is justified in the case of housing because a minority lack a sufficient income.

This suggests that housing is not properly a merit good at all. The problem is not that individuals are ignorant and therefore do not decide to purchase the right quantity, but rather cannot afford to purchase it *to the level deemed necessary*. The latter point is important in that it is not merely housing, but 'good quality housing' which is said to be the merit good. The normativity of the notion thus becomes obvious. A standard of housing is set which certain households cannot meet and therefore intervention is required to achieve it (however, there is no necessary correlation between the establishment of standards and their achievability). While health care operates in this manner to an extent, in that demand tends to increase along with technical advances, it does not *only* operate in this manner, as is the case with housing.

Hence the problem with treating housing as a merit good is that it rests on a differential view of human competence. Certain individuals and groups are deemed to be competent, and therefore able to fulfil their own housing needs, whilst others are not. This returns us to the discussion on group characteristics as the basis for social policy (see section 2.4, above), in that certain groups are seen to be competent while others are not. No attempt is made to differentiate between individuals within these groups, because national policy making is not possible without standardisation and the maintenance of certain basic stereotypes. Thus owner-occupiers are seen as capable and accordingly should be responsible for the maintenance of their dwelling, of dealing with disputes with neighbours and of making proper provision to ensure they can continue to meet their liabilities. Tenure becomes almost a badge of competence, regardless of the qualities and shortcomings of the individual households which comprise this rather arbitrary grouping.

But those unable to attain owner occupation are deemed to be incapable of meeting their own needs and thus housing policies have to be concocted to ensure they receive 'good quality housing'. Moreover, when they achieve the status of social housing tenants they are still deemed to be incompetent and therefore issues such as neighbour disputes and maintenance are dealt with by housing professionals. Yet, upon purchasing their dwelling, using their right to buy, this incompetence disappears, as does the responsibility of housing professionals. Competence is apparently to be determined by one's ability to service a mortgage debt. There exists therefore a form of tenure apartheid (King, 1996) which determines competence by tenure group.

This differential view of competence also operates at the individual level in that individuals in receipt of welfare services are deemed to be passive and incapable of taking decisions which affect their predicament. Because of structural constraints the poor are unable to assist themselves and thus they must receive direct assistance to relive their poverty. However, the assumption is that this assistance has a neutral effect on behaviour. Therefore it is presumed that there are no incentive effects within welfare provision. One can restate this presumption as a belief that the poor are ignorant of the nature of their predicament and are incapable of affecting their situation.

As we have seen in section 2.4, Murray (1984) takes issue with this view. He believes that individual recipients of welfare are no less competent to take rational decisions than tax paying citizens. He contends that the behaviour of the poor is rational in that they seek to maximise their own interests. The problem comes in assuming that what constitutes rationality at one economic level can be generalised to all other levels. Additionally, it is an error to see rational decisions as those based on the long term interest. Instead we should seek to explain the behaviour of the poor on the basis of their perceptions and situations:

> The objective is to establish what the incentives *are* (or were), and how they are likely to affect the calculations of a person who has few chips and little time. It is also important to put aside the distant view of long-term rewards that we, surveying the scene from above, know to be part of the ultimate truth of self-interest, and instead to examine the truth as it appears at ground level at the time decisions must be made. (p. 156, original emphasis)

In attempting to explain individual behaviour Murray suggests that we see rationality as a subjective process rather than an abstract notion separated from the particular circumstances of the individual. According to Elster (1983, 1986) rationality not only involves action but belief. One acts because one believes it is correct or in one's interest to do so. Rationality can be seen as purposive action based on beliefs about the world. However, it is not necessary for these beliefs to be correct. A decision may be perfectly rational even though it is based on false premises. Furthermore, rationality does not have to involve the conscious achievement of the actual outcome. This is partly because the belief might be false, but also because decisions are made under uncertainty (Anand, 1993). The main causes of this uncertainty are imperfect information and the fact that decisions are not taken in isolation. In particular one's actions will not be passively received, but will be reacted to. This means that rational decision making involves the calculation of the decisions and likely action of others. Therefore welfare recipients act on the basis of their beliefs and a calculation of their consequences in the light of the actions of others, in particular the actions of welfare bodies. This does not mean that they will be better off in the long term as a result of their actions, but they can receive an immediate benefit from certain actions which further embed them into welfare dependency.

If one assumes that welfare recipients are rational, and in consequence as competent as anyone else, one can more readily understand why welfare spending and the number of recipients has increased at the same time as economic growth. Murray suggests it is rational for a lone parent not to marry or to take up employment, as this will lead to a reduction in benefits (Murray, 1996). Individuals are actively reacting to the incentives presented in front of them. This is not because they are more evil, dysfunctional, or even more coldly calculating, but because they operate in the same manner as any person seeking to maximise their own interests. What differs is that, in the case of the poor, the options are limited.

Therefore, the mistake on the part of policy makers is to assume that there are no incentives which operate in social policy. The point is that individuals are exercising their capabilities. This behaviour becomes a social problem because the capability to take decisions has been uncoupled from the responsibility for the outcomes of that decision making. This arises because policy makers deny the capability in the first place, preferring to rely on structural explanations for poverty.

Murray, having offered his explanation of how social policy actually helps to magnify the problems it seeks to solve, goes on to discuss three so called 'laws' about the nature of social policy. He proposes that there are three laws present within social policy which can act as a guide to understanding policy failure as well as helping to design social programmes which might work. His first law is that of *imperfect selection*, which states, 'Any objective rule that defines eligibility for a social transfer program will irrationally exclude some persons' (p. 211). Murray suggests that there will be an 'epistemic error' in constructing social policy. This is the 'inevitable gap between quantified measures and the concept they are intended to capture' (p. 212). It is not possible to objectively and comprehensively define the 'truly needy' and to separate out the deserving from the undeserving. Murray suggests that this leads to the broadening of welfare programmes to include more people than strictly necessary. Indeed '(i)f persons are not to blame for their plight, no real harm is done by giving them help they do not fully "need"' (p. 212).

The second law is that of *unintended rewards* which is defined as, 'Any social transfer increases the net value of being in the condition that prompted the transfer' (p. 212). Murray suggests that a social programme seeking to ameliorate a problem, 'however unintentionally, *must* be constructed in such a way that it increases the net value of being in the condition it seeks to change – either by increasing the rewards or by reducing the penalties' (p. 213). He excludes those who are in that situation completely involuntarily, but suggests that these are few in number. For the majority the condition one is in is materially affected by the provision of benefits to try and relieve the problem.

Murray's third law is that of *net harm*. This states that, 'The less likely it is that the unwanted behaviour will change voluntarily, the more likely it is that a program to induce change will cause net harm' (p. 216).

Murray argues that the single most crucial factor in determining whether a social programme will succeed is 'the price that the participant is willing to pay' (p. 216). The greater the preparedness to make the necessary changes in behaviour, the greater flexibility there will be in policy design. Conversely, the smaller the price that participants are prepared to forfeit, the greater the constraints on social policy. The problem in the latter case is that inducements will have to be almost entirely positive, with little possibility for negative reinforcement. Furthermore, if the positive inducements are large, the programme will entice onto it participants who do not strictly need it. It thus makes the initial situation – say, long term unemployment – a more desirable state to be in, when the intention was to reduce or eradicate it.

Murray also suggests that social programmes have a wider affect than merely the particular beneficiaries. Programmes alter the conditions, norms and incentives operating within a community and make it harder for those seeking to be independent to break out of the consensus. Thus certain types of behaviour become seen as normal and this affects the social norms within a community. Hence norms of behaviour are created which separate these communities from the wider society.

One of the main themes running through Murray's argument is that policy makers misunderstand the incentive effects of social programmes. Therefore social problems such as poverty and dependency are as much a result of, or at best made worse by, government intervention. The premise is that individuals are constrained and that they are unable to make choices which might materially affect their position. Murray suggests that an important part of any explanation of social problems is the role of rational choices. It is therefore worth exploring this area in some detail.

2.7 Choice and responsibility

The majority of households in Britain have some choice over their housing. They are apparently able to provide for themselves through a market and they thus have a degree of choice about where and in what they live. This choice, of course, is constrained by issues such as employment, income, family ties and so on. But within these constraints the majority are able to exercise a considerable choice. I do not believe therefore that it is particularly controversial to suggest that housing is amenable to choice.

This is not to suggest that there is no imperative attached to housing, even where it is provided via a market. Housing, as Turner (1972) has discussed, is an existentially significant activity, and this is the case regardless of the standard of amenity enjoyed by the household. This means that when considering housing the concept of need is also apparent. In conventional policy terms housing need is used to refer to those households unable to provide for themselves. As I have discussed elsewhere (King, 1996, 1998a, 1998b) this is to confuse need with its fulfilment. My contention is that need should not be seen as a lack of something, but as a necessity. This means that the need does not diminish even when it is fulfilled.

But this view of need means that it is overlaid with the issue of the *means* of fulfilment. I would suggest that the crux of this issue is the amount of choice which households are able, or deemed able, to exercise. Those unable to fulfil their own needs are lacking choice in that they must rely on others. However, I would argue that the distinction between self-fulfilment and fulfilment by others is not an empirical condition, but one determined by the particular nature of provision and the normative understanding of the role of social institutions. It is perfectly possible to determine policy instruments which can maximise choice and thus permit households to fulfil their own needs.

Of course, this presupposes that individuals are competent to make rational choices. If individuals are not competent – if they are ignorant of the repercussions of their actions – then one would not wish them to make choices. As we have seen, this is precisely the premise upon which the merit good argument is based. Individuals are not aware of their own needs – they simply do not know what is best for them.

I wish to contend that individuals are competent and that social policy ought to be based on that assumption. I then wish to explore the consequences of choice, in particular the responsibility which flows from choices.

Housing is not a merit good precisely because the need for it is predictable (King, 1998b). We are aware of the need for housing and that is the case regardless of our current conditions or whether we have housing or not. We are all aware of what are the prevailing standards of amenity and are thus able to assess quality. If there is a 'housing problem' it is not one of knowledge, but of quantity and access (and I shall deal with this issue when I discuss subsidies and policies in sections 2.9 and 2.10). The predictability of housing means that it is an instrumental rather a basic need. For most of us our current housing is a consequence of previous choices we have made in terms of employment, financial commitments, relationships, children, and so on. Thus our current need – and our ability to fulfil it – is instrumental on these basic choices throughout the life cycle. Housing still fulfils a basic need, but this is not what determines the acceptability of our housing. We cannot fulfil our instrumental needs without fulfilling our basic ones, at least not without taking a particularly perverse decision.

This means that housing is a condition of personal choice in which competent individuals are able to determine their needs and how to fulfil them. This condition will apply regardless of current tenure and income. Indeed this assumption implies that access to housing is simply a matter of sufficient income, rather than about the more complex epistemic condition suggested by the merit good argument.

I have suggested that one should assume that individuals are competent. I am aware that this leaves me open to the rejoinder that some individuals quite clearly are not. Indeed, some individuals, because of mental disability, are not capable of deciding for themselves. My premise, however, is to suggest that there *ought to be a general presumption of competence,* rather than the belief that individuals are not competent and need government support. There will inevitably be individuals who are not able to determine their own interests, but these will be exceptional and readily identifiable. There is no necessary difficulty in meeting the needs of these people as exceptions. It would be possible to support these individuals (assuming they are not already part of another household) more sympathetically where there is not a standardised national system of welfare which is incapable of individualising the means of fulfilment. A general presumption of competence, rather than being callous, would seek to enable individuals instead of simply providing for them.

In any case it is necessary to make a distinction between those able to choose how to fulfil their needs and those who genuinely cannot. The presumption that individuals are competent would lead to a situation whereby it is generally assumed that an individual's predicament has arisen as a result of their own action: they have chosen to be where they are. I would suggest that one can presume a level of voluntarism will be present in most actions. This is a position diametrically opposed to the structural argument which sees individuals as hemmed in by forces beyond their control (see section 2.4). Instead of seeing individuals as passive victims of impersonal social forces, I see individuals as responsible, rights bearing agents capable of taking decisions. This capability may be constrained by factors beyond their control. An individual may be made involuntarily unemployed, but this does not mean that they do not have any choices. They can retrain, move to another area, take a low paid job, or decide to survive on state benefits until the right offer comes along.

Likewise, the overwhelming majority of pregnancies arise from voluntary acts between consenting adults. Most couples are aware of the potential consequences of sexual behaviour and therefore can properly be said to have chosen a particular route. There are exceptions to this, such as rape and incest, but these again should not be the model from which general policies are derived, precisely because they are exceptional.

My aim here is not to be censorious and try to prescribe certain actions. My belief is that individuals are capable of determining their own interests and how they go about achieving them. It is a matter for personal choice whether an individual takes a particular job or whether a couple decide to have a child. However, this should not imply that anyone but them should bear the responsibility for that action. If individuals are competent and capable of determining their own needs, it follows that they should be held to account for the consequences of their actions.

Choices have consequences and this instrumentality is unavoidable. However, social policy, in its refusal to apportion blame, seeks to move the responsibility for these consequences onto the state. But this leads to precisely the problem Murray identified in his Law of Unintended Rewards in that certain behaviour is encouraged by 'rewards' from the state.

My aim here is not to suggest that certain households should not be helped, but rather to suggest that social policy which is blame free has had disastrous consequences for personal responsibility and for the role of the state. It has perpetuated the view that individual actions are free of any personal consequences and has placed that burden onto the state. As a result, irresponsibility has grown along with dependency (indeed these are really two ways of describing the same condition).

The issue of personal responsibility is now firmly on the political agenda. This is seen by some as a reaction against the supposed individualism of the 1980s and early 1990s which placed individual rights over responsibility to the community (Bell, 1993; Etzioni, 1993, 1997; Gray, 1995b, 1997; Sacks, 1997 and Selbourne, 1994). These communitarian writers have argued that social and economic libertarianism have created an atomistic culture in which social institutions are collapsing. They see issues such as anti-social behaviour and a reluctance to work as examples of this and attempt to devise social and public policies which will re-create the lost sense of community or civic order. Their argument is that individuals have a responsibility to others and that the role of the state is to ensure that this is maintained. Individuals thus have a responsibility to others. While this sense of solidarity and responsibility was also present in more old fashioned collectivist views, the difference with communitarianism is that it states that individuals have a responsibility to others. Thus the concentration is not so much on state provision of needs, but on ensuring that individuals act in a responsible way (it being possible, according to communitarians, to state what the proper way to behave is). We can see some of these ideas taking effect in housing with such issues as anti-social behaviour and the use of probationary tenancies. Individuals are 'encouraged' to act in certain ways on pain of sanction.

The implication here is that it is possible to determine the 'correct' way to behave. Moreover, there is an assumption that government has a legitimate role in correcting behaviour which doesn't meet up to the required standard. This means that punitive action is taken against certain individuals and groups, at the same time, as we have seen, as other forms of behaviour are tolerated and even encouraged by government policy. It also means that, despite a rhetoric of individual responsibility, the role of government remains central. Government is assumed to be acting on behalf of the community and its values.

As I discussed in section 2.5, the state should be neutral towards its citizens, whom it has a duty to protect equally. It is not for the state to apportion benefits for some and punishments to others (unless those punishments are in response to coercion and violation of the rights of others). The problem for the citizen is that there is no recourse beyond the state itself and so the citizen is left without protection.

An individualist approach to responsibility would be to reject the notion that one can state an objective notion of the public good or the needs of the community. Rather, one should take a personal responsibility for oneself and for others because of the side constraint placed upon one to protect the interests of others (Nozick, 1974). This means that the recognition of the rights of others is grounded on their recognition of mine. The ends of diverse individuals might be incommensurable (Berlin, 1969) and this will mean that the rights of individuals will be in conflict. However, these rights cannot be overridden by force or authority, but only set aside by voluntary agreement by public discussion and compromise. Certain acts, such as paedophilia, theft, violence and murder are quite clearly infringements of the rights of others and require punitive action. However, legitimate disputes about lifestyles and choices are not. The role of the state is to be a neutral upholder of certain agreed abstract and general principles, not to take sides in terms of what behaviour is acceptable and what isn't.

My aim here is not to suggest that 'anything goes', or that certain forms of behaviour ought to be permitted unchallenged. My view is that it is not for the state to adjudicate between rival views of the good life and to interpose on the choices which competent individuals make. On the other hand, it is not for the state to shield individuals from the consequences of their actions. If individuals are competent, as I believe they are, they should take responsibility for their actions.

I am aware that the effects of such a view would be quite far reaching in terms of social policy and the expectations of many people currently dependent on welfare services. I am also aware that what I have outlined above is an ideal position, which would have to be hedged around with caveats to deal with particular situations which might arise. However, as a general principle – that individuals are competent and capable of taking responsibility for their actions – it can form the basis for a root and branch reform of welfare services including housing provision. But before discussing possible reforms I wish to add a further argument to my critique of collectivist arguments, namely the belief that an inevitable consequence of government action is government failure.

2.8 Government failure

Collectivist views of welfare tend to see individuals as being less than competent to determine their own interests. They may not know what is best for them, and accordingly some intervention is necessary to ensure that individuals are as well off as they ought to be, free of the structural constraints which currently hamper them. This implies that the state is competent. Collectivists appear to believe that the state is capable of directing the national income, of determining comparative needs and of attaining a greater degree of equality through redistribution. The criticism levelled at government by commentators such as Hills (1997) is not that government is incapable, but rather that it might not be committed enough or is taking too timid a stance to achieve what it is capable of achieving.

But what is not in doubt is the premise that government is capable of doing the job of distribution better than an uncoordinated process such as a market. There is, of course, an extensive literature on market failure, which has been countered by an equally extensive range of material on the notion of government failure. My aim is not to review this debate, but to pick out one argument that I believe is particularly important and upon which the whole debate might be seen to rest. This is the problem of how government can possibly coordinate the needs of millions of disparate individuals with incommensurable aims.

This problem can be stated in terms of an epistemological 'gap' between the intention of centralised planner and the resultant outcomes. Hayek (1948, 1967, 1978, 1988) is concerned to correct what he considers the fallacy of *policy constructivism* which he suggests pervades collectivist approaches to social and public policy. He states that there is a belief within collectivist approaches that, as all institutions have been made by human action, they can be remade by further deliberative action. This, according to Hayek, is a fundamental error on the part of policy makers. Institutions have developed in a particular way out of the uncoordinated interrelationship of millions of individual actions, none of which were of fundamental significance. According to Hayek, institutions and entities such as language and markets have developed *spontaneously* (1960, 1982) from human action rather than by any particular design or plan. It was the interaction of millions of individuals pursuing their own interests which has led to the current formation of institutions within a society.

However, it has become common since the Enlightenment to believe that what has been created by humans can be remade or recreated to suit a different purpose (Hayek, 1967, 1988). The problem, however, as noted by Mises (1981), is that the means to calculate the interests of the individuals within this society cannot be collected centrally. There is no satisfactory manner in which the interests of individuals can be differentiated by a large bureaucratic planning entity and the result is standardisation based on certain universal principles which are deemed to apply. In consequence, the spontaneity of human interaction is hampered and denigrated. Thus, for Hayek, the problem of policy constructivism is that the very belief that policy can direct human action appears to stifle it. This, of course, merely serves to make the constructivism ever more necessary.

But as Popper (1989) has discussed, 'it is one of the striking things about social life that *nothing ever comes off exactly as intended* (p. 124). He goes on:

> Things always turn out a little bit differently. We hardly ever produce in social life precisely the effect that we wish to produce, and we usually get things that we do not want into the bargain. Of course we act with certain aims in mind; but apart from these aims (which

> we may or may not really achieve) there are always certain unwanted consequences of our actions; and usually these unwanted consequences cannot be eliminated. To explain why they cannot be eliminated is the major task of social theory'. (p. 124, author's emphasis)

Popper goes further, to suggest that, 'the characteristic problems of the social sciences arise only out of our wish to know the *unintended consequences*, and more especially the *unwanted consequences* which may arise if we do certain things' (1989, p. 124, author's emphasis). The task of social theory is thus to explain how unintended and unwanted consequences arise. This has been recognised in a recent compilation on contemporary housing policy (Williams, 1997).

In his introduction to the text, Williams (1997) contends that housing researchers do not fully understand the interactions between different elements of housing processes. This leads to unintended consequences, a worsening of the position and consequently further intervention. One of the reasons for this is that, 'government might be the starting point for change but in reality policy is actually implemented by a range of organisations . . . and through the actions of individual consumers' (p. 2). Government has to rely on others for the implementation of policy and, as a result, the process is much more complicated than if government could exercise total control (and, of course, this is why it tries so hard to do so).

Williams suggests that the problem is that policy, and by implication discourse on it, is concerned with the short term. Policy is made to get to, and past, the next election, or to deal with an immediate dilemma. Williams argues that we should seek to make policies which are more sustainable and long term. We should seek policy which breaks out of the short term cycles of politics (although he offers no reason to suggest where the incentives for this should come from).

While Williams is clearly correct to point to the effect of unintended outcomes, I believe he errs in his prescription. He sees unintended consequences as a matter of not knowing enough about the interrelationships which occur in a complex social order. It is not that government is not competent, but that it has not proved capable *yet*. In short, for Williams, there is no questioning of the ability of policy makers to formulate the correct policies eventually. Unintended consequences are seen as being due to the system not operating properly. The task of social science is therefore to refine our understanding to the point where we can understand all the connections and consequences, and thus allow policy makers to make policy with greater confidence in their outcomes.

However, I would suggest that unintended consequences are due to the nature of the policy process itself. As Popper (1989) suggests it is not possible to rid the system of unintended consequences. But this is not because the policy makers and researchers currently do not know enough, but because they can *never* do so. Assuming the level of complexity remains (and social orders tend towards greater complexity than less), there is no way in which the diversity of interests and subjective expectations within a complex social order can be modelled accurately. In a sense, therefore, the problem is not one of unintended consequences, but the belief that we are capable of pre-empting them and constructing a social reality free of unwanted effects. This, of course, has far reaching effects for both policy making and the attempt to understand housing through social theory.

For the purposes of this debate, this argument suggests that there are limits to what government may attempt, because it can never have sufficient awareness of the complexity of social life to eradicate unintended consequences.[5] It is not unreasonable, therefore, to suggest that government will fail to achieve its objectives because of an essential lack of competence. The debate, I would suggest, can thus be seen to centre around the relative competencies of individuals and government. My view is that there are clear limits to the competence of government and that this is an epistemological rather than merely an organisational limit. Instead, it is my contention that individuals are rather more competent to determine their own interests and fulfil their needs than they are given credit for. It is precisely the mistaken belief in governmental competence and individual incompetence, compounded by a misguided belief in structural determinants and the necessity of greater equality of outcomes, that has led to dependency.

If individuals are competent, and government action is epistemologically challenged, what are the implications for housing policy? My task is now to try and answer that question by building on the more general discussion on the failures of collectivised welfare. I shall firstly look at the changing pattern of housing subsidies across much of the world, concentrating on the shift from object to subject subsidies. I shall argue that generally this shift is to be encouraged, but that there is the need for certain reforms, particularly to deal with fraud, perverse incentives and producer capture. Whilst I shall be concentrating on financial issues, I hope it shall be clear that the reforms which I propose will have broader effects on housing management, housing organisations and the housing profession.

In this essay I try to restrict my comments to the current structure of housing supports and to make some suggestions for reform. This is a limited (but nevertheless complex and controversial) task of critique followed by alternative proposals of reform which I see as attainable within current political structures. I would not pretend that I see the proposals to be discussed below as being the end point of reform. As I have discussed in my book, *Housing, Individuals and the State* (King, 1998), I would seek housing provision further deregulated than I have suggested here. My ideal would be for a voluntary system based on charitable organisations and mutual aid. In that book I have argued at some length that such an ideal is a long way off and will unfortunately be difficult to obtain.

The problem is in proposing a realistic means of achieving my ideal from where we currently are. Some libertarians, such as Friedman (1989) and Rothbard (1970, 1978), appear to rely on an abstract rationality to convince their fellow citizens of the veracity of their arguments – that as soon as individuals realise the virtues of a libertarianism they will adopt it as doing anything else would be irrational. I see this type of argument as little better than the Marxian view, that as they have discovered human nature and the motive force of history, it is for the good of humanity to force individuals into a particular form of social organisation.

However, the essence of libertarianism, even in the form expressed by Friedman and Rothbard, is based on the illegitimacy of coercion. It is the belief that individual liberty is the most important entity there is. To suggest that individuals are faced with a choice of libertarianism or else is, for a libertarian, absurd.

I suggest that, if one is consistent about a perspective which is non-coercive and based on voluntary association and exchange, there are limits to how far one can make changes which fall outside of current political practice. Revolution is by definition coercive, whilst reform can, at least in theory, be consensual. But this means that we can only make changes from the inside, by a process of evolution. Any changes are likely to be piecemeal and long term, involving many steps and potential detours. It means engaging with institutions one would rather did not exist and with those with whom one finds little in common. It also risks getting lost or being taken for a ride. There is though no practical alternative but to aim for reform from inside current institutions and structures.[6]

I see the proposals in this essay as being one step on the way towards the ultimate goal of a libertarian society based upon mutual self help, voluntarism and market exchange. I believe that the proposals can be seen as self-contained and as forming part of the crucial debate about the reform of housing and welfare benefits. But this should not be taken as meaning that these are the only changes we ought to make.

2.9 Shifting patterns of subsidy

Up to the late 1970s the emphasis in housing policy had been on alleviating perceived shortages. The priority had been on building new housing to meet unmet need. In consequence, government subsidy took the form of supply side or capital subsidies. However, since the later 1970s the perception of the housing problem has changed, largely because there is a crude surplus of dwellings over households. Therefore, as Boelhouwer and van Heijden (1992) have shown, the emphasis shifted towards quality and access issues. The problem now was not one of shortages but of ensuring that households gained access to dwellings of sufficient quality. Boelhouwer and van Heijden see this trend being manifested across Europe. Most European countries have followed a similar pattern of shifting from a concentration on the supply side towards issues of quality and access which necessitate a concern for the demand side.[7]

Kemp (1997) shows that this concern for the demand side can be seen beyond Europe, particularly in the housing policies of Australia, New Zealand and the USA. These countries have attempted to withdraw supply side subsidies, allowing rents to be set by markets. Demand side subsidies are then used to supplement income to allow these rents to be afforded. In Britain, whilst direct subsidies to housing organisation still exist, the trend has been towards a greater emphasis on personal benefits whch will allow households access to the existing stock.

Kemp offers three reasons for this general shift away from capital subsidies. Firstly, the end of massive housing shortages meant that a reassessment of the housing problem was needed. The problem was now seen as one of a shortage of income, which prevented access to quality housing, rather than a shortage of housing itself. Secondly, the perceived 'fiscal crisis' of the welfare state in the 1970s and 1980s created the belief that the welfare state was unaffordable in its current form. Personal subsidies can be targeted better and thus can be said to be more efficient in that more individuals can be helped for a given sum of money. Thirdly, the period also saw a general belief in market solutions emphasising the consumer over the producer. Kemp argues rightly that these three issues were international in their impact and therefore it is understandable that governments across the developed world shifted the emphasis of housing policy towards the consumer.

Whilst perhaps a majority of commentators would argue for the persistence of supply side subsidies, I would argue for the intrinsic efficiency and effectiveness of demand side subsidies as policy instruments (see King (1998) for a fuller discussion of this debate). I see a number of advantages in demand side subsidies which, assuming a properly constrained form of subsidy system were in operation, could lead to the individualisation of housing policy and set the conditions for further deregulation in the future.

Firstly, personal subsidies can be specifically targeted to those in need. One of the problems with supply side subsidies is that they cannot easily be withdrawn when the household's income increases. This isn't the case with personal subsidies which are dependent on income. Whilst it is possible to propose systems which offer time limited or reviewable tenancies subject to personal circumstances, they are likely to be politically difficult to enforce. Moreover, the withdrawal of subsidy as earned income rises is less disruptive and socially divisive than withdrawing a tenancy. One could also suggest that the possibility of losing one's home would have a more significant disincentive effect than means tested benefits already have. A system of personal subsidies can be devised (as I seek to do in section 2.10, below) which eradicates the current work disincentives inherent in the housing benefit system. The threat of the withdrawal of a tenancy as income rises is an either/or which it is difficult to finesse. There are other reasons, however, for preferring demand side subsidies.

The second advantage is that demand side subsidies can offer the household some choice in the housing market. This, of course, will be limited by the major constraints of income and availability, but the choice will be superior to that presented to applicants for social housing. Choice is, however, always relative and it is rare for any household not to be constrained by these factors. But what compounds the problem for low income households is the relative position across the tenures. The possible choice in the private sector is limited by unfair competition from the social sector (due to supply side subsidies) and the restrictions placed on landlords by the tax system (social landlords are exempt, but private landlords are taxed on income and profits). Moreover, currently in Britain it is only in the private rented sector that benefit entitlements are limited. The removal of these restrictions would go some way to increasing choice. A more fundamental change would be to remove supply side subsidies entirely so that all rented sectors operated according to the same conditions and freeing up subsidy for those who currently are unable to exercise a reasonable choice in the market.

A third advantage of demand side subsidies is that they can be tenure neutral and allow easy access across sectors. While this is not the case in Britain, where housing allowances are limited to tenants and mortgage interest tax relief has been substantially reduced, it is possible to devise a system which is tenure neutral, being based solely on the income of the households concerned.

Fourthly, the unpopularity of social housing funded by capital subsidies is an issue. There is not always a linkage between supply side subsidies and quality (Page, 1993). Indeed, as Power (1987, 1993) has demonstrated, much of the stock of dwellings built in the 'golden age' of social housebuilding has proved to be the least efficient and popular. This was partly due to the imperative of building quickly to deal with shortage. But I believe the principal cause was the 'top-down' nature of the process which assumed that the needs of individual households could be met centrally by experts. The problem was that individual choice was ignored and overridden by collective notions of the good.

Fifthly, demand side subsidies have the potential towards anonymity and thus might avoid any stigma which is attached to social provision. Income supports allow households to compete with others of a similar income. They are not instantly categorisable as the recipients of government handouts as is the case with those residing in social housing.

I believe therefore that there are benefits to a demand side system[8] and the withdrawal of supply side subsidies. Britain, however, still has a hybrid system which provides both forms of subsidy. The two systems obviously interact, in the sense that the reduction of capital subsidies leads to higher rents and consequently higher subsidy. The situation arises because 77 per cent of the recipients of demand side subsidies are social housing tenants (DSS, 1997) even though social housing makes up only 68 per cent of rented housing. This situation arises for two reasons, one obvious and one not so. The obvious reason for the high number of benefit recipients is because of the withdrawal of supply side subsidies necessitating greater support to tenants. Thus there is a direct correlation between the withdrawal of supply side subsidies and the increase in demand side subsidies. This is an obvious correlation, but it is not an inevitable one. Demand side subsidies have been in decline since the mid 1970s, and as Wilcox (1997) demonstrates, the rate of decline is not noticeably quicker in the 1990s than in the 1980s. However, the rate of increase in housing benefit in the 1990s was 11 per cent compared to an average of 4 per cent throughout the 1980s. I would suggest therefore that the problem is not one of the withdrawal of subsidy *per se*, but is rather one of system design.

There are two particular elements of the design of the current benefit system which have created this increase in costs and a heightened dependence on the part of social housing tenants. While this is a less obvious cause of the increase in benefit costs, any attempt to deal with the problem of increasing costs must aim at eradicating these particular design faults. The first design fault is that much housing benefit is paid direct to landlords and can therefore be used as a *de facto* revenue subsidy. Local authority tenants make up 60 per cent of benefit recipients and all of this subsidy is paid direct to landlords. Additionally, housing associations and private landlords can insist on direct payment when tenants fall more than eight weeks in arrears. However, tenants can voluntarily request direct payments and this is doubtless 'encouraged' by landlords when signing up the tenancy agreement.

The second issue is that the British system is an open-ended one, in that tenants are generally entitled to their full eligible rent as of right. While there are now rent ceilings for certain sectors due to local authority rent capping and local reference rents in the private rented sector, government still does not have full control over the system. In particular, of course, it cannot control the number of recipients. This is a difficult problem to solve as it depends on external factors. I believe that it would not be proper for government to limit benefit entitlements to a fixed number. However, it ought to be possible to reform the current system to create a greater certainty. The reforms I now consider below are attempts to deal with these design problems and to establish a deregulated system of housing subsidies based on individualist principles.

2.10 The reform of housing

As I have suggested above (section 2.8), it is always difficult to propose changes to existing systems without facing up to the law of unintended consequences. The history of housing offers many examples of policies which had fundamentally different effects from those intended, of which perhaps the most obvious is the introduction of rent controls on private rented housing. I am therefore all too aware that any proposals might have a fundamentally different effect when implemented from that intended.

This might lead one towards a form of fatalism which suggests that, if we are not able to fully forecast the outcomes of policy (which I believe is and will continue to be case), then we should not even try to do anything. This might superficially appear as a tempting proposition, but it is one that is ultimately unfulfilling. One can seek to maintain the purity of one's position, but this will not necessarily lead others to hold their fire as a mark of respect. That one rejects activism does not guarantee anything but marginalisation. Moreover, it is not as if we are at present in a position where considerable social engineering has not already taken place. Much policy is merely a form of re-engineering of past failures. Therefore, I believe that one should seek to reform policy structures, *but* always with full cognisance of the possibility that unintended consequences will create a situation that was not sought. What this means is that I cannot be certain of the full effects of the proposals I outline below. All I can suggest is that they are intended to deal with a number of specific problems and are aimed to reduce the amount of harm caused by government intervention. They are not intended as the last word on the subject, but rather to further develop the debate on the role of government supports to housing at a time when there is an apparent consensus that the current system of high rent levels and open-ended subsidies cannot continue. I also believe that one can only reform institutions and structures *from the inside* (King, 1998b and see section 2.8, above). If one believes in the overriding principle that coercion is illegitimate, then one can only reform with consent. This means that any changes are likely to be incremental. My aim here then is to suggest where we might go from the current position, but realising that the outcomes of these proposals are not necessarily where I would wish us to end.[9]

In this part of the essay I shall discuss the following issues. Firstly, as my aim is to cover all aspects of housing policy, I shall briefly discuss the liberalisation of the owner occupied sector and suggest ways in which policy might become more tenure neutral. Secondly, I shall discuss ways of dealing with supply side subsidises. A key element in this is the decentralisation of housing supports. My third area of concern is to discuss the reform of personal subsidies so as to alter the incentives which operate on households and housing providers.

2.10.1 Owner occupation

The majority of households in the UK are in the owner occupied sector. While the ostensible engine of this sector is market transactions, government has had a considerable influence over owner occupation. In particular, the Conservative governments in the 1980s pursued a policy of positive support for the sector which was both rhetorical and material. Margaret Thatcher frequently spoke of the property owning democracy and the part housing could play in this (Daunton, 1987; Saunders, 1990). This rhetoric was backed up by substantial tax expenditures, in the form of mortgage interest tax relief (MITR), and Right-to-Buy (RTB) discounts. By the late 1980s the 'cost' of MITR to the Treasury exceeded the amount spent on all other housing sectors combined (Wilcox, 1997). While one can debate whether allowing households to keep their own money is a really a government subsidy at all, one cannot doubt the effect that MITR has had on the housing market. Like a direct payment, MITR has cheapened the cost of owner occupation and thus increased the demand for it.

This in itself would not necessarily be a problem, were it not for two other issues germane to the sector. Firstly, housing costs for owner occupiers (and indeed the same is true for most renters) are usually the largest single item within the household budget. Secondly, government has used the relative significance of personal housing costs as a means of controlling consumer demand and inflation. Thus we saw in the early 1990s the successful way in which interest rates were used to dampen inflation through their effects on mortgage payments. However, we also saw several unsuccessful attempts made by the Major government to reverse the downward pressure on house prices as a result of this policy (King, 1996). Therefore, I would suggest that the problem is not merely that housing demand has been artificially inflated, but that government has sought to manipulate housing costs further in order to attain its broader macro-economic goals. Owner occupation, unlike rented housing, is an important political and economic lever which government has found it impossible to ignore. The effect of this intervention has been heightened volatility and instability in the market.

It is the combination of MITR and continual government interference and 'management' of the sector which creates the particular problem. MITR and RTB discounts have encouraged marginal income groups into the sector who have been particularly susceptible to increases in housing costs. As a result, the 1990s have seen an increase in repossessions and the apparently new phenomena of negative equity (Wilcox, 1997). I believe that the correct direction for policy with regards to owner occupation is to limit the possibility of this interference occurring.

Of course it is not possible, nor is it desirable, to decouple owner occupation from the wider economy. However, it is possible to reduce the impact which government action has on housing costs. Whatever the particular virtues of the tenure, the role of the government ought not to be one of encouraging households into it, but rather to be creating the conditions for stability which enable households to make proper choices and for a market to operate without the wild fluctuations of the past twenty or so years. Both the Major and Blair governments appear to have recognised the folly of specific interventions in the housing market. What has been more successful has been a more stable policy towards interest rates (no doubt helped considerably by sterling's departure from the ERM in 1992) pursued by both Kenneth Clarke and Gordon Brown. The passing over of responsibility for interest rates to the Bank of England is a further positive step towards greater stability and freedom from direct government intervention for political purposes. In addition, I believe that there is now a much wider recognition of the effect of exogenous factors on the housing market, particularly unemployment and job security.[10]

The role of government towards owner occupation ought therefore to be concerned with creating economic stability and not with encouragement and subsidisation. I would agree with the continued phasing out of MITR so that households bear the full cost of their mortgages. I would also propose the abolition of the Right-to-Buy allowing social housing tenants the right to purchase their property at a discount. If one is serious that government ought not to be encouraging one particular tenure, it is only consistent that the policy should be abolished. My view is that any landlord, public or private, should have the right to sell their assets (subject to safeguards with regard to the refunding of past public investment), but that they should not be forced to do so in order to achieve the ideological ends of government, and this applies *regardless of merits of the particular policy*. I should state at this point, and it will become clearer below, that my aim is not necessarily to support the interest of local authorities. My point is simply that the role of government is to offer stability to the housing market, not incentives to join it.

As important as stability is consistency. Government, by being tenure neutral in its policies, would be able to provide a level of consistency for the market which has been missing for perhaps a generation. By removing subsidies it would remove artificial incentives to join the market and thus properly individualise the decision making process. There is hope to believe that the marginal households would be less likely to enter the market (or at least not in such numbers). In addition, consistency on the part of government could further encourage the development of fixed rate mortgage instruments which are cheaper and more long term than present arrangements.

These changes depend upon on a change in expectations. The total abolition of MITR is now planned for 2001 and has not been met with a popular outcry. What is more difficult is the creation of expectations of stability and consistency. These can only be created over time by the very existence of stability and a lack of change. I would suggest though that the reform of owner occupation, despite being the majority tenure, is much the easiest sector to reform. This is because the policy measures I recommend are merely further movements along a road which government appears to be moving and which most see as being sensible.

2.10.2 Dealing with the supply side

The first element of reform should be the withdrawal of all supply side subsidies. While subsidies to local authorities and housing associations have been considerably reduced over the last fifteen years, these organisations still receive subsidies allowing them to build new property, to renovate their existing stock and to assist them in repaying the cost of past development. Housing association development already utilises a considerable amount of private finance and associations have now almost ten years experience of dealing with the market. I would therefore propose that public subsidy is reduced according to a published timetable allowing associations to plan for their future development and to adjust to a new regime. This reform would merely be codifying the trend of the past decade, but allowing for transparency and consistency.

Housing associations should also be encouraged to reinvigorate their charitable roots (Whelan, 1998) and to seek donations and the establishment of trusts to help their work. To assist this government could offer specific tax exemptions for charitable giving to housing trusts. Again, the publishing of a timetable for the phased withdrawal of subsidy would allow associations the time to develop other sources of finance from the voluntary sector. The original strength of housing associations within the community was their voluntary nature. Many were managed by local people with the aim of making a material difference to their local community. The dependence of associations on public subsidy and the increasingly interventionist regulatory regime of the Housing Corporation, has destroyed this local base. Instead, housing associations have been encouraged to expand their geographic sphere of operation and to merge to make themselves better able to thrive in the environment of managed competition developed by governments in the late 1980s and early 1990s. The effect of the subsidy regime has been a trend towards larger, regional or national associations who can take advantage of economies of scale in treasury management and project development. The aim of reform should be to break this dependence on public subsidy and allow associations to take a more direct control over their own affairs free from government interference.

One of the aims of the reforms I propose here is to localise the management and control of housing, shifting the burden onto the local community. This places a renewed emphasis on locally elected bodies and the local tax payer. It follows from this argument that the Housing Corporation should be abolished with the emphasis being placed on the development of stronger local partnerships between local housing associations and local authorities. The Housing Corporation currently wields considerable power over associations. In particular, it maintains control over funding and over the review of performance. This means that associations are particularly dependent on the policies of the Corporation. The phasing out of supply side subsidies would leave the Housing Corporation with no role. It would have no funds to disburse nor could it continue to justify a monitoring role, which in any case could equally as well be performed by the Audit Commission.

The removal of supply side subsidies to local authorities would have a different effect, in that support is currently for the maintenance of the stock and assistance with debt repayment. However, the effect of the current revenue funding regime is to create a net government surplus on local authority expenditure because the amount authorities contribute to the cost of rent rebates is greater than the housing deficit subsidy. The Blair government has agreed to change this procedure whereby rent rebates are paid out the rent of other tenants (DETR, 1998). The aim is to remove rent rebates from local authority housing revenue accounts, although without increasing the total financial allocation to local authorities.

The removal of the so called 'tax on tenants' would eliminate one of the government's limitations on voluntary stock transfers. Under current rules, housing benefit payments to local authority tenants are subsidised from rent income, whereas the full cost of benefits to tenants of registered social landlords falls on the social security budget. A shift to personal housing allowances, which were tenure neutral, would remove this obstacle and allow for more stock transfers. This could be further facilitated by allowing local authorities to use 100 per cent of capital receipts from stock transfers.

However, while the transfer of stock would lead to an injection of private finance to improve the stock, I would not suggest that local authorities be totally divested of their housing role. The potential strength of local authorities is their democratic accountability. This sense of accountability has been denuded by the limiting of local autonomy and increasing centralism (Jenkins, 1995). I would seek to see a returning to local government of its autonomy and accountability, so that it is able properly to tailor its services to the needs and wishes of the local community. This might not mean direct provision by the local authority itself, but local decision making on how much and what is spent. If this leads to a demand for increased housing provision paid for out of local taxation, it is perfectly proper for that demand to be fulfilled. This might include the continuation of material support to local housing associations. The proviso to this is that any expenditure be paid for entirely out of local contributions and rents. Housing is an area of social policy which is amenable to subsidiarity to the lowest level of competence, and although this presents a reversal from past trends, this should be encouraged.

As with the housing association sector, supply side subsidies would have to be phased out over a pre-announced period to allow local authorities to plan the necessary changes. I am aware that these changes imply a considerable renegotiation of the role of local authorities and the controls which the centre exercises over the sector. But I do not consider centralised control as effective, efficient or desirable in itself.

One of the main objections to the removal of supply side subsidies is the effect that it has had, and would continue to have, on rent levels. Rents would rise to market levels which would exacerbate the poverty trap and encourage greater benefit dependency. In addition, it would merely lead to the transference of subsidy from the supply to the demand side and thus have no direct benefit to government. Indeed, if demand side subsidies are indeed harder to control,[11] then these reforms might actually make things worse. Therefore, these proposals cannot be made in isolation and without changes to the current system of personal subsidies.

2.10.3 The reform of personal subsidies

It is my belief that the current system of housing subsidies (along with subsidies more generally) creates perverse incentives for both landlords and households within rented housing. This is particularly the case with housing benefit. The biggest growing area of housing expenditure in the 1990s has been housing benefit. It increased from a total of £3.7 billion in 1986/7 to £12.4 billion in 1997/8 (Wilcox, 1997). This was a consequence of the policies of the late 1980s which saw significant rent increases and a reduction in subsidies. However, it can also be said to be due to the incentives which operate within the benefits system in its current configuration. In this section I shall largely be concentrating on the housing benefit system as it operates in Britain. However, while some of these comments are quite specific, I believe that the principles behind my proposals are sufficiently general to be applied more widely (always accepting the problems of attempting to overgeneralise with regard to international comparisons in housing).

Governments in Britain since 1995 have not been unaware of the need to change housing benefit. The effects of the Housing Act 1988 and the Local Government and Housing Act 1989 were to dramatically increase rents in both the private and social rented sectors. The avowed intention of this policy was a further shift away from capital subsidies and consequently a greater reliance on rent income to support landlords. The intention was that housing benefit could take the strain. However, the consequence, in fact, has been the quadrupling of housing benefit costs to a level that government clearly finds unaffordable. The cost of housing benefit has been rising by 11 per cent per annum since 1991 compared with an average of a 4 per cent increase in the 1980s (DSS, 1997). There was therefore a justifiable belief that housing benefit was running out of control.

As a result of this increase in expenditure the Major government attempted to alter the benefit system by using *local reference rents*. These are effectively local rent ceilings which aim to limit rents to a reasonable level and to take into account the suitability of the accommodation provided. Therefore, the suitability of the household to the dwelling is now considered to ensure that 'up-marketing' is discouraged. In addition, it was hoped that the system would lead to a change in behaviour on the part of both landlords and tenants which would in turn encourage a reduction in rent levels (Bevan *et al.*, 1995). It is possible to see this as a form of *administrative rent control* whereby government was again able to exert some downward pressure on rents. The danger, of course, is that landlords are under no statutory obligation to charge at the reference rent level and thus tenants may be expected to supplement housing benefit payments from their income support. Further changes were introduced in October 1996 to limit housing benefit for single persons under 25 to the rent of the single room. Thus, for benefit purposes, it would be assumed that young people would be sharing a house in multiple occupation.

While government dealt with the growing cost of housing benefit in the private sector by eroding entitlements, it has taken a different tack for social housing. It has sought to control the cost of rent rebates to council tenants since 1990 by offsetting notional revenue surpluses against housing benefit. Further controls were introduced in 1996 when so called 'rent capping' was used to limit rent rebate subsidy to the rent guideline increase determined by government. With regards to housing associations, target rent levels are now included as part of the development bidding process. Therefore the Housing Corporation is able to take rent levels into account when judging applications for Social Housing Grant. The point though is that, instead of reducing entitlements to benefit, government has attempted to use the control it exercises over the supply side to limit the growth of personal subsidies.

However, it is clear that these changes have not had more than a limited effect on the benefit bill. Nor do they deal with the issue of dependency on the part of households. The emphasis has been more on dealing with the dependence which landlords have on the benefit system by limiting their ability to increase rents. This has had some effect on reducing rent increases, but it will not of itself lead to a reduction in welfare expenditure, nor will it reduce the dependency on benefit of the current 4.7 million recipients (DSS, 1997).

Further reforms are therefore necessary and I would propose that three changes are required. Firstly, the differentials between tenures need to be eradicated so that the benefit system is properly tenure neutral. Secondly, any successful reform must break the link between rent levels and the amount of housing benefit paid. This is necessary to prevent landlords adjusting rent levels to benefit maximums. Thirdly, and this relates to the above point, a separate housing benefit should be abolished with notional housing costs incorporated into a reformed system of income maintenance. I shall deal with these three proposals in turn.

2.10.4 Removal of differentials

Under the current benefit system the various housing tenures are not treated equally. Local reference rents are applied to the private rented sector (and some housing association tenants at the discretion of the particular local authority) but not to local authority and most housing association tenants who receive all their eligible rent (even though the local authority might not be fully reimbursed for the cost). Owner occupiers are not eligible to receive housing benefit, receiving instead limited support for mortgage interest payments via income support.

Moreover, single persons under 25 receive less housing benefit than other households which reduces their choice in the private sector. This restriction though does not apply if a young person obtains either a local authority or housing association tenancy. However, single persons are not generally deemed to be in priority need by these organisations.

From the point of view of the landlords, only housing associations are able to set their rents and be sure of full payment from housing benefit. Local authorities are limited by the offsetting of notional housing revenue surpluses on rent rebate subsidy and, furthermore, by rent capping which limits their ability to increase rents. Private landlords are circumscribed by local reference rents which mean that they might not receive the full rent. They therefore have to reduce rent levels or ask tenants to pay the difference between the rent and housing benefit payments. Their ability to do this will depend on the alternatives available to their tenants.

The first point to make is that many of these distinctions appear to be arbitrary and thus unjustifiable. It is pernicious to treat individuals differently because of their tenure or because of their age. To limit housing benefit to someone aged 19 but not to someone aged 26 is arbitrary and lacking in logic. Likewise, to suggest that restrictions on payments to the under 25 s should only apply to private rented housing is also arbitrary and based on the entirely spurious idea that social housing exists to meet needs, while private renting serves some other purpose. There is no basis for this particular distinction other than prejudice against the private sector.

I would argue that a reformed benefit system should be tenure neutral and therefore support should be made available to owner occupiers. Whilst this would increase the cost, this would be more than offset by my later proposals limiting support to a notional level. The basis of support should be the level of income and not tenure. The criteria for support should be based on household income with no regard to tenure. This also means that the distinction between rent rebates for local authorities, offsetting rents charged, and housing allowances to housing association and private tenants, enabling them to pay the full rent, should be abolished.

The removal of supply side subsidies to social housing will help with this removal of differentials. The ability to charge a lower rent due to subsidised development costs means that the various tenures do not compete equally together. The price mechanism may operate after a fashion in the private sector, where there is some relationship between price and quality. However, supply side subsidies break any link between price and quality in the social sector and allow social landlords to offer better quality dwellings at lower rents. This situation is only further exacerbated by differential tax treatment whereby the income of private landlords is taxed while other landlords and owner occupiers are exempt.[12]

2.10.5 Breaking the link between rents and benefits

One of the key problems of the current benefit system is the manner in which rent levels can chase up housing benefit. This has occurred consistently since the introduction of housing benefit in the early 1980s. The attempts in the 1980s to set maximum rents for benefit purposes merely led to the majority of private landlords setting rents at this maximum. This was a perfectly rational thing for landlords to do as it maximised their income, caused no hardship to their tenants on benefit and allowed them to argue that their rents were reasonable because these levels had some official sanction.

A further problem is that housing benefit, at least until 1996, was based on individual entitlements. It was based on the income of the tenant, who as a result received a payment equal to their eligible rent. The effect of this system was twofold. Firstly, as rent levels did not effect benefit claimants, landlords could increase rents with relative impunity. Thus council rents in the 1990s have considerably exceeded government guideline increases. Secondly, landlords had an incentive to favour housing benefit claimants as tenants as they were guaranteed an income and greater freedom to increase rents than would have been the case had tenants had to fund the increases from their own incomes.

These incentive effects were compounded by the fact that much of housing benefit is paid direct to landlords. As I have discussed above, Council tenants make up 60 per cent of housing benefit recipients (DSS, 1997), none of whom receive benefit directly but rather enjoy rent rebates which offset some or all of their liability for rent. Other landlords can claim payments direct where tenants are more than 8 weeks in arrears, or where the tenant 'voluntarily' agrees to direct payments. Not surprisingly, landlords frequently present the necessary form before tenants at the same time as the tenancy agreement, giving the apparent impression that tenants have little choice but to sign. These practices may appear more efficient from the point of view of government and the landlords themselves, but it merely diminishes the personal responsibility of the tenant and means that, so long as they remain entitled to benefit and periodically reapply for benefit, rent levels are a matter of indifference to tenants.

I believe that a reformed benefit system should attempt to break this producer capture. This can be done by making all payments to applicants and not to their landlords. Landlords should not be able to receive benefit payments direct, but only from their tenants. This would re-establish personal responsibility on the part of the tenant and dramatically reshape the power relations between landlord and tenants. Landlords would have to deal directly with tenants based on their contractual obligation. It would also make rent levels a significant part of that relationship again, in that landlords would have to consider the response of tenants to rent increases rather than merely the limitations of the benefit system (this, of course, would depend on the further reform of basing payments on notional rather than actual housing costs which I discuss below).

The main objection to this proposal is that there is no guarantee that tenants will pay their rent if benefit is paid to them rather than to the landlord. By making direct payments the subsidy is assured of being used for its intended purpose, which is not necessarily the case if tenants are given control over their benefit. I see this argument as an essentially paternalistic one, which assumes that competence is related to tenure. It is based on the premise, discussed in section 2.6, above, that tenants are not competent to determine their own interests and thus should not be trusted to use their income responsibly. However, the outcome of such an assumption, when it is acted upon, is precisely to remove responsibility from individuals and to create the incompetence which is assumed. An essential element of a reformed system of housing supports should be to reinculcate a sense of personal responsibility. Tenants, like owner occupiers, ought to be fully responsible for the consequences of their actions. Landlords have the sanction of eviction for those that do not pay their rent and the certainty of the application of this sanction ought to be sufficient to ensure payment. I therefore do not consider the paternalistic argument anything other than a self-fulfilling one. What is needed is for landlords to accept that tenants should be responsible and are indeed competent to manage their own affairs.

I am aware that there will be some individuals who are not capable of managing their own affairs. However, these are individuals who would normally be in need of specialist support or are in a transitional stage between this support and independent living. I would argue that the focus ought to be primarily one of social care based on clinical decisions which are beyond a landlord's control. These cases are clearly exceptional and identifiable, and thus capable of specialist treatment.

What is important here though is that the proper care of these individuals should not be used as an argument to preserve the general assumption of incapability apparently institutionalised in social housing.

The breaking of the linkage between rent levels and housing benefit is therefore an important requirement. However, the reforms I have discussed above would not be sufficient of themselves to achieve this requirement. What is also needed is the transformation of housing benefit into a notional allowance within a general system of income maintenance.

2.10.6 The end of specific housing subsidies

Housing is treated differently from most other goods and services deemed necessary for the poor. The majority of goods and services are made available to households through income support payments which are based on notional expenditure on certain necessary goods and services (food, clothing, utility bills, transport costs, etc.). Other goods, usually defined as welfare goods, such as health care and education are provided at the point of need and without direct cost to the recipients. Whilst housing has been provided in the form of a welfare good, support for housing costs is now primarily in the form of a specific allowance which, as we have seen above, is frequently paid directly to the landlord. Housing costs for the poor are thus distinct in being covered (partially or totally) by a specific allowance. This might be justified on the grounds of ignorance, in that individual households may be unaware of the benefits of good housing, or because of the expense of housing, in that it is the largest single item in the household budget. However, whatever the reasons might be for the development of separate housing supports, I would suggest that there is no particular reason now why housing should be treated differently from any other necessary good or service. My key proposal with regard to rented housing is therefore that housing benefit be abolished and that it be replaced by a notional element to cover housing costs within income support payments.

This proposal would involve increasing income support payments by a notional amount to assist with housing costs. Such an allowance should be tenure neutral and thus based on costs across all tenures. A simple version of this proposal would be to arrive at a notional level based on national average housing costs and an agreed proportion (say, 90 per cent) which ought to be covered by subsidy. However, even in this most simple of systems, the majority of properties would have to be excluded from the calculation as they would beyond the means on those on moderate to low incomes.[13] A reasonable calculation might be based on current local reference rents for the rented sector and mortgage costs based on Right-to-Buy valuations before discount (along with a notional element for maintenance costs). This would give a benchmark figure upon which to base the initial uprating of income support.

But the main problem with this simplistic scheme would remain: namely, that there are considerable disparities in housing costs across the country. This is a phenomena which does not really apply to anything like the same extent to the other areas of expenditure covered by income support. Thus setting a national average would appear over-generous in some areas and some tenures, while in others households would struggle to find any reasonable accommodation at all. Those taking a robust view of the operation of markets might suggest that over time there will be an adjustment in housing costs as a result of these payments. This is certainly plausible in the rented sectors, especially if there is no longer any differentiation between the treatment of social and private rented housing. The aim should be to ensure that all landlords, be they social or private, compete against each other on a level playing field. If this could be maintained (and it does imply changes to the allocation mechanisms of social landlords), over time, rents would adjust to the levels dictated by the available income of potential tenants. The particular problem here would be the owner occupied market where housing costs would not necessarily fall as they are linked to historic house price values and interest rates. Moreover, prices in the lower value sectors of the market can be affected by changes in other parts of the market. Thus while the rental system might be more of a closed system and thus amenable to changes in internal incentives, this is less so with owner occupation.

For this reason I would suggest that instead of a notional level being set across the country, it would be more sensible to establish a system based on local housing costs. I would suggest that such a modification be only transitional with the clear aim of shifting towards a single national rate. This could be achieved by a damping mechanism with differential increases in income support. However, a target date for the ending of the transitional system should be announced to ensure that the damping mechanism has the necessary effect on incentives and minimises the propensity of households to move to areas of higher housing costs in order to benefit from an apparently more generous level of support.

Kemp (1998) has argued for a system which not only differentiates by area, but also according to tenure on the grounds that rents in the private sector differ from the social rented sector. This is superficially appealing, but would have the effect of creating incentives for and against particular tenures at the local level. It would merely maintain the current inflexibilities between tenures. I would therefore argue against any such attempt to offer different levels of allowance to different tenures.

I see this proposal of incorporating housing costs into income support payments as having several distinct benefits. Firstly, of course, it will assist in the eradication of the producer capture of personal subsidies by landlords. Payments would not only be direct to the tenant, but would also be 'hidden' within a more general allowance. Rents would therefore have to be set according to the ability and preparedness of potential tenants to pay and not on prevailing benefit and subsidy levels. It would thus ensure landlords managed their costs according to the prevailing market conditions, and established a more equal contractual relationship with their tenants. Tenants would no longer be merely a passport to subsidy, but customers deemed able to exercise choice.

Indeed, choice is the second advantage of this scheme. By not tying subsidy to a particular tenure, tenants are given the prospect of choice across all sectors. But also, by incorporating a housing allowance within income support, households would be able to choose how much of their income they wished to commit to housing costs and thus the quality of housing they received. Housing could then properly become one choice of many in terms of how the household used its available income. This would be an improvement on current circumstances where the quality and price of accommodation is largely set by the landlord. Households ought to be able to trade off quality and price and the system proposed here is better able to facilitate this.

Thirdly, there is the important point that households become more aware of the real cost of their housing. This, of course, is an important prerequisite if rational choices between available dwellings are to be made. Payments direct to the landlord ensure that rent levels are a matter of indifference to benefit recipients. Prohibiting the landlord from receiving payments direct would ensure that rent levels were relevant to households. This awareness of cost would serve to prevent 'up-marketing' and allow a more genuine market to develop.

Fourthly, payments direct to households makes it clear that they are responsible for their contractual obligations. They would be directly responsible for making payments to their landlord or mortgage lender and would not be able to pass this responsibility onto an impersonal bureaucracy.

Fifthly, this system of subsidy eradicates the whole issue of tapers and benefit withdrawal which contribute towards the poverty trap by reducing incentives for work. Hence it is a system which can be incorporated much more satisfactorily within mechanisms such as the Working Families Tax Credit, which is likely to be hampered by the effect of the current benefit tapers. Of course, with regard to work incentives more generally, the absolute level of the notional housing allowance would have an effect. Thus this incentive effect will have to be taken into account when setting the notional level.

The proposed system therefore has a number of crucial advantages over the current system and these benefits would only be magnified by the other proposals I have made. I have made no attempt to determine the financial consequences of these proposals. Clearly setting notional levels for the housing allowance gives government more control over total expenditure. However, it does not allow government to control the number of claimants and thus it can only ever estimate expenditure. I would suggest however that these estimates could be made with much greater confidence than can be made at present. My main aim though in this essay has been to discuss the system more in terms of its moral effects. The ability this system would give government to control expenditure is doubtless a boon, but it has not been my principal aim.

These proposals are based on the premise that individuals are competent; that they can be responsible for their own affairs, and consequently ought to be. The aim of welfare benefits should be to instil independence and encourage individuals to take care of themselves. This means that any scheme should be *limited*. Indeed, the attitude of government ought to be to take every legitimate opportunity to reduce its interference in the lives of its citizens. My proposals in this essay seek to show how government could successfully withdraw. Moreover, by encouraging independence the enactment of these proposals would demonstrate the competence of individuals to determine their own ends. It could therefore open up the opportunity for a shift towards more voluntary forms of provision based on mutual aid and charitable organisations.

I am aware that these proposals might appear somewhat pragmatic when set beside the individualist principles with which I began this essay. But as I suggested in section 2.8, above, these principles cannot be achieved other than by consent. If coercion is illegitimate then libertarians cannot seek to impose their political ends on others. We must start from where we are and work within current structures and argue against current orthodoxies. This might mean that our methods differ strictly from our principles. What it does not mean though is that the principles are not worth upholding or are negated. Nor should it mean we ignore the realities of current debates in public and social policy.

The more one considers collectivist arguments for welfare provision the more one is taken by the pessimistic assumptions of human nature which underpin them. A set of beliefs which seeks to liberate humanity from want, merely endorses the belief that individuals are ignorant and incapable. It is, of course, easy to caricature the views of individualists as being hard hearted towards the poor.[14] But this is to misunderstand the tenor of individualist arguments which seek to extend potential and not to circumscribe it. I believe that individuals are competent and capable of responsibility for themselves. But this does not mean they are not co-operative and altruistic. Individuals clearly have a responsibility for others. The problem of collectivist arguments though is the belief that this altruism can be displaced onto the state or the community. However, once this assumption is realised, individuals lose any need to be altruistic and to co-operate, because their responsibility is passed onto others. As Levinas (1969) has stated, we have a responsibility to the Other (be it our neighbour, a homeless person in the shop doorway or a stranger who presents herself before us). This responsibility is a moral absolute, but it is *personal*. We cannot pass it over to a collective body: it cannot be conveniently displaced onto some supervisory organisation acting for us. I believe that social policy should encourage personal responsibility and not seek to denude it by doing what individuals can quite capably do for themselves. This applies just as much to our responsibility to others.

3
Governments and Social Welfare

Michael Oxley

3.1 Introduction

In order to make an essential distinction between my approach and the arguments by King in Chapter 2, the substantive part of this chapter begins with an analysis of the difference between individual and collective decision making. Individual decisions are seen to rely strongly on market processes while collective decisions depend in large measure on the actions of governments. The case for a significant role for collective decisions, which are essential to welfare in a complex society, is set out. It is suggested that the dichotomy posed by a division into market activity and government activity is false and that markets rely on strong government activity. A welfare economics framework, with an emphasis on the concept of market failure, is used to present a rationale for public policy which reacts to the inefficiencies of markets and individual decisions. There is an examination of the connections between housing and specific 'externalities' issues, such as health, education and crime, which, it is argued, can require important reactions by government. In contrast to the rejection of redistribution by King, this chapter argues strongly that redistributional policies are inextricably linked with housing policy. The interactions between the distribution of resources and housing provision are examined and the case for a housing policy with clear redistributive components is set out. Some illustrations of housing policy in practice, based on western European approaches are provided. The changing nature of governments' relationships to housing markets is explored. The counter arguments to King's propositions are summarised and an alternative agenda for housing policy reform is presented.

3.2 Individual and collective decision making

For housing policies to exist, there has, at some point, to have been a decision to take collective as opposed to individual action to influence the provision of housing. Collective action, if driven by rationality, will have some aims, and the instruments to pursue those aims will have been selected with respect to the probability of them achieving the given aims. The decision to take collective action might be seen as a decision by society to take action, or to allow some sort of agent to act on its behalf. Policy implies the possibility of social decision making and beneficial policy requires that the social decision making is, in some respects, better than individual decision making. Since much of the preceding chapter relies on arguments about the supremacy of individual over collective decision making, it will be useful to make the case for social decision making and to examine the limitations of individual decision making. It is important to stress, at this stage, that the case for social decision making is different from the case for collective provision. Thus, to argue for a housing policy based on some decisions taken by, or on behalf of society, is not to argue that society, or an agent of society, should be the owner or the supplier of the housing. There is a case that can be made for social housing, but this is not the same as the case for a housing policy with social objectives. Economists sometimes call individual decision making atomistic decision making. Such decision making involves lots of uncoordinated decisions being taken with a view to enhancing the self-interest of the individual. Without any social controls, such a situation is one of chaos. If chaos prevails, there can be no useful predictions about the outcomes in terms of individual or collective well-being. In a situation of chaos, the lack of order produces arbitrary distributions of rewards and access to resources.

It has been unusual for proponents of political economy to argue for total atomistic decision making, for the resultant chaos is easily predicted and most often disliked. It is more common to argue for a reliance mainly on atomistic decision making with some social decision making. Such a situation was seen by Adam Smith (Smith, 1776) to lead by the intervention of an 'invisible hand' to a state where each individual pursuing self-interest would maximise benefits for the society which was composed of those individuals. However, Smith saw the need for society to decide on the provision of some goods and services. If one accepts a presumption in favour of atomistic decision making because of, say, individuals being the best judge of their own welfare, it is the exceptions to the rule which have to be justified. I will argue in section 3.3 that there are several exceptions to the rule (which, adopting the reasoning of modern welfare economics, provide a case for social decisions) but it is instructive first to challenge the very notion of an absolute division between atomistic and collective decision making.

In economic analysis, atomistic decision making has been preferred and defended by economists who favour a free market approach. Beneficial atomistic decision making is, in fact, seen to be synonymous with a competitive market economy. There is a standard 'proof' that a 'perfectly competitive' market economy will produce an efficient utilisation of resources (Winch, 1971, pp. 77–99). In this competitive state the allocation of all productive resources and all goods and services is predicted to be *Pareto Optimal*. With this optimality there can be no improvement in the well being of any individual without reducing the well being of others. Given the power of this analysis and its influence on twentieth-century policy making in the western world, I will expand on the analysis and the associated caveats in section 3.3. However, for now, the significant point to stress is that markets cannot function efficiently without social decision making.

Markets are social constructs. They are not 'natural phenomena'. They are not, as is often assumed, the example *par excellence* of the operation of individual action. The decision to buy or sell, in a 'free' market, may certainly be taken by an individual, but that individual takes a decision knowing that the action is endorsed by a wider society. In a market it is not physical items which are traded, but rights. These *property rights* are protected by an agency acting on behalf of society. Let us, for the moment, adopt the usual convention of calling this agency the state. The state performs essential property right enforcing, underwriting and protecting roles which allow markets to function. Without the performance of these roles, no one would engage in market exchanges because they would have no certainty of holding on to goods and services acquired through polite exchange processes. Without property right protection, underwriting and enforcement it would be open to anyone to seek to take property from another by the use of force or other methods of persuasion that might prevail in a situation of chaos. It might be argued that the apparatus of the state may not be necessary if individuals realise through enlightened self interest that respect for property rights is mutually beneficial, but the operationalisation of this realisation immediately requires a collective decision and an agent to take and apply this decision.

The question that may be immediately posed is 'can there be markets without the state?'. Relatively unsophisticated markets can exist without complicated rules regarding the definition and protection of property rights. But even in unsophisticated markets it is essential that the right of the individual – who has gained property through a market transaction – to benefit from the property is recognised if trade is to occur. Thus, at least some simple form of collective agreement to recognise these rights is necessary. This agreement requires, at a minimum, a simple form of the state. With more complex markets and more complex property rights, more complex documentation, protection and enforcement of property rights may be necessary.

Property rights in housing which bestow the opportunity to occupy, or to pass to others the opportunity to occupy, must be clearly defined and accepted if markets in rented or owner occupied housing are to exist. The legal payment by one person to another for the right to occupy a house is not simply an agreement between two parties. It is an agreement endorsed by the state and by society and enshrined in a system of law which has been established by collective action. Individuals take advantage of a system of laws which enable markets in housing, and markets in all items, to operate. From time to time laws are changed and property rights are moderated. These changes influence the deals which are struck between individuals in the market. Thus laws which change the security of tenure which a tenant has relative to a landlord will change the rent which each party is willing to accept. If laws have regulated this rent, the state has moderated the market considerably. Many changes in laws and regulations have subtle but very significant effects. A wide range of changes in property rights as a result of building regulations or planning requirements alter the value of the rights and influence what will be paid in the market. If a planning change gives a right to build houses in a field previously only available for growing potatoes, a major change in the price which governs the right to use the field will result.

The current configuration of property rights in housing within any country is not necessarily the result of a careful set of decisions by the state, but the state does need to endorse that which is acceptable. The markets which follow from any configuration of property rights are thus implicitly or explicitly legitimised by the state. Hayek (1967, 1978) claimed that markets are the result of spontaneous processes rather than any particular design or plan. The result however, whether what has gone before is spontaneous or carefully constructed according to deliberate principles, must be endorsed if it is to flourish.

As I have used the term 'state' as an agent of society, I shall use the term 'government' to mean an agent of the state. Without the state's endorsement, protection, enforcement and sometimes alteration of property rights in housing, through the agent of government, there would be no markets in housing. Housing markets, like any markets, are not mystical happenings which are separate from the activities of the state or from governments. They are social constructs which rely on the state. It is therefore wrong to conceive of the state 'interfering' in markets or of governments 'intervening' in markets. This is, however, the language which is frequently used to describe the activities of the state relative to markets. Even economists who support a strong and active participation by governments in housing markets write of the case for 'government intervention' in housing markets (e.g. Barr, 1998; Robinson, 1979). It is not a question of intervention. It is rather one of government activity in relation to markets. Challenging the accepted language is important, for the words that are frequently used describe a separation of markets and the government. This is as if the market has its own territory and government has its different territory elsewhere. Sometimes the language used suggests that the territory of the market is superior to that of government, or that it is legitimate while the territory of government is not. Government is thus seen to 'intervene' in markets or to invade the territory of markets. The dichotomy which this language enforces is completely false. One can no more separate markets and the state than one can separate the heart from the brain and have a healthy body. The nature of the relationship between markets and the state (and which decisions take place atomistically through markets and which decisions are made by governments) is important but there should be no pre-assumed superiority of one sort of decision making over another.

If markets and government inhabit similar and not separate territory, it is not the interference of governments in markets which should be examined and neither should we speak of a boundary between collective and individual decision making. We should, rather, consider how markets function and the relationship between atomistic and collective decision making. It has been claimed that 'The entire history of political thought is riven by the great dichotomy between organicism (holism) and individualism (atomism)' (Bobbio, quoted in Rothstein, 1998, p. 31). The great mistake is to view as a dichotomy that which is a symbiotic relationship.

The mistake is compounded by viewing individual decisions as 'free choice' decisions which inevitably enhance the well being of the individual and are thus always superior to collective decisions, which are viewed as dictatorial or as constraining individual well being. There is very little practical unconstrained free choice in a complex society.

Freedom to do as you will is freedom to drive on the wrong side of the road, to steal and to kill. Constraints are imposed in the interests of others. Individual choices impact on the welfare of other people. The ability to exercise effective choice is also effected by the resources at one's disposal and the information one has. What decisions to leave to the individual, which constraints to try to modify and which decisions to deny the individual are thus the important questions which must be addressed. Individuals are not, in practical terms, in a position to make free unconstrained choices about where they live and what sort of housing they occupy. They make constrained choices. These constraints are sometimes set by governments and almost always by the resources at the individual's disposal. More broadly, the constraints might be seen as the consequences of historical processes, acts of nature, or simply the practical circumstances in which individuals find themselves. Judgements may be made on which of these events or circumstances are of the individual's own making, or are factors for which the individual should take credit or be given blame, but ultimately the options are few. Either individual choice is accepted within the existing constraints, the constraints are modified, or collective decisions are made. It will be argued here that each of these options has merit in different sets of circumstances. Sometimes individual decision making has considerable merits but there are also merits in moderating the constraints and in sometimes taking collective decisions. The arguments can be advanced by considering the issues within the framework of modern welfare economics. This will allow us to pursue more rigorously the issues of atomistic and individual decision making and the success and failures of market processes.

3.3 Welfare economics, governments and housing

Economics is about choice. It is also about well being and satisfaction. At its broadest level, welfare economics is about the use of resources to maximise the well being of society. A succinct definition states that 'Welfare economics is the study of the well being of the members of a society as a group, in so far as it is affected by the decisions and actions of its members and agencies concerning economic variables' (Winch, 1971, p. 13). The economic variables include the factors of production, the goods and services produced from these factors and the distribution of these goods and services and the associated benefits. Welfare economics recognises the significance of the objectives of society as a whole rather than the private objectives of its members. It also recognises that private and public interest can conflict and that some actions make some people better off and others worse off. Whether, on balance, such actions are desirable can only be answered by referring to the interest of society rather than the interests of individuals. Thus, the use of a welfare economics framework might be seen to involve a considerable departure from the position taken by King in chapter two where it is stated that 'I believe there is no social or common interest as such, merely an aggregation of individual interest' (p. 13). However, the departure is dependent partly on definition, for we may simply choose to call the aggregation of individual interest the social interest. If we determine that the social interest is something different from this, because we acknowledge that simply adding individual utility functions ignores the interconnectivity between utility functions, we have the possibility of a social wellbeing which is different from the sum of the wellbeing of those who compose the society. Such a proposition is not complex for it involves simply accepting that one person's decisions may impact negatively or positively on the utility of another.

A policy may be seen as a deliberate course of action designed to improve the welfare of society. For such action there must be objectives. Welfare economists have traditionally sought to make important divisions between what welfare economics can and cannot say about policy objectives. It has been argued that 'It is not possible for economic analysis to determine what the objectives of society ought to be, nor whether a particular social state is better than another. Such questions are the subject matter of moral and political philosophy' (Winch, 1971, pp. 13–14). Welfare economics attempts, according to this perspective, only to advise on the appropriateness of actions to achieve these objectives not on the appropriateness of the objectives themselves. The implied separation between policy objectives and policy instruments can, however, be highly misleading. Suppose that the welfare economist is told that an objective of society is to limit the increases in rents that tenants pay. The recommended course of action might be to control or fix rents. Rent control, as a policy instrument, might however be predicted to lead to unwanted consequences such as shortages of accommodation. By questioning the given objective and asking why rents should be limited, the welfare economist may discover that rent limitations are pre-conceived to be the means to some other end such as 'preventing exploitation' or 'making housing more affordable'. The economist has a role in questioning the objectives as well as prescribing possible instruments. The questioning should lead to a clarification of the objectives as well as a better specification of the instruments. The clarification of objectives and a statement on what the *aims* of policy are is essential to any useful policy debate. If policy aims are agreed, the debate is about the most appropriate methods or instruments to achieve these aims. A political economy approach to housing policy is concerned with debate about both what the aims of housing policy are and what the most appropriate instruments are to achieve these aims. This approach is exemplified in the analysis which follows. It will be important to ultimately disentangle differences of opinion between King and myself on, firstly, the aims of housing policy and, secondly, the instruments of policy.

Barr (1998) makes much of the distinction between aims and methods. It is suggested that 'There is general agreement that the major aims of policy in western societies include *efficiency* in the use of resources; their distribution in accordance with *equity* or justice, and the preservation of *individual freedom*' (Barr, 1998, p. 4; emphasis in original). These aims, it is acknowledged, can be defined in different ways and accorded different weights. The answer to the question, 'What are the *aims* of policy?' is argued to be 'explicitly normative and largely ideological' and is in marked contrast to the question, 'By what *methods* are those aims best achieved?' which 'should be treated not as ideological but as technical – that is it raises a *positive* issue' (Barr, 1998, p. 4). The very example which Barr gives to illustrate his point does however expose the difficulties and the limitations of the aims/methods and normative/positive distinctions. He suggests that the question, 'How much redistribution of income, wealth, power, etc. should there be?' is 'clearly ideological and normative; it is an aims question and so properly the subject of political debate' but 'How should the economy best be run (i.e. the market system, central planning, or a mixed economy)?' – is largely a question of method and a positive issue 'more properly the subject of technical than political discussion' (Barr, 1998, p. 4). However, it will be worth exploring whether redistribution is not an aim in itself but the supposed means to some other end. If, for example, redistribution is predicted to improve housing conditions, an improvement in housing conditions might be the true aim and the connection between redistribution and housing conditions is properly the subject of positive and empirical investigation and not a normative issue to be discussed only in terms of ideology. Likewise, the choice of central planning or a mixed economy will be correctly influenced by ideological stances about degrees of individual decision making which are seen to be compatible with aims of individual freedom, equity and justice as well as positive issues about the efficiency of alternative regimes.

It will thus be necessary not just to separate aims from instruments but to clarify exactly what the aims are, why they are policy aims, and to examine the normative and the positive issues involved in the choice of policy instruments. I will return to these issues and examine the problems involved in closely specifying the aims and instruments of housing policy in section 3.4, but it is instructive first to examine the prescriptions of welfare economics in relation to the all-embracing aim of maximising the welfare of society.

The maximisation of social welfare is conventionally analysed using the framework established by the Italian social scientist Vilfredo Pareto (see, for example, Winch, 1971, pp. 27–71). The analysis is founded on explicit value judgements which state that, firstly, the individual is the best judge of his or her well being or utility; secondly, society can be examined as the sum of the individuals which comprise society; and thirdly, the welfare of society is increased if the utility of one individual can be increased without reducing that of another. When no such increases are possible there is a 'Pareto Optimum'.

When, with given tastes, technology and resources, an economy is organised so that it is not possible to make anyone better off without making someone else worse off there is an efficient allocation of resources. The notion of such an efficient economy or a *Pareto efficient* economy has had much appeal. The relevance of Pareto efficiency is dominated by the link to a competitive economy. A central theorem in welfare economics is that, subject to a number of qualifications, universal perfect competition will result in *Pareto Optimum* (Cullis and Jones, 1998, pp. 1–8).The extent to which this theorem is accepted is of much significance to the type of economic system, and the associated political system, which is supported within a society. It does, in turn, provide the paradigm within which the aims and instruments of housing policy might be formulated.

A perfectly competitive economy is one in which there are markets which are not dominated by the power of specific buyers or sellers, there is perfect information and there is freedom to enter and exit markets. If the conditions necessary for perfect competition hold and there is a competitive and enterprise-driven economy, the argument suggests, there is no need for governments to become involved in the provision of specific goods and services. Production and consumption decisions can be left to individual firms and individual consumers acting in a competitive and self-interested fashion. There is indeed an accordance between the optimality of Pareto and the 'invisible hand' of Adam Smith (Barr, 1998). Each individual will by pursuing self-interest promote economic efficiency and the well being of society if the Pareto and Smith propositions are accepted. The idea that 'market success' results in economic efficiency is a powerful and persuasive notion in promoting the concept and the practice of free market economies with lots of atomistic and minimal collective decision making. Challenging the notion of market success by the development of the concept of 'market failure' is thus central to the case against unfettered individual decision making and the case for some collective decision making.

There is a large literature on market failure (see, for example, Cullis and Jones, 1998) and here only some of the essentials are set out in order to emphasise that individual decision making and competitive markets cannot be relied on to promote an efficient allocation of resources. Some aspects of market failure apply more strongly than others to the production and consumption of housing and it is these aspects which will receive the most attention (for discussions of market failure and planning, including the planning of housing, see Oxley, 1975, and Bramley *et al.*, 1995). Thus the emphasis below is placed on externalities, public goods, merit goods, information problems and the concept of equilibrium.

Externalities exist whenever the decisions of individuals impose costs or bestow benefits on others which are not reflected in market transactions. More formally, 'an externality is said to be present when the utility of an individual depends not only on the goods and services the individual purchases and consumes but also on the activity of some other individual' (Cullis and Jones, 1998, p. 31). Externalities are a wide ranging and pervasive feature of any society. They emphasise the interdependence rather than the independence of individuals. Economists distinguish between technological and pecuniary externalities (Cullis and Jones, 1998, p. 132). The former directly effect utility and production functions whereas the latter take effect through changes in prices and wages. It is the former that are the true market failure in that the market may simply not take account of these effects. Positive externalities bring benefits and negative externalities impose costs. The production and the consumption of housing involves a wide range of positive and negative externalities. Some of these are trivial and some are of the utmost importance to the well being of millions of people. The trivial might amount, for example, to minor disputes between neighbours; the major might involve people affected by epidemics of infectious disease consequent upon the slum conditions of the housing of others.

The production of housing inevitably involves external effects. A poorly constructed house poses a danger not only for the purchaser and occupier but also for the passer by. Governments do not usually allow housing of any standard, as decided by individuals, to be constructed. They do not give individuals the freedom to trade in dangerous buildings. Atomistic decision making is restricted and controlled by laws which limit individual freedom but enhance public safety. The pure external effect is, in this example, compounded by the problem of information. The perfect information requirement of perfect competition cannot realistically be achieved in housing transactions. Information about poor foundations or impending subsidence is easily concealed. Property rights cannot be exchanged efficiently if the property rights are not clearly known. Markets in this case can be helped towards greater efficiency not by governments standing back and relying on individuals to voluntarily provide information and to keep to explicit standards but by them taking positive action. Governments do regulate for minimum standards of construction to improve information and to reduce negative externalities. Financial institutions recognise the information problem by, for example, requiring surveyors' reports on dwellings against which loans are secured. Not all aspects of information deficiencies thus demand government action but when a lack of information puts power in the hands of some at the expense of others, or contributes to an externality problem, governments may decide to act.

The construction of new housing inevitably affects the neighbourhood in which it is built. The potential negative externalities imposed by housing blocking a view or impeding light have long been tackled by planning controls. The positive externalities which well designed and appropriately located housing can provide have similarly been promoted by planning measures. One could elaborate on many examples of housing through its design, location, construction and maintenance bringing positive or negative effects to individuals other than those who decide on the design, location and other matters. Where these effects are significant, governments in virtually all countries, for many years, have concluded that unfettered individual decision making is inappropriate. This does not mean that governments make these housing production decisions themselves. It does mean that they regulate and seek to influence the decisions of individuals.

If it can be demonstrated that housing which has particular attributes in terms of its physical standards, design and location has positive effects on the well being of a wider population than those who inhabit the specific units considered, there is a powerful case for promoting these positive effects. There are three areas in particular that have received attention with respect to these wide positive externality aspects of what we will, for the advantage of shorthand, call 'decent housing'. The three areas are *health, education* and *crime*. The connections between these three areas and decent housing which are relevant for the current discussion are essentially a matter of empirical evidence. That is, the only (hopefully uncontroversial) normative propositions here are that less ill health is better than more, higher educational standards are better than lower standards and less crime is preferable to more crime. The issue to be dealt with by evidence is then whether these phenomena are influenced by housing conditions. I do not intend to review the growing body of empirical work in these areas but rather to make the point that if there are strong cause and effect relationships there are important externalities. These externalities will not be recognised and acted upon in atomistic decision making processes.

The health and housing connection has often been examined in the negative as well as the positive sense. That is, the proposition that poor quality housing causes ill health has been expounded, as has the proposition that good quality housing promotes a healthier population. Slum housing as a breeding ground for disease was a fear of Victorian Britain. The case for government action to improve housing standards was promoted not only, or even mainly, in terms of the benefits to the slum dwellers but to the neighbouring populations who would enjoy the benefits of improved health prospects (Conway, 1999).

There is a wealth of research which links specific illnesses in modern times with housing quality. The connections between poor quality housing and health problems are not necessarily straightforward, as much of the research acknowledges, and a simple uni-causal relationship between a health problem and physical housing conditions may ignore the role of other variables such as income, class and age. However, if an improvement in housing conditions can bring significant improvements in health, the quality of housing becomes not just a private but also a public matter. The nature of the public action that should be taken in the light of this finding is not determined by the finding itself. It does suggest, however, that some collective action will be appropriate if individual decisions result in a housing stock which is of an unacceptably low standard; that is a standard which contributes significantly to health problems. As with the issues of the construction and planning of housing more generally, the issue of setting standards arises. This important issue will be the subject of more discussion in due course. The lowest standards of housing are achieved by homeless people. The links between homelessness and poor health have been well documented:

> Homeless people generally suffer more health problems than the rest of the population. It is common for them to have skin ailments, respiratory infections, traumatic injuries and chronic gastro-intestinal, vascular, dental and neurological disorders. Homeless people are at greater risk of trauma, road traffic accidents and violent crime. Mortality rates are increased at least 3 fold in homeless populations. The life expectancy of a homeless person is 42 years.
>
> (Leicestershire Health Authority, 1999, p. 72)

In relation to housing and education, the first question is again an essentially empirical issue. It is whether an improvement in housing quality can bring about an improvement in educational attainment. The evidence is not as extensive as that for housing and health and the results less clear. A report for Shelter in 1995 claimed that thousands of children's education is undermined by homelessness (Power and Whitty, 1995). It noted the disruption of frequent school moves faced by children in homeless households and the lack of somewhere to do homework for children in bed and breakfast accommodation. It is not a general improvement, in the sense of an increase in the average quality of the aggregate housing stock, which may bring gains but rather changes in the housing circumstances of a selection of the population which may bring about the necessary improvement in welfare. The problem with this approach, more so than with the housing and health connection, is that a naive physical determinism can be substituted for more thoroughgoing analyses of the complex causal factors. One does not need to support crude physical determinism, or to be convinced by comprehensive multi-factorial analyses of the determinants of educational attainment, to accept that some changes in housing circumstances can have some positive effects on educational achievement.

The notion that certain types of crime are more concentrated in some housing areas than others is also well documented. Again, the cause and effect relationships are less easily proved than is the case with health. Much of the literature on housing and crime focuses on 'problem estates'. It is clear, on such estates, that as well as significant levels of certain types of crime there are high incidences of unemployment and low incomes (see, for example, Page, 1993, 1994 and Power and

Tunstall, 1997). The causal effects of these phenomena and the attributes of the housing should ideally be disentangled. There has been a long-running belief amongst some academics that the design of housing has an effect on behaviour and that certain types of crime are more likely with certain forms of housing than others. One does not need to accept the extremes of physical determinism, that can be found in some analyses, (e.g. Coleman, 1985; Newman, 1973) to acknowledge that some housing designs and layout may be more conducive than others to lower rather than higher rates of crime. Given that there might be no specific incentives for private decision makers to opt for the preferable designs, there is a case for public encouragement of such designs. The weakness of individual decision making is thus once more revealed.

The existence of significant externalities makes a case for some sort of public action. The presence of externalities suggests that individual decision making in matters related to the design, construction and maintenance of housing can be inefficient. There is not, however, a necessary case for collective provision that is thus made. It is rather a case for some decisions to be made by some form of government rather than by individuals. The options regarding these decisions will be considered later.

Another part of the armoury of market failure is public goods. Public goods pose a problem for markets and individual decision making because there is no incentive for private decision makers to demand or to supply public goods. Public goods are defined essentially with respect to their technical characteristics. Public goods exhibit three technical characteristics: non-rivalness in consumption, non-excludability and non-rejectability (Barr, 1998, p. 104). A formal definition suggests that a public good is one 'which all enjoy in common in the sense that each individual's consumption leads to no subtraction from any other individual's consumption of that good' (Samuelson, 1954, p. 387). The phenomenon of public goods illustrates the point that markets work well when individual property rights are well defined and enforceable. With public goods they are not. Private profit maximising entrepreneurs are thus not interested in supplying public goods. If when individual A consumes the good, the amount available for individual B is not diminished and it is not possible to provide the good for A without providing it for B, the entrepreneur cannot provide exclusive bundles of the good. There will thus be some difficulty in extracting a payment for a public good. Consumers will have every incentive to conceal rather than reveal their preferences for such goods. Once they are provided all can consume but no one will wish to pay. Like many aspects of welfare economics there is a large literature on public goods. The essence of the technical ramifications and the associated work is summarised in Cullis and Jones (1998, pp. 45–70). There are few practical examples of pure public goods which display all of the technical characteristics set out above. There are, however, many goods which display some of these characteristics. The free market does not necessarily supply optimum amounts of these goods. Such 'quasi-public goods' are, furthermore, often supplied jointly with other private goods.

Housing is not a public good. Dwellings clearly can be supplied exclusively. There is rivalry in consumption, and private property rights in housing are created and traded. Dwellings are, however, usually jointly supplied with quasi-public goods. The consumption and the value of housing is enhanced by the provision of proximate quasi-public goods. For example, most dwellings benefit from access to a road and to street lighting. Roads and street lighting are quasi-public goods. Given that both of these items display some of the attributes of public goods it is unlikely that atomistic market decision making will result in efficient levels of output. There is an opportunity cost involved in production but not in consumption. In order to produce the good for one household it is necessary to produce it for many households. However, the lack of exclusivity in provision will make it difficult to extract individual voluntary payments. Individuals are likely to attempt to be free-riders. The provision of such items therefore tends to rely on public expenditure. There is a tendency for both public finance and public provision. With public and quasi-public goods, the failure of price signals to suggest appropriate levels of output tends also to mean that decisions on how much to produce, and indeed when and where to produce, involve public sector decision making. There is usually, in short, some planning involved which means that decisions are made not at in individual level but at a societal level. It follows, as a practical proposition, that decisions on the provision of quasi-public goods such as roads and street lighting have to be linked to decisions about where and when to construct housing. One could extend the examples of quasi-public goods to include sewerage and drainage and a whole range of physical infrastructure. Thus, although houses are not public or quasi-public goods, their provision is inevitably closely linked to the provision of such goods, and decisions on their production cannot be made efficiently without a linkage to social decisions on the provision of infrastructure. Efficient housing production thus requires a degree of social and collective decision making.

A further cause of market failure, well recognised in welfare economics literature, is the case of merit goods (see, for example, Barr, 1998, pp. 89–90; Cullis and Jones, 1998, pp. 67–8). Acknowledging the existence of merit goods involves suspending the assumption of consumer sovereignty. Thus one accepts that in some circumstances the individual is not the best judge of his or her welfare. In these circumstances there are goods which individuals should consume even though they decide not to consume, or not to consume in quantities which are sufficiently large. Merit goods have been defined in this way: 'If the consumption of a good by the voluntary decisions of individuals, given their incomes, is deemed deficient/excessive not due to the existence of externalities or pricing inefficiency, it is a merit/demerit good' (Ng, 1992, p. 286). To accept a paternalistic stance in which governments know better what is good for them than do individuals involves strong normative assumptions. Whether or not a good is a public good is essentially a technical and positive issue, but whether a good is a merit good is essentially a moral and normative issue. Why should an individual not be the best judge of whether or not to consume a good, and in what circumstances might governments know better than individuals? Two sets of circumstances are sometimes cited. One relates to a lack of information and the other to a lack of competence. Each may require some social action but the nature of the appropriate action will be different in each case. If individuals fail to demand adequate housing because they do not have information that tells them that adequate housing will reduce the likelihood of them suffering from a given illnesses (which we can assume in this instance is not contagious and thus does not involve an external cost) the answer might be to improve the provision of information. If they lack competence because they lack maturity, or have a mental incapacity, or their judgement is impaired by drink or drugs, the impediment is likely to relate to a range of considerations, and not just housing, and the appropriate action is unlikely to involve making only a housing-related decision. When individuals lack competence in the ways described, economic theory has some difficulties in modelling both the nature of the problem and reactions to the problem. This is because of the all-pervading assumption of rational decision making. If individuals are not, for whatever reason, rational decision makers the idea of them making decisions to maximise anyone's utility, be it there own or someone else's, fails to have any value.

If a drug addict fails to see the benefit to him or her of medical treatment, there may be a case for arguing that the treatment is a merit good and that the individual should be encouraged or forced to have such treatment irrespective of personal decisions. The proposition, and what it implies for a denial of individual liberty, is of course highly debatable and not one from which general principles should be derived.

The idea of children as incompetent decision makers is again problematic for economic theory because it implies that they are unable to take rational decisions in their own self-interest. Economists often 'get round' the problem by considering households and not individuals to be the decision makers. Societies tend to ascribe responsibilities for decision making for children to someone else: parents or guardians. Only if they fail to act responsibly does society in a wider sense tend to intervene.

It is unreasonable to treat housing like drug medication or to assume a general lack of responsibility for decision making on behalf of children. It is thus wrong to argue that housing should be treated generally as a merit good. It is equally wrong to argue that housing of some minimum standard is a merit good. This is, however, the stance of several attempts to justify social rather than individual decision making for housing and to argue for promoting individual housing consumption above what it would otherwise be. As Barr states, without explicitly supporting the proposition, there is an argument that 'housing is such an important part of community welfare that individuals should be compelled to consume at least some minimum quantity. This is the merit good argument in its pure form' (Barr, 1998, p. 373).

It may be seen that there is here a degree of agreement between what is argued in by King in Chapter 2 regarding the conclusion that housing cannot be defined as a merit good. However, the important point is that housing cannot appropriately be regarded as a merit good if there is adequate information and the interests of children and other individuals who lack competence are catered for. The analysis does, however, mean that merit good arguments have to be clearly separated from externality and inadequate resources arguments. There is a case on externality grounds for promoting the consumption of decent housing but this is an argument about the benefits to others not the benefit to the consumer in question. There may also be a case for reacting to an inability, rather than the incompetence, of individuals to consume adequate housing. This inability may relate to insufficient resources and is an aspect of an equity rather than an efficiency argument. Equity issues will be examined in relation to redistribution in section 3.4.

Before moving to equity issues, another efficiency issue should be considered. This relates to the concept of equilibrium. The welfare economics theorem which links Pareto efficiency to perfect competition seeks to show that perfectly competitive markets *in equilibrium* produce the desired result (Winch, 1971). Equilibrium is a complex concept. In its *general equilibrium* sense it means that there is simultaneously a balance between demand and supply in the markets for all factors of production and all goods and services. The reality of markets is that there is a constant process of adjustment. This process has consequences for individual utilities which may be positive or negative. One can argue for accepting these consequences as temporary phenomena which are of little lasting significance, or one can see them as serious impediments to the acceptability of market processes. If one takes the latter view, another important challenge to market operations and to their atomistic decision making processes is posed.

Housing markets can adjust towards new equilibria very slowly and with much personal cost. An increase in housing demand because of increased employment opportunities or the sudden influx of population to an area will tend to raise house prices and if the market is at work the increased prices will ultimately bring forth more supply. That is the theoretical position. If there are no barriers to increased housing production, and house building resources are widely available there is no reason to assume that events on the ground will not follow the predictions of the model. But all of this will take time; possibly a long time. In the meantime, some people may pay very high prices for housing and some may go without decent housing. Problems of housing shortages, of slum housing and of homelessness can be viewed as problems of adjustment to equilibrium. If one believes that it is best to let markets work and find their way to new points of equilibrium, one will see in this situation no case for collective action, no case for social action, only a case for waiting for equilibrium. In fact, to do anything other than wait for a new equilibrium can be seen as taking action which impairs the efficient allocation of resources and is thus wasteful.

Taking action which results from impatience with waiting for equilibrium does not mean replacing the atomistic decision making of the market place by collective decision making. It might mean investigation of the causes of the slowness of adjustment to new equilibria and tackling these causes. It might also mean ameliorating the consequences of short-term disequilibrium by some form of compensating action which requires collective decision making.

Housing markets inevitably involve market failures. In particular, housing involves significant externalities and its provision is essentially linked to the provision of quasi-public goods. Add to this the tendency of housing markets to linger in disequilibrium and we have important reasons to doubt the individualistic decision making capacity of housing markets to deliver efficient outcomes. In support of efficiency one may therefore seek alternative arrangements for the provision of housing if these are likely to involve a better utilisation of resources. These alternative arrangements do not necessarily involve collective provision or the suspension of market forces but they do involve a variety of mechanisms which rely on social rather than individual action. The arrangements and mechanisms are considered in subsequent sections.

Just as markets can fail so can governments. There is an extensive and growing literature on government and non-market failure (see, for example, Cullis and Jones, 1998, pp. 352–73; Wolf, 1987). Government production and allocation can be inefficient, and merely replacing markets by governments does not necessarily lead to improvements even if there are considerable market failures. However, governments do not inevitably fail to do better than markets, in some circumstances, and some types of government activity are likely to be better than others. The literature on government failure should no more lead us to believe in the supremacy of the market than the literature on market failure should lead us to believe in the supremacy of governments. Rather, judgements about appropriate activity for each should be made in the light of specific circumstances.

To advocate the pursuit of an efficiency objective is not necessarily to argue for the supremacy of any particular ideological perspective. In fact, Barr (1998, pp. 73–7) argues that efficiency is entirely compatible with several views of society including libertarianism, utilitarianism and socialism. Barr argues that given that an increase in efficiency can raise welfare under many theories of society, 'The aim of efficiency is therefore common to all these ideologies, although the weight attached to it will vary when its achievement conflicts with distributional goals' (Barr, 1998, p. 103).

The action which is taken on efficiency grounds will depend on one's ideological position with respect to the redistribution of resources and the connections which one acknowledges between housing issues and the distribution of resources in society. Views on distribution, and the place of redistributional policies relative to housing policies, are at the centre of political economy of housing arguments and the discussion in the next section will show some important points of departure with the position taken in the previous chapter.

3.4 Redistribution

The market based outcomes in a society organised to achieve Pareto Optimality can include large differences in the utilities accruing to different individuals. Some individuals will have much larger incomes than others and some will be able to consume much more than others. This distribution can be accepted by society or there can be social decision making which is designed to change this distribution. There is no good reason why the given distribution should be accepted as in any way 'correct' or 'natural'. It will be the consequence of an initial endowment of property rights, demands for goods and services and market trading. The process of market trading involves, as set about in section 3.2, the state protecting, enforcing and underwriting property rights. The state thus bears the responsibility for the resultant distributional outcomes. There is nothing sacrosanct about the distribution of incomes or goods and services, nor is there any 'value free' position which can be established with respect to the role of government in relation to distribution. To accept the existing distribution of utility involves a normative presumption in favour of the *status quo*, and a decision to change the status quo involves a normative predisposition against the status quo.

In favour of the *status quo*, it might be argued that individuals have inalienable rights of ownership of what they have and – as long as they have acquired what they have legally – no one, including governments, has any right to tax it away. If this is an absolute position, governments can obtain no taxation and so they have no finance and so they cannot exist. The absolute position is, in short, one which favours chaos. It may also be claimed, as is argued by King in Chapter 2, that individuals create income and wealth and thus individuals are the just recipients of their labours. It is not, however, individuals who create wealth. It is interactions between individuals which create wealth. In isolation individuals cannot trade and they cannot receive incomes which accumulate to become wealth. The creation of incomes and wealth is a social not an individualistic activity. The creation is a consequence of social processes. If the creation is such a consequence, is not the distribution necessarily such a consequence? Individuals have economic resources as a consequence of the property right endowments and the trading activities which society promotes. The maintenance of this society requires government and governments require income. Once the need for governments to raise taxation is accepted, the relevant issues become: how much is to be collected, from whom, and how, and on what are the proceeds to be spent. The actions consequent upon the answers to these question inevitably involve redistribution. The concept of a government which does not redistribute resources is thus an oxymoron. The belief that a government should seek to preserve the distribution resulting from market outcomes is to ascribe to market forces some sort of 'correctness' or 'justice' which they do not have.

Governments sometimes may take action not to improve the efficiency with which resources are allocated but to improve the equity or the fairness with which resources are distributed. An explicit equity objective is a redistributional objective. It is important to state that this has nothing whatsoever to do with equality. Attempting to achieve an equity objective does not involve attempting to achieve an equal distribution of income or of utility. It involves attempting to achieve a distribution which is judged according to specific criteria to be just. Governments might also redistribute resources in an attempt to achieve some other specific objective. Such an objective might be an improvement in the quality of housing occupied by some households.

There are thus at least two sets of relationships between redistributional policies and housing policies. In one, redistributional policies have an equity objective and the execution of the policies has consequences for the consumption and production of housing. In the other, a change in housing circumstances is the objective which can be advanced by a redistribution of resources.

It will be useful to examine the equity and the housing objectives in more detail. The equity objective can be associated with any of the following principles: firstly, maximising utility; secondly, promoting just rewards; or thirdly redressing the consequences of market power.

Utility maximisation and a case for redistribution can be linked simply, following the logic adopted by Pigou (1932), through the principle of diminishing marginal utility. As more of most commodities are consumed, the argument suggests, the additional satisfaction or utility gained from consuming an extra unit falls, even though total utility may continue to increase. At lower levels of consumption, extra units of consumption, or acquisition of a commodity, add more to utility than they subtract at higher levels. The principle has even been applied directly to money. In a crude form it provides not just a defence of, but a positive case for 'Robin Hood' activities which take from the rich and give to the poor. Such a case would be rejected out of hand by strong advocates of a Paretian approach for they would, like Pareto, argue that all interpersonal comparisons of utility should be rejected. Thus utility is seen as a purely introspective concept which cannot in a cardinal sense be measured and compared between individuals (Ng, 1983).

A just rewards approach to redistribution challenges the right to large rewards achieved by some and contrasts this with the lack of justice in the small rewards received by others. The debate here concerns a mix of judgements about what factors do, in practice, determine the income and the resources to which an individual has access and what principles should ideally determine what each individual receives. If one believes that rewards should be determined by, say, effort or needs and not be influenced by, say, inheritance or luck then one may support redistribution to make actual distribution accord more accurately with these principles. Any dispute around this approach then becomes one of the value of the beliefs and the efficiency with which the proposed redistributive methods will achieve a distribution which accords with a stated set of values.

Redistribution can be supported as a means of curbing or counteracting excessive market power. Thus if firms have supernormal profits because of their monopoly power or individuals get very large wages or salaries because their earnings contain a large element of economic rent, there may be a case for taking some of this excess from them. If, indeed, the reward does include economic rent this can be removed without affecting the production of goods and services. Economic rent is, by definition, a payment over and above the reward required to keep a factor of production, be it labour, land or capital, in its current occupation. In a housing development context, this is the essence of the classic case for betterment or economic rent taxes on land which soars in value when it is set for development from, say, agricultural to residential use. If one believes it is wrong for economic rent to be received, this becomes a specific case of the promotion of the just rewards case for redistribution, but one which has particular strength because of its additional support on efficiency grounds. The arguments against redistributive policies which target economic rent are often refuted not on grounds of principle but on grounds of practicality. The major practical limitation is the difficulty of identifying and separating the economic rent element of rewards from the 'transfer earnings' element which is essential to the continuation of a factor in its given use. This difficulty, and the connection with long run equilibrium and efficiency, can be particularly important in housing markets. If, for example, rents rise substantially in an area after demand for housing has risen, how much of the extra rental income is the landlord's transfer income and how much is economic rent? That which is economic rent could usefully be removed from landlords according to the principles enunciated above. However, will such removal be a disincentive to an expansion of housing supply which would be accompanied by the eventual long run removal of the rental surplus? The answer can only be determined empirically. The issue is whether higher rents can, in the particular set of circumstances, produce more supply and how the adjustment to a new equilibrium will come about.

If, because of a desire to promote equity, governments wish to promote a redistribution of resources, the consequences for housing provision depend on the policy instruments which are to be used to promote the redistributional objective. Three broad and distinctive, but not mutually exclusive, policy approaches, each with a set of policy instruments, can be identified.

One approach concentrates on taxation and expenditure and uses income transfers to give more spending power to those on low incomes. It is essentially money which is redistributed and the use of the money is left to the choice of individuals. If more housing consumption is chosen then some improvement in housing conditions may result, but the actual change in housing circumstances in a market framework will depend on the responsiveness of supply to the higher prices which will result from the increased demand. This responsiveness is what economists call the price elasticity of supply. With inelastic supply much of the gain will go, at least in the short run, to housing suppliers and not to housing consumers. Prices will increase without a proportionate increase in supply.

A second approach uses the proceeds of taxation to provide selected goods and services at zero or sub-market prices to those who are deemed to be in need of these commodities. If housing is a selected good, this approach clearly has major consequences for housing provision. Indeed if it is one of the major selected goods, housing provision becomes a significant instrument of redistributive policy. The important questions for discussion in this case are: why should housing become a selected good, how is housing need to be determined, how is housing to be allocated and how efficient is this method of redistribution in kind in achieving an equity aim? These questions in turn relate to a wider debate about the efficacy of money redistribution verses redistribution in kind and in this context they will be debated in section 3.6.

A third approach is potentially more fundamental. It seeks to address this question 'what are the causes of the inequitable distribution of resources?' It then involves prescribing and undertaking action which ameliorates these causes. Thus if, for example, poor educational life chances, a lack of personal power, poor information, discrimination on grounds of gender, race or disability are seen as root causes of inequity, policy instruments which seek to address these issues are adopted. This approach can be seen in a social inclusion approach to poverty reduction which tries to tackle the causes of poverty rather than to simply redistribute income or immediately consumable goods and services. The consequences of this approach for housing provision are contingent upon whether or not housing circumstances are viewed as a cause of social exclusion. If they are, some direct action to improve housing conditions for some households becomes a key part of a 'combatting social exclusion' agenda. If housing provision is not deemed to be such a component of social exclusion, then changes in housing conditions become a less direct and longer term consequence of a reduction in inequity rather than a shorter term instrument of change. The extensive links between housing and social exclusion and the roles which housing providers may play in reducing poverty are examined in Brown and Passmore (1998). They suggest that 'In tackling poverty, social housing organisations must focus on both core and non-core activities. The latter include employment and training initiatives, supporting local community groups, and promoting education projects' (Brown and Passmore, 1998, p. 7). They argue that 'housing organisations cannot ignore the issue of poverty. Traditional core activities such as housing management and development may exacerbate the problems, or they can be used to alleviate potential difficulties. They are not neutral in their effects . . . (and) more radical and innovative approaches can be developed by housing organisations, by acting strategically and involving other bodies, especially local communities' (Brown and Passmore, 1998, p. 9).

If policy makers aim not to improve the overall efficiency in the use of resources in society or to achieve equity in the distribution of resources but rather simply to improve housing conditions, the relationship between housing and redistribution is potentially one where redistribution becomes the means rather than the end of policy. If housing conditions are inadequate, it might be concluded that this is because some households are unable to demand housing of an acceptable standard. If this inability is due to a lack of resources, then resources might be redistributed to those who lack effective demand. The redistribution could take the form of additional income or housing supplied at sub-market prices. In this analysis, a lack of effective demand due to a given distribution of resources is seen to be at the centre of a housing problem which should be resolved. Housing policy should then be orientated towards the resolution of this problem.

This is a view of housing policies which sees a lack of effective demand and the relationship between demand and need as a key concern of policy. Housing need is often poorly understood and ill defined. The term 'housing need' is used in a variety of ways which adds to the confusion. Here the following definition is adopted:

> Housing need may be defined as the quantity of housing that is required to provide accommodation of an agreed minimum standard and above for a population given its size, household composition, age distribution etc., without taking into account the individual household's ability to pay for the housing assigned to it.'
>
> (Robinson, 1979, pp. 56–7)

This is a definition of aggregate housing need. The 'agreed minimum standard' should be such that housing above this standard, which we may call 'decent housing', is the only housing which is acceptable. Decent housing would provide adequate shelter to households and produce no negative externalities, as defined in section 3.3. Individuals have unmet housing need when they are unable to exercise effective demand for decent housing. Effective demand involves a willingness and an ability to purchase. Purchase here could mean to buy or to rent. There is no necessity to ascribe to decent housing the status of 'merit good' for since any lack of effective demand may not be due to individuals failing to recognise the benefits of decent housing but rather a lack of resources. The case for society satisfying housing need is not essentially one of over-riding individual choice in a paternalistic fashion but rather of empowering individuals so they can occupy decent housing irrespective of their ability, but not their desire, to pay for that housing.

Viewed in this way, housing problems are essentially problems of a lack of effective demand for decent housing. Markets work on the basis of effective demand. To have effective demand for decent housing, an individual must have the desire and the ability to acquire such housing. The tenure arrangements are not of any great significance here. It could be an ability to rent or an ability to purchase in the housing market which is under consideration. It will be useful to identify ten types of response which governments might have to the problem of a lack of effective demand for decent housing. Each involves a redistribution of resources but each involves the use of different policy instruments and thus different distributional means and consequences.

3.4.1 Increase household incomes

The first response involves trying to increase effective demand by raising the incomes of selected households or individuals with low demand. This means using some sort of income supplement. With the extra income, individuals may chose to purchase more housing but they may choose not to do so. The extent to which extra income results in extra housing demand depends on the income elasticity of demand for housing. That is, it is a matter of individual choice and preferences for housing compared to other items. The extent to which the extra demand is effective in increasing the supply of decent housing depends on the price elasticity of supply of such housing. Whether or not supply is very responsive, that is elastic, and a large volume of additional decent housing results, is dependent on the conditions in the housing market and the institutional arrangements for organising supply. These institutional arrangements will be considered more fully in section 3.7.

3.4.2 Provide housing vouchers or housing allowances

The second response involves increasing the demand for decent housing by subsidising its consumption. This means tying additional income to the consumption of housing. There are several variants of how this can be done in practice. It could be done by using housing vouchers which can be used to purchase certain types of housing. This was the essence of the section 8 housing allowance programme in the USA, although it is an approach which has not found favour in Europe. (Howenstine, 1986; Oxley, 1998). Here the common variant is the use of some form of housing allowance, like housing benefit in the UK, which meets part of the cost of housing consumption. Some of the benefits of subsidy will, as with the first approach, end up with housing suppliers: how much depends on supply elasticity.

3.4.3 Housing consumption credit support

Given that the majority of house purchase decisions rely on borrowed money, the demand for housing can be raised by making this credit cheaper and/or more easily available. There are a variety of methods by which this might be done. Borrowing costs from private sector institutions can be subsidised, borrowing from such institutions can be guaranteed and thus risk and interest rates reduced, or borrowing could be made available at sub-market rates from public sector providers of finance. If the objective is to only selectively enhance effective demand, the benefits of cheaper finance should be targeted at households with inadequate demand and the arrangements for credit subsidisation and supply orientated to this goal.

3.4.4 Addressing non-financial factors which impede effective demand

It is usual for economists to assume that lack of income is the cause of insufficient demand. The favoured ways for enhancing demand are described in 3.4.1 and 3.4.2 above. In addition, the significance of interest rates is sometimes acknowledged and so the method discussed in 3.4.3 is supported. It is rare in economic analysis for additional personal factors to be recognised as constraints on demand, for their recognition tends to violate the assumption of rational decision makers. However, in practice, individuals may be unable to demand decent housing not because they lack the financial capacity, but because they are constrained by other personal attributes including mental and physical incapacity. It has been suggested that at least 30 per cent of the homeless population suffer from mental illness:

> generally rates of mental illness are twice those of the domiciled population and are of a more severe nature. The rate of alcohol misuse is about 3–5 times higher amongst homeless people. At least a fifth of hostel residents can be expected to have both alcohol related problems and mental illness. Drug misuse is becoming more frequent, particularly amongst younger hostel users. About 1 in 5 homeless people have both a mental illness and a drug problem.
>
> (Leicestershire Health Authority, 1999, p. 72)

Many households fail through ignorance or the complexity of provision to claim financial benefits to which they are entitled. This is a case of not being able to cope with the way a system works. For those who cannot cope with the complexities of housing markets, simply providing them with cash to enhance their effective demand may be inappropriate or insufficient. They may need other help if they are to exercise effective demand.

3.4.5 Subsidise supply without price and allocation conditions

The fifth approach subsidises supply directly, rather than demand. Thus housing suppliers receive incentives to increase supply and to reduce the price of decent housing so enabling more households to afford the commodity and to exercise effective demand. A variety of subsidies which reduce house builders' and landlords' costs are possible in principle. The consequences of this approach are dependent on the effectiveness of the subsidy in reducing the price of decent housing and the reaction of consumers to the lower price. The price elasticity of demand is therefore influential in determining how much more housing will be supplied and the price at which it will be made available to consumers.

3.4.6 Subsidise supply with price and allocation conditions

A sixth approach, like the fifth, subsidises suppliers, be they housing developers or landlords, and encourages them to reduce prices and increase supply. However, rather than leaving the degree of price reduction and the degree of supply increase only to the consequences of market demand and supply, the subsidy is conditional on specified rent levels and production levels. The subsidy can also depend on the personal circumstances, including the income, of those who occupy the housing. Through subsidising supply conditionally governments may influence the allocation of the housing and thus suspend market determined allocation.

3.4.7 State supply with market allocation

Each of the approaches above involves working with market processes and there are still individual consumption decisions. There is individual choice in housing consumption but the constraints on choices are moderated. There is also choice by housing suppliers. They can take the subsidies on offer but they do not have to. A seventh approach rejects reliance on the market and replaces market supply by state supply. This means that the state or an agent of the state becomes directly involved in the supply of housing. In principle this could be state supply of an amount sufficient only to bridge the gap between what households can effectively demand and what they are deemed to need or it could be all of the supply of housing. The state supplied housing will have to be allocated in some way. In principle it could be assigned prices and allocated according to ability to pay. This would, in effect, mean a state supply and a market allocation process. Ability to pay should be enhanced if the net effect of the extra production is lower prices. If effective demand is appropriately expanded through lower prices, housing need will be met.

3.4.8 State supply with non-market allocation criteria

Governments could decide to supply housing directly or to use some sort of agent of the state (a local housing authority?) to supply housing and it could seek to determine the allocation of this housing according to some sort of needs criteria so that ability to pay is not a barrier to access to decent housing. The volume of housing which the state supplies, directly or indirectly, could be either an amount to bridge the gap between market demand and social need or it could be total housing supply if the government determines that it wishes to eliminate private sector production.

3.4.9 Change the definitions of housing need and decent housing

A more cynical approach by government involves trying to change the volume of housing which is needed. This volume is, as the definition of housing need used above makes clear, a function of acceptable standards of housing. What is acceptable and what thereby constitutes decent housing is a matter of public policy determination. Governments may simply try to reduce total need by lowering the standard and may seek to make need correspond more closely, or ultimately to coincide, with market demand and supply.

3.4.10 Use a mixture of approaches

Rather than taking any one of the nine approaches set out above, governments could combine elements of two or more of these approaches to produce some sort of mix of approaches. As will be shown in section 3.5, this is, in reality, what European governments, and indeed most governments throughout the world, have done. Governments in practice do not stand to one side and leave housing entirely to the individual decision making of markets.

The relative merits of the approaches discussed above will be considered further in section 3.5, in the context of what now happens, and in section 3.7, in the context of what might ideally happen in future. It is at this stage worth re-emphasising that governments may take any of these approaches with a housing policy objective in mind, not a redistributional aim, but the consequences of the policy will involve redistribution. In fact, if governments have a housing objective which requires that housing need is satisfied, and there is an inadequate supply of decent housing, they must by means of the approaches above engage in redistribution. As previously argued, if the aim is redistribution, consequences for housing provision will follow. There is, in short, inevitably a very significant set of relationships between housing provision and redistribution.

Some approaches (3.4.1 and 3.4.2) involve, essentially, redistribution in the form of income transfers and others (3.4 and 3.4.8) involve a transfer of goods. The question often posed is: 'which in principle is best, income transfers or transfers in kind?' This is a general question in social policy, but one which has a particular importance for housing policy because it is of relevance to issues such as: 'should there be state provided housing (e.g., council housing) or should there be only extra cash for those in need?' Before examining some of the pros and cons that have been identified in the policy literature it is worth making the point that many housing policy actions (e.g. 3.4.3, 3.4.4 and 3.4.5, above) do not readily fit one of the usually polarised alternatives of cash or housing.

The case for cash transfers rests mainly with the notions of consumer sovereignty and consumer choice. It is argued that if individuals are left to decide how they wish to spend money they can make choices which best promote their welfare and so such transfers are likely to increase utility more than will transfers in kind such as the direct provision of housing (Robinson, 1979, pp. 117–20). Why, if this is correct, should governments ever do anything more than make cash transfers? Why in particular should they get involved in the provision of housing?

It may be desirable to override consumer sovereignty if individuals lack information which may push their preferences in favour of housing and improving information is too costly or too impractical an option. In practice these circumstances are unlikely. More persuasively, consumer sovereignty may not prevail if the recipients of redistributed resources lack the competence to make optimum decisions. Thus if there is a link to 3.4.4 above, provision in kind may be more efficient. Without violating consumer sovereignty, there is an argument for provision in kind if the utility of the provider of the redistribution as well as the recipient is considered. If the provider considers that more housing consumption is better than, say, more alcohol consumption because of the wider benefits to society from more housing, the provider will be happier with housing provided in kind if this reduces the risk of more alcohol consumption being the main result from an income transfer. The provider may therefore gain more satisfaction from a housing transfer of a greater money cost than an income transfer. More taxation spent on housing may be preferred to less spent on income transfers. Recipients may reach higher levels of satisfaction with generous housing transfers than less generous money transfers. As it has been succinctly put, 'Social welfare might be higher with in-kind transfers, despite the absence of any efficiency reasons for public production or allocation, simply because both rich and poor prefer it that way' (Barr, 1998, p. 90).

If the objective of policy is more housing consumption and production, this may be achieved more cheaply with public supply if there is significant inelasticity in the supply of housing. In such circumstances, income transfers which lead consumers to chose more housing consumption may raise house and land prices, provide economic rent to landlords and landowners and provide very little extra housing. There might in specific supply conditions thus be an efficiency reason for public provision. A significant expansion in council housing took place in the UK in the 1950s under a Conservative government largely because public sector production was seen as the most efficient way of quickly reducing a considerable housing shortage. But, it must be stressed, public provision does not necessarily mean public allocation. There are many ways of allocating housing which do take account of need while allowing significant elements of consumer choice. An example from the Netherlands will be considered in section 3.7.

The conclusion from the discussion of money transfers versus in-kind transfers of housing is that while the 'in-kind' arguments are very strong for health and education they are relatively weaker for housing, for housing it is in only in restrictive circumstances that a case can be made for provision in kind on either efficiency or equity grounds. There is thus a selective, and important, but not a general case for redistribution in the form of housing.

An additional question of principle regarding distribution is 'does it have to be government which organises the redistribution or could it be done by individuals?' Government redistribution can be seen as compulsory and individual redistribution as voluntary. It may not have to be government in the sense of *the* central government which does the redistributing but there are many benefits of the redistributive process being socially organised and compulsory. The elementary point is that if there is a redistributive goal, or a housing aim requires redistribution, the redistribution may simply not occur if left to the chances of voluntary effort. An aim can be too important to be left to the risks and vagaries of voluntary giving. Voluntary effort may be noble and well meaning and achieve much if all donors give in adequate amounts, but if they do not, the problem of inadequate resources at the disposal of others remains. Potential donors, who face no penalty for not contributing, may be tempted to be free riders and not give, expecting that others will carry the burden for them. If decent housing is important enough a goal it is too important to be left to the risks of charity.

Empirically, there are clear links in the UK between poor housing conditions and low incomes. A report published by the Joseph Rowntree Foundation compared the connections in 1974 and 1990 and suggested that 'housing conditions have improved for all income groups, but remain worse for those with low incomes' (Hills, 1997, p. 68). It was found that low income households were more likely to lack basic amenities and to live in over-crowded conditions. Improving the quality of housing consumed by those on low incomes should be an aim of housing policy.

3.5 Housing policies in practice

Western European housing policies were geared in the aftermath of the Second World War to reducing housing shortages. Housing production was clearly an aim of policy in most countries in the 1950s and 1960s. Social housing systems developed in response to shortages. It has been argued that:

> The social housing systems that were developed in the 1950s and 1960s have some common features. First, social housing was seen primarily as a construction rather than a management responsibility. Secondly, policy was mainly concerned with the number of units built; quality and variety were minor issues. Thirdly, the development perspective focussed on housing estates. Little attention was devoted to the residential environment or any linkages with the local economy, the local community or existing amenities. Last but not least, the market did not come into the picture. Social housing was predominantly a matter of bureaucratic planning and allocation processes . . . (and) . . . there was a general tendency to finance and subsidise property rather than give direct support to individual households who need help in paying their housing bills.
>
> (Priemus and Dieleman, 1999, pp. 624–6)

Subsequent developments put increasing emphasis on improving the quality of the stock and on improving the distribution of subsides so that they were 'better targeted'. In the 1990s most governments have tried to reduce public expenditure on housing in the light of improving housing conditions and budgetary pressures related to the control of inflation and compliance with European Monetary System convergence criteria. There is growing evidence of increased concern with allocation processes and the need to make these more responsive to consumer preferences. This is an area where new initiatives are required in the UK if social housing is to both contribute to a continuing inability of some households to occupy decent housing and is to be fully utilised.

There are wide differences between countries in institutional arrangements and housing subsidy systems but the governments of all European Union countries have adopted and continue to apply, even in times of strict public expenditure constraints, much influence on the provision of housing. In no country has a free market approach with much reliance on individual determination in the demand and supply of housing been allowed to prevail. It will be useful to refer again to the methods of redistributing resources, identified in 3.4, and consider the applications in practice. Nowhere do we find governments relying on a general increase in household incomes as the means for raising effective housing demand. There are, however, many examples of governments, especially from the 1970s onwards giving considerable emphasis to housing allowances to relieve household budgetary pressure and to support housing demand. There was a decisive switch in favour of housing allowances in a period in which supply subsidies were being reduced and more emphasis was based on market forces. It is important to recognise that the systems in several countries were trying to ameliorate the consequences of rising rents and inconsistent pricing where rents varied widely without any clearer association with housing quality (Oxley, 1987).

Support for the costs of housing consumption has typically taken the from for tax allowances for interest payments. The once very generous mortgage interest tax relief in the UK has now been phased out but variants of this form of subsidy continue in many European countries. As a means of supporting housing demand such measures have been heavily criticised on both efficiency and equity grounds. Large benefits, without appropriately designed systems, can go to those on high incomes. As a means of promoting home ownership, tax exemptions usually fail to target marginal purchasers.

Supply subsidies have most usually been given with conditions attached. Such 'conditional object subsidies' have been a principal means by which social housing has been promoted in western Europe. A significant distinctive feature of the UK is that such subsidies have gone in large measure to support local authority housing and thus large municipal landlords have been the main supplier of social housing. The emphasis in the last two decades, on housing associations as the key social housing developers has not greatly depleted the predominance of local councils as owners of the social rented stock.

In Germany, in contrast, social housing subsidies have been available to a variety of private and public sector landlords who have been prepared to meet rent and allocation criteria. In several countries, including Greece and Spain, social housing subsidies have supported owner occupation not social renting. An article entitled, 'General trends in financing social housing in Spain' (Pareja Eastaway and San Martin, 1999) is entirely about specific forms of subsidised home ownership. It is shown that, 'One of the characteristics of social housing programmes in Spain is that they have historically encouraged the buying of a house as a means to get access to housing' (Pareja Eastaway and San Martin, 1999, p. 710).

Supply subsidies have generally declined in importance relative to demand subsidies largely as a reaction to changing perceptions of the housing problem which is being addressed. The more housing has been seen as a problem of distribution and low incomes, rather than as a problem of production, the more has been the emphasis on housing allowances and the less has been the emphasis on object subsidies. It has been shown that in western Europe 'There has been rapid growth in targeted assistance in the form of housing allowances and housing benefits since about 1980. That development entails a dramatic shift away from property subsidies towards income linked subsidies' (Priemus and Dieleman, 1999, p. 627). However, this has been seen to have serious drawbacks 'First and foremost, housing allowances have much less impact on the supply side of the residential construction market and the housing market. If the main goal is to mobilise the supply, property subsidies would be more effective than housing allowances' (Priemus and Dieleman, 1999, p. 627). In the light of this, support for housing supply is still important in several countries and is likely to remain so as long as there is a lack of confidence in the ability of consumer subsidies to fully deliver affordable housing of an acceptable quality. Governments have thus in practice tended to rely on a variety of approaches which redistribute resources through subsidising both housing producers and consumers.

The European Union has no direct responsibility for housing provision. There cannot, according to the principle of 'subsidiarity', be a European housing policy and responsibility for housing issues rests with the member states. There is thus supposed to be no European housing expenditure and the only budgets for housing should be national, regional or local.

However, where housing investment, which improves the quality and quantity of the housing stock, also promotes economic growth, urban regeneration and increased prosperity, there is no reason why such support should not, in selective cases, come from EU funds. This would not amount to abandoning the principle of subsidiarity but it would amount to a pragmatic recognition of the very significant links between housing investment and wider aspects of well-being. This would, however, require a change in the rules regarding EU finances (Stephens, 1999) and the probability is that there will continue to be no explicitly European housing budget and national government will continue to bear the responsibility for housing issues. The actions which national governments take and the degrees of freedom they give to individual choice in housing matters will continue to be significant policy issues.

National policy actions have involved the range of redistributive options set out in section 3.4. Support for housing demand, relative to housing supply has increased in recent decades and the emphasis has been on the financial rather than the non-financial impediments to effective demand identified in section 3.4. Supply side subsidies, which have been used as the principal means of supporting the development of social housing, have had more explicit price and allocation conditions attached in countries such as Germany, France and the Netherlands than has been the case in the UK. A greater reliance on direct state provision in the form of local authority housing has also been a distinguishing feature of the UK's institutional arrangements. It is the allocation mechanisms for social housing which are now receiving fresh attention in several countries, including the UK. It is on this issue that the role of individual decision making has particular significance and where further changes can be expected.

3.6 Juxtaposition with Chapter 2

Before engaging in some policy prescription in section 3.7, it will be useful to review the substance of the arguments thus far in this chapter and contrast them with the position taken by King in Chapter 2.

It has been argued that there is a false dichotomy between market processes, with atomistic individual decision making, and governments engaging in social decision making. Rather than being opposing alternatives these two sorts of decision making are necessarily complementary. Without government decision making there can be no markets.

Housing markets, like most markets, work because the property rights traded in the market are protected, underwritten and enforced by governments. It is wrong to conceive of governments intervening in housing markets. Government activity is an essential component of markets. The nature of that activity can in the interests of market efficiency usefully include actions which compensate for market failures. Thus governments become involved, via regulations, in the planning and production of housing. They may also usefully promote the production and consumption of decent housing because of the wide positive externalities arising from decent housing. The nature of government action depends on the purpose of that action. If government action is intended to enhance the demand and supply of decent housing it will necessarily redistribute resources. There is nothing in the propositions advanced in this chapter which would judge such an intention to be in any sense illegitimate. The methods by which governments achieve their housing objectives should be determined by the efficiency of the policy instruments and the acceptability of the trade offs with other policy objectives.

In responding to some of the specific points in Chapter 2, I am not attempting to defend a position that could usefully be defined as collectivist, if collectivist means provision by the state. What exactly is meant by collectivised provision is not entirely clear. Certainly state provision is not a necessary component of a welfare state. The enhancement of individual welfare can be undertaken by many means other than state provision and housing provision can be enhanced by a wide range of social actions. A fundamental difference of approach which I have in comparison with King is that I do not seek to promote any specific beliefs as absolutes which then govern and constrain all subsequent actions. I would thus totally reject such statements as, 'I believe that the liberty of the individual should override all other concerns' and, 'I believe there is no social or common interest as such'. (Ch. 2, p. 13). When one argues about beliefs, one can simply say that the difference of opinion as to what matters is a matter of pragmatism, or see that a given position is held as a sort of act of faith and one has no faith in that position. On these two points, I would take both stances. If individual liberty overrides all other concerns, everything other than individual liberty can be sacrificed and no action which impedes individual liberty can be taken. As a practical matter, constraints on individual liberty are essential if chaos is to be avoided and the constraints imposed on individual liberty can enhance the well being of others. Pursuing a social interest which results in different outcomes from the atomistic decision making which is coincidental with self interest is an essential function of government. Both the competence and the ability of individuals to provide for themselves is argued for by King. I can agree that most people could, arguably, be competent decision makers in that they can be judged to act, within the constraints of their limited resources, in their own best interests. However, this competence has two important limitations, the significance of which is minimised in Chapter 2. Firstly, many do not have such competence because they lack mental attributes, skills and information. Such impediments to competent decision making may be dismissed as not the general rule or as applying only in a minority of cases, but it is necessary to have actions to take account of significant minority cases. Secondly, and quantitatively more significant, the vast majority of persons will be unable to predict, or will not be influenced by, the external costs and benefits of their actions. The external costs and benefits of housing decisions are, as argued in section 3.3, a major reason for rejecting absolute individual liberty and its associated atomistic decision making. The ability of individuals to provide for themselves is, furthermore, limited by the resources at their disposal. These resources are financial and personal. Unless one sees these resources as being endowed to individuals by processes which are absolutely correct according to some higher principle, then any change in these resources may be good or bad depending on the circumstances. I cannot subscribe to the 'correctness' of any such higher principle and thus believe that changes in the resources at individuals' disposal can significantly improve individual and social well being. Changing these resources does not necessarily imply providing individuals with housing. The limitations of the case for provision in kind have been acknowledged in section 3.4. The case for *some* provision in kind will be reexamined in section 3.7.

King has argued (Ch. 2, p. 16) that three assumptions underpin the collectivists' justification for redistribution of income and property. I do not wish, I must again stress, to defend generally collectivised provision, but I do think that redistribution is a necessary and appropriate function of the state. The case for redistribution does not, however, depend on the 'three assumptions' stated in Chapter 2. Thus it does not depend on an assumption of *no enforcement and no confiscation,* nor does it relate to any particular *theory of poverty* and neither is it necessarily related to the objective of *producing equality*. There may be some who would seek to use these grounds but I would not. It will be useful to elaborate on and respond to the validity and significance of each of these assumptions.

The notion that redistribution involves illegitimate enforcement and confiscation is linked to the proposition that there is no national income, only individual income. Individual income, it is argued, is generated by production. The acceptability of transferring 'goods and services away from those who have produced them regardless of their consent' is challenged (Ch. 2, p. 18) and it is suggested that all income is individual income: 'It is not therefore legitimate to redistribute this income according some alternative notion of justice than that which has been arrived at by the process of production' (Ch. 2, p. 19).

There are several strands to the counter argument. First, goods and services are not produced by individuals acting in isolation. Individuals cannot produce income and wealth on their own. It is the processes of interaction with others which produces income and wealth. Individuals do not determine their own rewards. In a market economy, the rewards which individuals obtain as factors of production are dependent not just on what goes into the productive process but also the demands for the products. Producers cannot control these demands. Individuals combine with others to produce, and the share of the proceeds which 'belong' to some individuals in this productive process and what 'belongs' to others is not something which can be determined by the application of absolutist principles. Individuals are, of course, not powerless to influence their wages or profits but they do not determine or control them. The determination of rewards is a social not an individual process. Furthermore, both production and exchange influence what individuals receive and each is dependent on a given distribution of property rights. As argued in section 3.2, markets work through the exchange of property rights. Why should one accept that the prevailing distribution and configuration of property rights is in any sense 'correct' and more acceptable or more legitimate than any other? Its only salient factor is that it is what it is. It is the *status quo*. Why is this acceptable? As argued in section 3.2, property rights exist and are tradable as a consequence of social action. Only in a society where property rights are protected by the state is trade worthwhile and only then does production have value. Property rights and the subsequent trading are parts of social processes.

If one rejects any redistribution because what we have is what we have and what we have legitimately earned, one would have to ascribe legitimacy to the *status quo*. There is no good reason to do this, either with respect to 'high' or 'low' incomes. The receipt of large rewards in the form of 'economic rent' (section 3.4) is the consequence of a degree of power which a factor of production has to promote a reward over and above that which is necessary to ensure production. Economic rents are not determined by the actions of the owners of the factors of production. They are socially determined. The farmer who sells his field for housing development and gets a reward five times the agricultural value has not determined this new value and thus secured economic rent on his own. He has done so because he is part of a society which recognises his right to hold the original property rights in the agricultural land and to sell the new property rights in the residential development land. The demand for the housing on the land has not been created by the farmer. It has been socially determined. This is not to say that the farmer has done nothing of value and does not deserve some reward but there is no reason why he should get what he gets, because that is what it is, rather than he should get something else.

Individuals do not receive rewards which they irrevocably 'own'. They obtain socially determined rewards. There is no more a case for arguing that consent is required to change these rewards than there is to argue that individual consent is required for any other actions which governments take on behalf of society. What must be 'legitimate' here is the process by which government has gained and continues to exercise its powers. This is an issue of the nature of the constitution which governs the state. Other than expressing a personal preference for a constitution which involves some form of democracy, I do not intend to go into the ramifications of the options which are possible. What is impossible, from a practical point of view, is obtaining the universal consent of individuals to actions taken by governments. One can thus ascribe to a general principle of the legitimacy of government, and of action within the constitution, but beyond this not to the legitimacy or otherwise of each and every action a government takes depending on 'consent'.

In the context of the discussion of the causes of poverty in Chapter 2, King suggested that an explanation which relies on 'structural causes' suggests that 'the victims of poverty are blameless for the position which they are in'. The rejection of structural explanations can be seen to imply that those in poverty are to blame for their position and that they have the power to alleviate their position. It is not appropriate to respond by debating the merits of a wide range of alternative theories of relative and absolute poverty at length. I do, however, reject simple explanations which are based on seeing poverty as the outcome of either 'individual actions' or of 'structure'. The reasons why some people have less income than others, and by virtue of this are unable to exercise effective demand in the housing market, are many and complex. Generalisations are of limited value. For different people there will be different reasons. It might be possible to identify some reasons as being associated with the structure of the economy and the distribution of power in society, and some with individual attitudes or effort. Individuals have strictly limited powers to influence their own circumstances. This power is, on average, higher under some sets of social arrangements than others.

King has argued in Chapter 2, that in the light of an acceptance of a structuralist view of policy, some measures intended to reduce poverty actually increase poverty because they change individual behaviour in a counterproductive fashion. Some measures, some forms of benefits, do undoubtedly change behaviour. Some policy instruments are designed to change behaviour. If they do not have the desired effect in alleviating poverty because of bad design, the answer is to improve the design, not to conclude that poverty is individually determined and those in poverty are responsible both for their position and the change in that position. Some of the causes of poverty are the consequence of social actions. Society should be responsible for its actions as individuals should be responsible for their actions.

In section 2.5 there is a critique of the argument that income needs to be redistributed because of inequality and that redistribution is related to the aim of equality. Undoubtedly, there are some who do advocate redistribution in order to seek equality, and there are appropriate references in Chapter 2, but I would not seek to advocate an aim of equality, nor do I believe that the notion of equality is central to, or even a necessary part of, the case for redistribution. The case for governments redistributing, I suggest, has three components. Firstly, there is nothing sacrosanct about the *status quo* and therefore no reason for governments to protect it by not redistributing; secondly, an alternative distribution to that currently prevailing may be sought for reasons of equity (not equality!) or social justice; and thirdly, governments wish to alleviate the undesirable consequences of the current distribution.

The first component of the case is enshrined in what has been argued earlier in this section about the determinants of the distribution of rewards. They are a function of property rights which are endowed and protected by a mixture of individual effort, chance, laws and regulations. What is received is a function of social processes which determine the values of commodities and factors. There is no overriding authority which gives legitimacy to this distribution of rewards but no other.

The second component is linked to what has been argued in relation to equity in section 3.3 where equity was argued in terms of maximising utility, promoting just rewards and redressing the consequences of market power. The pursuit of equity can be seen to be compatible with the pursuit of social justice. The analysis of the determination of rewards presented above makes it clear that Hayek's view (Ch. 2, p. 33) that market outcomes within the law cannot be judged to be just or unjust is rejected. However, one can agree with Miller (1976) that a completely general theory of social justice is logically impossible. Miller argues that social justice has three elements: *rights, deserts* and *needs*. Rights could include liberty and equality before the law. Deserts implies that rewards should be in accord with individual contributions and needs implies that there is entitlement to certain commodities. In a pure market economy, justice will be defined in terms of rights and the requital of deserts. A collectivist approach, it is suggested, favours distribution according to need. Miller argues correctly that rights, needs and deserts involve conflicting claims. The relative weights attached to each will vary between societies. No one principle can claim supremacy. One can conceive of a notion of social justice which acknowledges the trade-offs between these elements and involves judgments about the degree of compromise of one that can be accepted to achieve the other.

The most compelling argument for redistribution in relation to housing provision is, however, that redistribution will alleviate some of the undesirable consequences of a lack of resources by some persons. This involves an objective which is difficult to define and to measure with precision. This lack of precision and the difficulty of quantification does not make the redistribution wrong. Not to redistribute but to allow suffering as a consequence of a lack of resources is not a superior position to redistributing.

This is not redistribution for the sake of a distributional curve with a particular shape which is better than others. Redistribution is not the end: it is a means to an end. The end is an improvement in the well being of some people.The improvement requires resources and the resources have to come from somewhere. Who should provide the resources? The answer is those most able to without an unacceptable diminution in their own well being. No abstract and absolute principle determines the degree of enhancement in the welfare of some, or the degree of diminution experienced by others, for there are trade offs involved. There must be some judgement on what trade offs are acceptable to society.

This third aspect of the case for redistribution is a case for a redistribution of resources to promote the effective demand for decent housing where this lack of effective demand is the reason for a disparity between housing demand and housing need. In marked contrast to King's arguments in Chapter 2, redistribution is seen as an essential and inevitable part of an effective housing policy. However, redistribution, whether it be in income or in kind, while it is a *necessary* part of housing policy may not be a *sufficient* policy instrument. This is the case if the impediments to effective demand lie with factors other than income. In other words, there are circumstances in which simply giving people money and telling them to 'go and play the housing market' or giving them a house and saying 'that's it – job done' will not be enough. There are several reasons why such redistribution may be insufficient. First, it will not remove inefficiencies and housing market failures of the sort examined in section 3.3: these will require other measures. Secondly, it will not remove the non-income related impediments to a lack of effective demand. These are the sort of issues usually ignored or underplayed by economists which are mentioned in sub-section 3.4.4 under the heading of *addressing non-financial factors which impede effective demand.* These include personal attributes which make individuals unable to cope with market transactions but also discrimination on grounds of, for example, race, gender or disability which adversely affect their power in the housing market. There is a strong link here to the concept of effective citizenship. Those who lack effective citizenship may lack effective housing demand. The links between welfare, housing and citizenship and the concept of 'differentiated citizenship and housing experience' are examined by Kennet (1998). Differences in access to the rights of citizenship leave some excluded and unable to participate. It is not just income but power and the rights of citizenship which require adjustment according to this thesis. The point is made in the wide context of the connections between housing policy and 'citizenship, choice and control' in Marsh and Mullins (1998).

There is an alternative important perspective here which views individuals not as producers or consumers who are active, or not, in a market but as citizens with rights and obligations. However, it is a perspective which is compatible with seeing some individuals in poor housing not because of a lack of income, but because they have been denied effective access to decent housing by other socially determined processes.

A third major reason why income redistribution will be insufficient is that it will not address the causes of the lack of income. This is where a wider social inclusion policy may be adopted to embrace superior longer term policy instruments. This does not deny the importance of other redistributive measures in the shorter term.

King has argued in Chapter 2 that, 'In place of the notion of equality ... I would seek to put the notion of neutrality at the centre of this debate' and, 'This means being strictly neutral between the interests of citizens, except where individuals are being coerced in some way by others' (Ch. 2, p. 34). Being neutral means accepting the *status quo*. I have already argued why I think this is unacceptable. However, the exception to neutrality which is advanced in the quotation above may be a very important exception. There may be many and diverse ways in which some citizens exercise explicit or implicit coercion over others.

A further point on the disagreements regarding redistribution relates to the ideals proposed in Chapter 2 and the practical proposals for reform. Despite expressing a thoroughgoing dislike for redistribution, the actual reform measures proposed involve subsidies. It is not the abolition of subsidies which is proposed but changes in the design of the housing subsidy system. The details are presented as a sort of interim solution on the way to some other ideal. It is not suggested even in the long-run that all subsidies should be abolished. Subsidies involve redistribution. There is thus a wide gap between the principles propounded by King and the reality of the proposals. If subsides are accepted, so is redistribution and the debate becomes one about an appropriate design of an effective housing policy. I shall return to this in the light of my agenda for change in 3.7.

Two further aspects of the arguments from Chapter 2 are firmly rejected. These are a liking for charitable and voluntary activities, giving them an important role in assisting with social problems, and a preference for local over national activity to influence housing provision.

I reject a strong role for voluntary and charitable contributions mainly on the grounds that they are too uncertain in their generosity and outcome. If redistribution is required to improve access to housing, it is far too important to leave to the vagaries of charity. There should be some certainty that adequate redistribution will occur. This will require the power of government.

If redistribution is to occur at the local level rather than the national it will be less effective and less equitable redistribution for inevitably some localities are richer than others. Redistribution amongst the rich and redistribution amongst the poor, but not between rich and poor, is not much redistribution at all.

3.7 An agenda for change

Policy aims are rarely expressed with any degree of precision. Governments in the UK have used several variations of the broad aim of 'a decent home for all households at a price within their means'. The terms 'decent home' and 'a price within their means' typically go undefined.

Housing policy has sometimes been much narrower than it is now. In Britain in the two decades after the Second World War, it was quite clear that the aim of housing policy was to build more houses. There was an acknowledged housing shortage and political parties tried to outbid each other with their promises of how many houses would be built if they were elected. Housing policy was housing production policy. With an aggregate shortage allegedly eliminated, by 1977, Labour's Green Paper could refer to the need to remove only local and particular housing shortages (DoE, 1977). There has been much tenure bias in UK policy with the idea of promoting home ownership under the slogan of 'a property owning democracy' elevated to a housing policy aim rather than recognised as an ideological aim with no necessary connection to improving housing conditions.

Housing has widened the range of considerations which it encompasses and has become more explicitly attached to other social policy objectives. The Minister for Housing set out in 1998 some 'Principles for a New Housing Policy'. It was more about *what* the government intended to do and *how* than *why* the government was acting. It was, however, made clear that 'housing is at the centre of the Government's social policy. This Governments's housing policy will take more account of broader social impacts and, in particular, will focus on strengthening the family, tackling social exclusion and meeting welfare to work objectives'. There was to be 'a more comprehensive and integrated approach. . . . At the local level this means housing authorities working closely with their partners . . . tenants, residents, people in housing need, businesses, lenders, housing associations, community and voluntary groups and other statutory agencies . . . to develop real, comprehensive housing strategies and the partnerships necessary to put them into practice' (Armstrong, 1998, p. 13). Housing was seen to be about standards: 'We will pay more attention to improving the standard of housing, in new build and in improving conditions in existing housing'. The link, however, to social exclusion is strong and was re-emphasised: 'In line with the Government's approach to social exclusion, we will give priority to changes which help those least able to operate effectively in the housing market, the disadvantaged, homeless people, tenants of the poorest quality homes and other vulnerable people in our communities' (Armstrong, 1998, p. 13).

Housing, in the current government's approach, therefore, contains the instruments of some wider objectives but it also contains its own aims and instruments. Thus housing is used, for example, as a means to achieving more social inclusion. There is nothing new in this. Housing has in the past, when Keynesian economists have had the ear of government, been used as a means to boost the economy and promote economic growth. When housing improvements are promoted as part of urban renewal schemes, the policy aim may be seen to be more 'urban regeneration', with connotations of encouraging local economies, rather than on more explicitly improving housing provision. Physical housing improvements can also be related to an environmental agenda and to conservation and energy saving objectives.

To analyse housing policy objectives more closely it is useful to reconsider a narrower focus. This is a focus which puts an improved enjoyment of good quality housing and a reduction in the consumption of inadequate housing as the central aims of policy. Measurable reductions in homelessness, a fall in the volume of households occupying housing deemed to be unfit or in need of substantial repairs and improvement and an increase in the volume of households occupying adequate housing then become the criteria against which the 'success' of housing policy should be judged. Focusing on such aims makes housing policy less abstract and allows its faults and achievements to be more easily evaluated. This is not to say that there will not be less 'social exclusion' or 'more choice' or an 'improvement in well being' or more 'efficiency' or 'social justice'. These concepts do, however, become part of the context rather than explicit aims. They help to define an environment within which the choice of policy instruments will be made.

The search for appropriate policy instruments then focuses on an analysis of why some people are homeless and why some people occupy inadequate housing. This means reconsidering the formulation of the problem as a lack of effective demand, by some households, for decent housing. The policy aims are then specified as increasing the consumption of decent housing, reducing the consumption of inadequate housing and reducing homelessness. Ten possible responses, in principle, involving different sorts of policy instruments, have been set out in section 3.4 and some statements on the use in practice by European governments have been made in section 3.5. Now there is an attempt to provide some comments on an appropriate mix of instruments that might more effectively achieve the policy aims defined above. I shall divide the instruments into those targeted on the demand side of the problem and those targeted on the supply side.

A lack of effective demand is most usually associated with a lack of income. There is little doubt that those in the worst housing circumstances are on low incomes and that there is a high degree of association, throughout Europe, between low incomes, poor housing and homelessness. In these circumstances, one policy instrument to be used is an appropriately constructed and operated housing allowance system. This should, as advocated by King, be tenure neutral. It should be payable to households in all tenures and should be a function of household income, household size and housing costs. It should promote maximum choice by households in the type, tenure and location of the housing they occupy. Its structure should minimise any 'poverty trap' effects. There is a good case for making a link with notional and not actual housing costs for the reasons given by King in section 2.10. In short, and without debating the details of each point, I am in agreement with some of the changes to the British housing benefit system which are advocated in Chapter 2. The main points to question are the link between the payment of a housing allowance and housing costs and who receives the payment, the consumer or the provider? Whilst the link exists, there is a good case on practical grounds for relating payments to house price indicators. This will avoid the problem of determining housing costs for home owners when some have bigger mortgages than others and some have no mortgages. Given the tenure neutrality objective, one cannot discriminate between home owners' and tenants' costs, and house prices provide an approximate regionally variable indicator. Why have any link at all with housing costs? One reason is that the subsidy is designed to promote housing consumption not consumption generally. The other is that without this link, the allowance would, in practice, be much more generous in low housing cost than in high housing cost locations. The first reason highlights most clearly the individual choice verses promoting housing consumption dilemma. If housing consumption can be promoted effectively through other measures including supply side reforms it might be possible to give preference to maximising the choice as to what the household does with extra income. The acceptability of this notion is, then, contingent on these other measures. Similarly, if other changes eventually bring about large reductions in regional housing cost differentials one can imagine a cogent case being made for the abolition of housing allowances in favour of an income supplement which could be used for any purpose.

While housing allowances, as opposed to general income supplements, remain in place, an important issue is to whom in the rented sector they should be paid to: tenant or landlord. King makes a strong case for payments to tenants to promote individual responsibility and choice. With respect to 'responsibility' there are significant issues to be addressed which confront the difference between the ideal and real situations. Ideally, all tenants would be responsible and use their housing allowance or income-related housing supplements to pay the rent but what should be the reaction to either irresponsibility or to the inability to manage personal finances? If rent arrears grow and evictions follow should the response be that this is the acceptable consequence of handing more responsibility to tenants or should we be more cautious? A good deal of help and advice may be necessary to promote responsibility and much more may be needed to overcome inabilities related to a lack of personal management capacity. The reality may be that a long term shift towards payment to individuals, with much short term continuation of payments direct to landlords, and considerable support and advice in understanding the processes of coping, may be needed for a limited set of households.

The reality of consumer choice in housing is related partly to how the housing is priced and how it is supplied. The pricing of rented housing, especially social rented housing, does not follow consistent principles in the UK. I have shown (Oxley, 1987) that housing allowance systems in western Europe have developed not only as a reaction to low incomes and high rents facing some households but also as a reaction to 'inconsistent pricing' where rents vary arbitrarily as a consequence of historical costs, political decisions and financing oddities. Any change in housing allowances should be linked to addressing the question, 'What should rents represent and how should they be determined?' They are likely to promote individual choice better if they reflect the value that households place on the attributes of dwellings. This means that rents will be higher for popular dwellings and lower for less popular dwellings. In short, consumer demand will have an influence on rents. Reforms which promote this objective would form part of a desirable agenda for change but this does not mean that all rents and all house prices would immediately be determined by unregulated forces or crude demand and supply. Housing pricing reforms for all sectors would need to be related to a major appraisal and transformation of public policy with respect to housing supply.

Providing reformed income related assistance across all sectors, as the main instrument of housing policy, would correctly acknowledge that housing issues are income distribution issues which need to be addressed by redistributive measures. However, the real consequences will depend on the supply of housing. This means both the physical aspects of the housing and the terms on which access is available. It also means the responsiveness of supply to changes in demand.

The objective of decent housing will not be achieved simply by giving people more money, hoping they spend some of it on housing and hoping that the supply-side response to more demand is increases in the quantity and quality of dwellings available. The inability of individuals to express effective demand for decent housing is partly a function of the lack of such housing. Problems of damp, poorly insulated, badly designed and poorly located housing for rent and sale will not disappear because of more individual spending power. Eventually, in a market situation with good information and the impediments to inelasticity removed, this is predicted to happen in equilibrium. The adjustment to equilibrium, as argued in section 3.3, may be long and painful.

The supply side of housing policy should be geared to increasing the quantity and quality of decent housing. It should thus be a housing investment policy and a quality assurance policy. It should be geared to improving the efficiency with which housing is supplied. It should involve using the power of the state to regulate and to encourage. It could involve some limited volume of direct housing provision by the state but this would not be essential. The state's concern should not be limited to a sector called 'social rented housing'.

Some regulations to promote minimum standards in the production and supply of housing already exist through, for example, building and planning controls and public health legislation. There is a case for more action to improve standards in rented housing by the use of improved and strengthened legislation. In an ideal situation, with a more even balance of power between landlord and tenant, one can imagine standards being forced up by poor quality being rejected. In the absence of this situation, landlords of all sorts can usefully be required to supply a product which conforms to basic requirements. Standards should be enforced.

The supply of housing can be promoted by government supporting a variety of housing suppliers. These do not need to be the local authorities or housing associations which have dominated the traditional institutional arrangements for the supply of social rented housing in the UK. There is much that could be learnt from adopting the German approach which treats social housing as a form of finance rather than as a form of tenure. Thus a variety of providers including private sector firms, individuals and non-profit enterprises have been able to receive subsidies in return for complying with quality standards, keeping rents within specific limits and adopting allocation policies which give preference to households with low incomes. There can be housing with a social purpose without social ownership. Variations of this approach can be found in other European countries but the clearest expression is in Germany (Oxley, 1995). This form of provision has, with the complementary use of housing allowances, been adopted in Germany and rationalised using the sort of arguments I have used above:

> Housing markets are in a state of imbalance or at least experience recurring periods of supply deficits. Market power is tilted towards the suppliers of housing services; disadvantaged are those consumers with small resources relative to their consumption needs or those with socially stigmatised traits (minorities, immigrants, etc.). These outcomes of a purely private housing service system seek to correct these equity deficits by giving the disadvantaged consumer groups a 'second chance' through special markets with a subsidised supply, through income supplements designed to improve individual purchasing power, or through other policy instruments. These policies are designed to correct the equity outcomes of private market transactions and server a redistributive purpose.
>
> (Konukiewitz, 1985, p. 185)

The range of social landlords in the UK is expanding with the development of local housing companies and a variety of new registered social landlords but there is a case for further expanding the competition and increasing the variety of housing, and housing suppliers, from which consumers might choose (Oxley, 1999a). Such developments would result in a profile where there was less state owned housing but much housing with a social purpose and it would make the UK's institutional arrangements more like those in several other western European countries (Oxley, 1999b).

Landlords are likely to require some form of subsidy if they are to perform a social purpose. Subsidies may be defined widely to include a variety of mechanisms which reduce the cost of producing or consuming housing below what it otherwise would be (Haffner and Oxley, 1999). Thus support could take the form of tax concessions rather than the direct provision of funds from public expenditure. In the context of UK private landlords, there is one particular form of tax change which would stimulate supply and would put residential landlords more on a par with commercial property investors and, incidentally, make their fiscal arrangements more like those in several European countries. This would involve providing depreciation allowances which reduced landlords' tax bills and increased their rate of return. Landlords would need to sign up to a 'social housing contract' in order to get the concession. The contact would require them to agree to minimum standards and agree to promote specified access policies.

The central supply side issue should be the delivery on an acceptable quantity and quality of housing to meet the preferences of households and to provide housing with positive externality effects. The quality dimension should encompass design, location and, in the case of rented housing, management aspects. If private sector suppliers were able to meet all of these requirements, possibly with the help of some regulation and subsidy from government, better than other landlords, an important question would be, 'why do we need local authorities and housing associations as landlords?' There are two aspects of the response to this question. One, we do not know that private firms could do the job better and secondly 'social' landlords do more than supply 'bricks and mortar' housing and alternative arrangements would have to be judged with respect to the desirability and the ability of landlords to deliver on the wider issues. Taking these issues forward is at least as much an issue of empirical evidence as a matter of principle.

It is clearly wrong to group all social landlords together as a single form of supplier. There is a variety of organisational forms and practices not just between countries but within countries. As forms of non-profit enterprise, we know very little of the motivations and behaviour in practice of UK housing associations. We have 'theories of the firm' and theories of the way that government might work but there is very little theorising on the way that non-profit organisations work. With a lack of empirical information and a lack of theory it is difficult to surmise on the decision making processes of social landlords, the extent to which they exercise degrees of freedom and the extent to which they act as agents of the state. There are likely to be many organisational forms in practice with varying amounts of power exercised in a discretionary fashion by management boards, executives, tenants and regulatory authorities (for a related discussion see Maclennan and More, 1997).

Whatever the organisational form, there are two central decisions that have to be made. These are the production decision and the allocation decision. Efficiency can be promoted by making these decisions responsive to household preferences. Effective means for the expression of preferences should thus be an important part of the institutional arrangements for the supply of housing.

Social housing does not have to be housing which is allocated on the basis only of needs criteria which pay little attention to the type of housing and the locations which consumers desire. The Dutch are experimenting with social housing allocation procedures which give much more weight to personal preferences than is the norm in the UK. The 'Delft Model of Allocation', of which there are in practice many variants that have been developed since it was first used in Delft, involves vacancies in the rented stock being advertised and expressions of interest being registered by interested applicants. There is then an attempt to allocate, taking into account the characteristics of the dwelling and the applicants' preferences. It is a system which has proved popular with municipalities and tenants (Kuelberg, 1997). An allocation unit covers more than single social landlords and does in several instances attempt to match dwellings and households over several municipalities on a regional basis. There is a case for exploring the transferability of variants of the Delft Model to the UK.

Changes in allocation procedures need also to take account of the findings of a Joseph Rowntree Foundation Inquiry which stated that:

> The increasing polarisation of council and housing association housing, combined with the way in which much of it takes the form of large estates, is one of the major causes of the gradual increase in polarisation between areas which is taking place on the ground, with disturbing social consequences. For existing estates, local authorities should review allocations procedures to avoid allocations to a particular estate consisting overwhelmingly of those dependent on benefits. New developments should avoid large estates, and where possible there should be a mix of tenure types to ensure that even if most of the social tenants have low incomes, there are others in the same neighbourhood in different circumstances.
>
> (Joseph Rowntree Foundation, 1995, p. 52)

Alternative forms of provision should be considered. The use of a 'state agent' model has been mooted by Maclennan and More (1997). The model combines market production and state allocation:

> The 'state agent' model leaves the production and pricing of homes and services to market producers. The 'state agent' would then be responsible for securing market vacancies, of an acceptable quality, and matching them to qualified waiting list applicants. Subsidies would then be calculated in relation to household incomes and requirements and be paid directly to the landlord. A contract, for an agreed duration, would govern landlord–tenant relations.
>
> (Maclennan and More, 1997, pp. 540–1)

Maclennan and More suggest that this system could generate market signals and allow subsidies to be well targeted. They acknowledge, however, that in periods of shortage suppliers could extract scarcity rents. One way of tackling this, it is suggested, is to combine 'social agent' and 'not-for-profit' models. The 'social agent' would contract with not-for-profit providers who would be limited in their desire and ability to charge scarcity rents. However, the problem that would remain is efficiency and it is argued that 'the main challenges concern how not-for-profits can be made to behave as efficiently as possible' (Maclennan and More, 1997, p. 541).

Efficiency can be promoted through competition. This competition could be between a variety of housing providers both profit and non-profit making. If these providers are setting rents which reflect consumer preferences these rents also provide the signals for the new production that is required. In such a framework what would be the essential roles of government? Firstly, government would be helping consumers to express their preferences better by means of income related assistance. Secondly, it would through regulation ensure that the quality of supply is sufficient to provide sound, safe shelter. Thirdly, it would through regulation and supply side subsidy ensure that housing was supplied in sufficient quantity and quality combinations to ensure that positive externalities were promoted and negative externalities were avoided.

Would it be possible for this to be achieved without any non-profit suppliers? Ultimately, if regulation and subsidy are adequate, yes. However, one needs to consider all the 'no-bricks and mortar' services which social sector landlords currently provide in the UK. Registered Social Landlords are now involved in a wide range of services including, for example, training through foyers, care with sheltered accommodation, and information dissemination to help tenants get access to services to which they are entitled. One needs also to consider the scope of the activities that registered social landlords contribute to which may be broadly called 'combatting social exclusion' and 'promoting urban regeneration'. The community involvement which these involve may be encouraged in the private sector but it will not necessarily be part of the operating ethos which will prevail amongst profit makers. The value of the externalities implicit in these wider activities points again to the case for a diversity of suppliers.

To stress and elaborate on an important conclusion, access to decent housing requires a supply side response with new measures to promote housing investment. This investment is needed to replace poor quality and unpopular housing in both the rented and owner occupied sectors. It is also desirable in order to promote the positive health, education and possibly crime reduction externalities.

It would take a major change in emphasis in UK housing policy for increased housing investment to be a major policy aim. With such a change, much could be achieved through new financial and institutional arrangements. These would be geared to increasing the rate of return from investing in housing and widening the range of housing suppliers.

Given the economic and political constraints on more direct housing expenditure to support supply side subsidies, emphasis could be put on tax concessions of the sort that have been effective in promoting housing investment in other counties, especially Germany. The specific measures to be considered include depreciation allowances, capital gains tax concessions and changes in tax relief for rental income and operating costs.

Depreciation allowances could allow the initial cost of housing investment to be written off over, say, twenty years. A generous rate in the early years, tapering over time would ease the problem of the 'front end loading' of the costs of housing investment. The allowable initial costs would include any scheme which created new housing from new build and conversions or those which brought about significant improvements in the quality of existing housing. The provision of some form of depreciation allowance for housing would make the UK more like other European countries such as Germany and France and put housing more on a par with other forms of investment in productive assets. Special concessions on capital gains and rental income would go further and give housing an enhanced status compared to other investment activities.

Given the indexing of capital gains tax provisions, any changes for housing would have to be very generous to have a significant effect. Thus more emphasis on net rental income might be more effective. A simple approach which allowed maintenance and management costs as standardised proportions of gross income could be implemented.

The main purpose of these changes would be to enhance the net return from housing investment. These changes should be accompanied by major reforms in the institutional arrangements which govern the division between the private and public rented sectors. The lack of a clear division in some other countries is in marked contrast to the UK. The implication is the creation of privately owned housing organisations with a social purpose. These 'social housing enterprises' would be a new form of rented housing supplier. Taxation privileges would be given in return for agreements which governed the quality of accommodation and the terms on which it was allocated. The operations of such institutions would demonstrate that social housing need not be publically owned nor non-profit.

New housing providers could work alongside housing associations both as developers and suppliers. The development potential of housing associations could be enhanced by learning from the funding arrangements applicable elsewhere. In the Netherlands and France, loans to associations can be underwritten by some sort of guarantee scheme. In both countries, associations pay a premium for insuring their loans. This amounts to a pooling of risks. The Dutch system, with a combination of a Social Rented Sector Guarantee Fund and a Central Social Housing Fund provided the most sophisticated model. Loan guarantees reduce risks to the lender and consequently rates of interest are lower. If such a system was adopted in the UK the state need not act directly as a guarantor, although it could, as in the Netherlands, act as the underwriter of the guarantees funds.

A reduction in land costs could promote more housing investment. If land costs are high because of the premium associated with planning permission, there is a case for extracting some of the 'excess profit' of the landowner. There does, however, need to be sufficient incentive for the developer to supply land for development. This is the problem of taxing economic rent or betterment. The Dutch have the most comprehensive 'solution' in Europe. It involves most housing development land being acquired by municipalities and passed on to developers. This gives them considerable control over prices and surpluses. Such an approach would not be politically acceptable in the UK. It can be argued that in the UK planning agreements and obligations allow local authorities to negotiate away some betterment and use it for low cost housing. A more comprehensive and certain approach is, however, necessary to provide sufficient land at low prices. A tax like Development Land Tax, targeted specifically at increases in value resulting from planning permission could achieve this purpose. Housing investment would be further promoted if the proceeds of the tax were dedicated to housing.

Changes in land taxation could be used to promote more brownfield and less greenfield development. This would be in line with the present government's target of 60 per cent of new housing development on brownfield sites. The positive externalities from such development include environmental and sustainability advantages. Taxation on greenfield sites could be used to promote brownfield developments including conversions of non-residential property into dwellings. There could be different tax rates for different types of development in different locations.

These points on housing development and land supply reforms are given only as illustrations of the sort of measures which could, with a change in demand side measures, bring a fresh approach to both the production and allocation of housing. The product of housing policy, if these demand and supply side reforms were implemented, would be an improvement in the quantity and quality of housing and enhanced access to this housing. It would be a policy based on social action to address social problems but without unnecessary social ownership or restrictive bureaucracy.

4
Limiting the Role of Government

Peter King

4.1 Philosophy and economics

The two previous chapters have shown that there is a considerable gap between my perception of the capabilities and competence of individuals and those of Oxley, who chooses to emphasise the limitation of individual decision making and, in consequence, the need for social decision making. The two chapters have also shown the differences which our respective disciplines can bring to this debate.[1] I have tended to concentrate on the normative issues which underpin social policy and have thus judged policy in what could be broadly seen as moral terms. Oxley, however, has developed a critique of this position using the tools of economic theory and has developed a set of technical efficiency criteria with which to judge policy.

Some could, and doubtless would, argue that this difference in approach has limited the nature of the debate. The fact that we rely on different disciplines to justify our arguments means that we are not really talking to each other at all.

I find such a view deeply troubling, particularly for a field of study such as housing. Housing research does not fit into neat disciplinary boundaries; or rather, the complexity and ubiquity of housing issues does not allow for ready compartmentalisation within traditional disciplines. Housing provision and consumption has economic and political implications, but housing can also be seen as significant in psychological, sociological and architectural terms. No discipline has a monopoly of insights on housing and thus any cross fertilisation of ideas between disciplines is bound to be fruitful.

In terms of this debate the cross fertilisation of ideas allows for what are committed positions to be seen in a new light. I believe that the virtue of an economic critique of a philosophical argument (and hopefully vice versa) is that it opens up the boundaries of the position through tools which are not available within the latter discipline. It forces the political philosopher to face up to the limits of their discipline by presenting the debate in other terms. This is not the same as countering a different political or ideological position (although this is, of course, present in this case as well), but one of extending the debate beyond boundaries – of questioning why one sees an issue in a particular way and not in another which might be equally valid and be equally well grounded in the literature. Oxley's economic argument, therefore, has forced me to question the content of my libertarian argument, but also the very assumptions upon which my argument is based.

But a strong belief in the virtues of a cross disciplinary approach should not be taken as acceptance of the particular validity of Oxley's arguments in Chapter 3. The process of cross fertilisation can go two ways. Indeed, the relationship might well be an unequal one, where one side of the argument has more ground to give and more to learn from the other discipline. Perhaps naturally I believe that Oxley's economic approach has more to learn from my philosophical analysis offered in Chapter 2, both in terms of method and the substantive issues raised. It is not my intention then to concede much ground in this debate, even though I consider Oxley's arguments to be well put and offering a coherent defence of the welfare liberal position.

Before beginning my rejoinder, it might be useful to state what I consider to be the crucial elements of Oxley's argument. This will, I hope, be useful in that it is these points which I intend to focus on. I could, of course, offer another essay of equal length to Chapter 2, answering in detail all of Oxley's points and restating my own position. Space (and the reader's patience) does not allow this, so I have tried to select what I consider to be the important issues, which are often general to the argument, and to try and show their limitations.

Oxley's argument,[2] it seems to me, rests on two crucial elements. Firstly, there is the critique of the atomistic position in decision making which suggests that individuals operate in isolation from others or from any formal constraints determined by institutional arrangements, culture, tradition, and so on. He suggests that my discussion of individual competence is an example of this atomism or ontological individualism (Graham, 1988; Lukes, 1973), which accordingly allows him to criticise me for apparently espousing a distinction between the individual and any social entity. Oxley counters this atomism with a defence of what he calls social decision making, whereby decisions are made by some social entity and presumably grounded in some form of consensus. Allied to his argument is the contention that the division between the market and government is an artificial one in that markets are social constructions. Markets are not natural, but are social constructs and are thus made, at least partially, by government.[3]

Oxley's second key point is that markets fail, leading to a reduction in economic efficiency. He contends that the aim of economic efficiency is consistent with any ideology or set of institutional arrangements. He offers examples of market failure in a housing context concentrating particularly on the existence of externalities. He claims to show that the existence of externalities – which are observable empirically – necessitate government involvement.

Oxley discusses two other subsidiary, but significant matters, namely my apparent acceptance of the *status quo* position with regard to property holding and redistribution (although by this term he most certainly doesn't mean the current pattern of distribution) and my apparent mixing of an absolute moral position against redistribution and specific policy measures which appear to accept a redistribution of resources.

Finally Oxley discusses specific institutional arrangements which, whilst showing a greater dependence on demand side subsidies than is currently the case, are still clearly at odds with the position I have discussed at the end of Chapter 2.

These then are the key points which I need to answer. Partly I would suggest that Oxley's chapter tends to misrepresent my argument – this is particularly so when he relates my position to atomism – but also he offers substantive criticisms which, if proven, would seriously weaken my belief in the competence of individuals to decide for themselves. I therefore need to attend to these criticisms. In doing so I believe that my position will be further clarified, and, one hopes, strengthened.

4.2 Atomism and individualism

My first task is to deal with what I consider to be a serious misunderstanding of my position. However, in doing so, I believe I seriously undermine much of Oxley's argument. In section 3.2 he undertakes a considered critique of what he terms atomistic decision making. This apparently is where each individual makes decisions without regard for anything but their own self-interest. Much of Oxley's argument has merit, and if it were the position I had adopted in Chapter 2 I would indeed have been in serious trouble. Fortunately though I, like my colleague, would not subscribe to an atomistic position.

Political theorists tend to refer to the notion that society consists of nothing more than individuals as *ontological individualism* (Graham, 1988). If correct, this view is consistent with the belief that individuals operate without reference to any entity outside of themselves. Certain libertarians appear to adopt this position, particularly Friedman (1989) and Rothbard (1978). Rothbard consciously adopts what he terms the 'Robinson Crusoe' approach, which suggests that once we have discovered what decisions a rational individual actor will take we have solved the main problems of economic activity. Such a position denies the need for any central co-ordination and is consistent with an anarchist society. However, I am no anarchist, and I would dispute that my position is representative of this atomist view.[4]

I clearly believe, therefore, that the state has a role. However, this role should be a strictly limited one which does not seek to do for individuals what they are able to do for themselves. Moreover, I believe that individuals are capable of doing much for themselves, to the extent that the role of the state with regard to housing, as in other areas, is negligible.[5]

The form of individualism which I adopt does not necessitate the rejection of society. I rather seek to suggest societies are reducible to individuals, and that therefore the interests of individuals should override any so called social interest. My individualism has two distinct elements, one methodological and the other political.

Firstly, to deal with the methodological variety. As Elster (1993) states, methodological individualism is an essentially trivial notion which 'tells us to study the individual human action as the basic building block of aggregate social phenomena (p. 8). He suggests that as a doctrine it has been misunderstood and thus tries to clarify what methodological individualism is by what it is not:

> It implies neither an atomistic perspective (it grants that relations between individuals are not always reducible to their monadic predicates), nor egoism (it is compatible with any specific set of motivations), nor rational choice (here again it is perfectly neutral), nor the innate or 'given' character of desire (it is consistent with the view that desires are shaped by society, that is, by other individuals), nor finally with political individualism (being a methodological doctrine, it is compatible with any political or normative orientation). (p. 7)

It is not then an attempt to suggest that there are only individuals and nothing else, but that society can only be properly understood by reducing it to the elemental building blocks of human action. As Hayek (1948) suggests, 'there is no other way towards an understanding of social phenomena but through our understanding of individual actions directed toward other people guided by their expected behaviour' (p. 6).

The importance of Hayek's definition is that it does not suggest an isolated process, but one where individuals interact with others to try and achieve their ends. As Mises (1966) has stated, humans are fundamentally social beings and socialisation is an evident process, yet 'this process took place in individuals' (p. 43). Social change is due to human action, which of necessity means social interaction within groups whose composition and membership is not of our own choosing.

Of course, this does not mean that human action is not constrained by family, community and nation. However, these constraints are not *a priori* entities, but are themselves the result of past individual action. Society precedes and outlives any one individual, but this says nothing about how a society is determined. That a society outlives any one individual does not imply that society is not the result of individual actions.

But to adhere to methodological individualism is not to suggest that government has, nor should have, no role in the change process. Elster is indeed correct to suggest that methodological individualism is a doctrine which is compatible with any political and normative orientation. However, methodological individualism can be used in an attempt to analyse the role of government, by questioning how a society develops and whether it is therefore amenable to purposive intervention. It raises the relationship between the intentionality of social action and the outcomes which might derive.[6]

The importance of this doctrine is seen when one considers Oxley's argument that markets are social constructs which are not natural entities and which, moreover, do not exist independently of the state.[7] Methodological individualists since Mandeville and Smith in the 18th century have argued that societies have evolved by the uncoordinated actions of individuals. Some of these individuals might have had greater influence than others, but no one individual or act has been determinate. This, of course, means that all social entities, including economic markets, are social constructs. But it is not the case that all social entities have been constructed in a like manner.

Hayek (1978) distinguishes between what he calls constructivist and evolutionary forms of rationality and these can be readily adapted as explanations of the development of social entities. The constructivist argues that all human institutions are the result of human reason and human will. These institutions have been, and can be, constructed to a particular purpose. On the other hand, the evolutionary approach suggests that institutions (and our knowledge of them) grow and develop through individual action and experience, but in an unpredictable and unplanned manner. Instead of institutions being created deliberately they have evolved out of countless human acts and interactions. Quite clearly markets, along with language and common law, have evolved out of human action in an unplanned manner.

It is indeed true that markets have always been regulated (as language has been codified), but this does not mean they have been deliberately created. As Hayek (1960) has argued, it is only through the rule of law that individuals can be sure of the integrity of markets. However, Hayek is referring here to the evolving common law and not to statute law made by government. To suggest that one part of the state – the courts – have a role in protecting the interests and rights of individual is not to imply the wholesale control of markets by government.[8]

Therefore it is indeed proper to say that markets are social constructions, but this does not mean that they have been purposively made. It also should alert one to the difficulties in attempting to 'remake' markets through government action.

There is a further issue with Oxley's discussion of the linkage between markets and government which I need to discuss briefly here. He suggests that it is an error to talk of government intervention in markets as 'They are social constructions which rely on the state' (p. 74). There is therefore no separation between government and markets. There are two points to discuss here. Firstly, Oxley in the rest of his discussion proceeds expressly to insist on such a distinction, in that he is concerned to justify an extensive series of interventions in the market. Why would any justification be necessary if the relationship was as symbiotic as he suggests?

The second point is related but is more substantive. If it is improper to talk of 'government intervention', as it implies a separation between government and the market, are we to infer that the normative question of the level of government involvement is not a real issue either? The level of government intervention varies over time and between countries and this is frequently seen as the overriding consideration upon which all other political and economic questions rest. Oxley appears to want to downgrade this from a normative question of political debate to a semantic and methodological issue where there is no debate once the purported misunderstanding over language has been clarified. I would suggest, however, that the perception that the market and government are separate spheres is not accidental or due to a misunderstanding of social relations. It arises precisely because of the antithetical nature of markets and government action, whereby markets facilitate (however imperfectly) individual choice, whilst governments deal with imperative conditions where choice is deemed inappropriate (Levine, 1995). The separation between markets and government is therefore a key political distinction based on the perceived competence of individuals.

I have been more explicit with my political individualism, having relied on Nozick's classic statement of the sovereignty of individual and the neutrality of the state (Nozick, 1974 and see Chapter 2, pp. 18–19). I see political individualism as being where individuals are seen as being prior to society (Graham, 1988; Lukes, 1973; Macfarlane, 1978). Macfarlane (1978) defines individualism as 'the view that society is constituted of autonomous, equal units, namely separate individuals, and that such individuals are more important, ultimately, than any larger constituent group' (p. 5). It is where one generally assumes individuals are competent and able to determine their own interests and the means of achieving them. But what this position emphatically does not do is to deny the existence of society. It is rather to put the notion of society into its proper place. A society can be viewed as a construction aimed at serving the interests of individuals (Graham, 1988). Its existence can therefore only be justified in so far as it is furthers the self-chosen desires of its members. This is not to suggest, however, that any one individual is able to control a society, nor that it is possible to purposively design a particular type of society (at least not without violating the interests of other free individuals).

An individualist view of society suggests that there can be no interest of a society or social good as such, only the agglomeration of individual goods. Oxley argues that there is a distinction between the social and individual interests and this is because 'simply adding the individual utility functions ignores the interconnectivity between utility functions' (p. 76). Therefore:

> we have the possibility of a social well being which is different from the sum of the well being of those who compose the society. Such a proposition is not complex for it involves simply accepting that one person's decisions may impact negatively or positively on the utility of another. (p. 76)

However, Oxley's summation of social well being is merely the aggregation of these adjusted individual utility functions. So, assuming that utility is at all measurable, an adjusted individual utility function is still an individual one, no more and no less. What Oxley is aggregating is still the sum of individual utility functions. There is no other way of achieving such an aggregate.

My position therefore is not an atomistic one. I do not contend that individuals operate in isolation from others, or that there are not social entities which have a significant affect on individuals. I believe that individuals are competent and capable and this is a presumption which ought to form the basis of policy. Unlike Oxley (p. 72) I do not believe that policy should be made on the basis of exceptions, but on general assumptions about individuals. This is because, as I have already argued in my discussion on Murray, social policy changes behaviour and therefore to assume incompetence and dependency is merely likely to create it.

4.3 What is 'social' decision making?

Having defended the notion of individual decision making, and suggested that the distinction between atomistic and social decision making created by Oxley misrepresents my argument, I now wish to question the concept of social decision making which Oxley places at the centre of his argument.

When Oxley discusses social decision making he appears to be using the term 'social' as an alternate for collective. Indeed, he does refer to collective decisions. However, these notions are not formally defined. He does state that he seeks to use 'the term state as an agent of society' and 'government to mean an agent of the state' (p. 73). This implies that social or collective decision making is that which is made by government. Of course, this connection between society, state and government is not an unproblematic one, even if one accepts the homogeneity of a particular society.

But putting aside again the problem of what constitutes the state, there are three substantive problems with Oxley's conceptualisation of decision making. Firstly, I would suggest that collective and social decision making are not alternates for each other. The notion of the collective connotes a notion of co-operation and sharing. In this case it implies that a decision has been arrived at by a group and is owned by them. However, much of Oxley's argument, particularly when he talks of externalities, is based on the impossibility of perfect information. This, he suggests, means that individuals are not capable of informed decisions which optimise economic efficiency and equity. Yet the same informational requirements would appear to be necessary for collective decision making. Moreover, if the externality argument holds, individuals would not be aware of the benefits of mutual co-operation. Therefore why would they come together? Thus when Oxley talks of collective decision making he is not talking of mutual co-operation, but rather of decisions taken *because of the impossibility of such co-operation.*

The notion of social decision making does not imply ownership and collegiality. I would suggest that the notion can refer to either the means or ends of the decision making process. It might refer to the means by which a decision is taken, in that it is taken by society's representations. But it might refer to the intended end or purpose of the process of decision making. The process has a social end in terms of benefiting society, rather than an individual or group. In both cases, however, there is no implication of a collective end or purpose.

I believe that Oxley is using the term most frequently to refer to the ends of policy. Decisions are taken for the betterment of society, in the belief that any society is greater than the sum of its parts. He is not suggesting that decisions be collective in the sense that they have been consented to by all.

Thus the second substantive issue with regard to social decision making is precisely who takes decisions and on whose behalf. Oxley's notion appears to suggest that decisions are taken on behalf of a society by an elite who somehow or other are endowed with the necessary information and capability to decide on the interests of individual members of that society. Oxley, rightly in my view, suggests that the market has no mystical powers to ensure a particular outcome. However, for his model to operate, it is necessary for apparently supernatural powers to be accessible to an elite capable of making social decisions. If this knowledge is not supernatural one would be interested to know how it is not accessible to ordinary individuals when they are operating in the market.[9]

The third issue with regard to social decision making relates to the basis for an agreement on what is a social means or end. How does this elite of decision makers arrive at an outcome which can be termed social? Is it merely because of the process used and therefore is any decision taken by government a social decision in the same way that any dwelling funded by government subsidy is referred to as social housing? Or is a social decision one based upon the needs, wants and desires of a majority or a sufficient coalition of interests?

The problem with answering these questions is that there is no way outside of the socially determined process itself. Once one accepts the legitimacy of social decision making it becomes the vehicle which filters issues towards itself. It is this social process which determines what might be left to individuals and what is too important. The real problem of this type of argument is that what is seen as social is itself socially determined. Therefore once the principle of social decision making is ceded, there are no practical checks on the growth of this process. Indeed, as the Thatcher and Major governments showed, even the attempt to return decision making and choice back to individuals could only be taken by greater centralisation of resources and decision making (King, 1996).

Oxley's description is thus one where decision making is captured by an elite who take decisions based on the assumption that they are more capable or have more and better information. Oxley justifies this on the grounds that markets fail to operate properly. In particular he concentrates on the issue of externalities as the key fault with reduces the efficiency of market outcomes and thus places a limit on individual decision making. I therefore need now to attend to the issue of externalities. In doing so I also wish to comment on the assertion by Barr (1998), and apparently accepted by Oxley, that the positive technical questions of economic efficiency are applicable with any set of normative political arrangements.

4.4 Externalities: a one-sided view

Not surprisingly, as an economist, Oxley suggests that there are certain technical criteria which can be used to justify social decision making and redistribution. He concurs with Barr (1998), for instance, in stating that there is no necessary connection between an efficiency objective and any particular ideology. Barr defines economic efficiency as being about 'making the best use of limited resources given people's tastes' (1998, p. 70) and suggests, as does Oxley, that the standard techniques of welfare economics can be used to ensure efficiency. Barr argues for the need to separate aims and methods, claiming that aims are normative and reliant on ideological considerations whilst methods are a technical matter. He separates out the questions of, 'how much redistribution we wish' from, 'how should the economy best be run to achieve this'. The first question is a normative one requiring political discussion and resolution, '(b)ut, *once that question has been answered*, the second question is largely one of method (i.e. a positive issue) and more properly the subject of technical than political discussion' (p. 4, author's emphasis). Thus, according to Barr, the choice between market or government solutions to the efficiency question is a matter of technical efficacy dependent on the particular case.

Oxley, quite rightly in my view, shows a degree of scepticism with regard to Barr's division between the normative and the positive. He claims that redistribution might be the means to an end (in this case to improved housing conditions), rather than the end in itself. He is indeed right in seeing that the distinction between aims and methods is blurred. However, he is surely mistaken to suggest that because redistribution is the method rather than the aim it can then be seen as a positive issue itself where 'the connection between redistribution and housing conditions is properly the subject of positive and empirical investigation and not a normative issue to be discussed only in terms of ideology (p. 77). The blurring of aims and methods with regard to redistribution does not imply the supremacy of methods over aims. I would rather claim that the level of redistribution is indeed properly seen as a normative issue, *but that so is the choice of method to achieve that level.* As Oxley himself argues, the state cannot operate without a degree of redistribution through the tax system. One cannot have state provision without redistribution, whereas a predisposition towards markets implies voluntary exchange rather than an enforced reallocation of resources by the state. In welfare policy I would suggest that aims and methods are inseparable and that they are driven – quite properly – by normative considerations. I would therefore see technical arguments such as economic efficiency and externalities as having a justificatory purpose by placing an apparent positive veneer over a particular set of normative assumptions.[10]

But despite Oxley's scepticism towards Barr's artificial division between aims and methods he later relies upon this division and quotes Barr with apparent approval. Indeed Oxley himself states: pursuing 'an efficiency objective is not necessarily to argue for the supremacy of any particular ideological perspective' (p. 88). This quotation is intended to end his discussion on market failure and particularly his claim that externalities are pervasive in housing. Oxley may therefore be sceptical of the division between aims and methods, but not to the extent of discontinuing with it as a strategy.

The notion that externalities need government intervention to ensure a greater level of economic efficiency is central to Oxley's argument. Individual decision making, he argues, leads to externalities because 'the decisions of individuals impose costs or bestow benefits on others which are not reflected in market transactions' (p. 79). He goes on to suggest that '(e)xternalities are a wide ranging and pervasive feature of any society' (p. 79). In particular, Oxley suggests that there are three specific areas where there are 'proven' positive externality effects as a result of what he terms 'decent housing' (p. 81). These areas are health, education and crime. He suggests that, 'The connections between these three areas and decent housing which are relevant to the current discussion are essentially a matter of empirical evidence' (p. 81). Thus Oxley appears to be suggesting that if one can prove that health and education is improved and crime reduced by 'decent housing' government intervention is both efficient and desirable.[11]

Before discussing the issue of externalities in general there is an obvious problem with this argument. Oxley suggests that government intervenes to improve the quality of housing and thereby causes an improvement in health care and education and a reduction in crime. This then can be seen as a rationale for the provision of social housing. However, if this is the case, why then is social housing the locale of current efforts by the Blair government to deal with social exclusion? As Brown and Passmore (1998) state, one of the three targets of the government's Social Exclusion Unit are 'problem housing estates – its prime targets are the worst 1370 *social housing estates* identified by a range of indicators of deprivation . . . (p. 123, my emphasis). Therefore, in what sense has social housing actually offered any remedy to deprivation (which we must assume, along with Brown and Passmore, includes health, education and crime)? Can it not, in fact, equally be said that the social housing provision provided by government has created the very negative externalities its existence is meant to break down? What Oxley therefore has to account for is the *empirical* effect of government intervention. This, of course, does not mean that it might not be possible to derive positive externalities from social housing under different circumstances in the future. It does, however, create a degree of justified scepticism about the role of government and lead one to the conclusion that a reliance on governmental competence necessitates a leap of faith.

However, one can challenge Oxley's position on externalities on more fundamental grounds. In particular, I wish to discuss two counter arguments to the picture drawn by Oxley. Firstly, I wish to suggest that his picture is at best a partial or one-sided view in that, as Coase (1974) has shown, it is a logical necessity that the creation of a positive externality for one person or group can only be achieved by the creation of a negative externality for another. Secondly, I wish to discuss the subjectivist argument propounded by the Austrian School which has consequences for the significance and the measurability of externalities.

According to Coase (1974) what conventional analyses on externalities forget is that the problem is a reciprocal one:

> The traditional approach has tended to obscure the nature of the choice that has to be made. The question is commonly thought of as one in which A inflicts harm on B and what has to be decided is: how much should we restrain A? But this is wrong. We are dealing with a problem of a reciprocal nature. To avoid harm to B would inflict harm on A. (p. 119)

What this suggests is that there are two sides to any discussion on externalities, but the analysis given by Oxley suggests that the only worthy concern is that for the person harmed. The key insight of Coase, however, was to show that the solving of the 'problem' of externalities in reality relates to a weighing up of relative costs. The cost of curing the externality – the cost to A – has to be assessed relative to the benefits of reduced harm to B.

More fundamentally though Coase's argument suggests that the costs of externalities are in fact internalised in that both A and B are capable of assessing the costs of stopping or continuing the harm in question (Boudreaux, 1994). According to Coase, what prevents the proper internalisation of externalities are the transaction costs involved and the restriction on the enforcement of contracts. Hence we have the so called 'Coase theorem' which can be stated, following Friedman (1996) as, '(i)f bargaining were costless, inefficiencies due to market failure could always be eliminated by bargaining among the affected parties' (p. 268). What this means is that '(w)henever bargaining is possible, no government intervention beyond the specification and enforcement of property rights is required to achieve the socially optimal level of economic activities' (Bourdreaux, 1994, p. 179). What is required then to internalise an externality is the possibility of voluntary exchange between the parties involved.

The implication of this argument is that the role for the state is restricted to the proper enforcement of contracts, the restriction of monopoly power and the proper identification of property rights. If rights are invested in those who value the rights most highly (or, otherwise stated, whose harm is the greatest) then the externality can be properly internalised. This position offers a useful rejoinder to Oxley's argument in that it suggests that the problem is not one of a one sided harm inflicted on one party by another, but the proper attribution of property rights (or assessment of the relative level of harm).

However, one might respond to Coase's argument by suggesting that it is limited to those cases where property rights are unambiguous and where transaction costs are not too high. Barr (1998) suggests that there are examples such as air pollution (ambiguous rights) and traffic congestion (high transaction costs due to large numbers involved) which limit the usefulness of Coase's approach and which therefore require intervention. This may be the case (although Bourdreaux, 1994 disputes it), but this objection is not particularly relevant to the example of housing, where the external effects are likely to be individual or, at worst, local. In cases of externalities involving housing, property rights are likely to be unambiguous and the numbers involved not large. Bargaining, subject to proper legal supports and enforcements, is likely to be possible and thus the effects of externalities can be balanced by voluntary action without the need for government action. Indeed, as I discussed in Chapter 2, it is government action favouring one party against another which is likely to prevent efficient bargaining from taking place.

The second key issue with regard to externalities relates to the inability of government to determine the levels of harm externalities cause individuals. As Austrian school thinkers such as Hayek and Mises have shown, government does not have access to the relevant knowledge. This knowledge is rather held by individuals and is essentially a subjective calculation based on an individual's assessment of their own interests. The existence of externalities implies a measurable opportunity cost either to third parties, in the sense of a negative externality, or to the particular decision maker in the case of a positive externality (in the sense of a charge for use which it is not possible to collect). However, if decisions are made on the basis of subjective criteria, these costs can never be assessed by an outside observer (Rothbard, 1970; Shand, 1990). Thus 'any attempt to assess costs is hypothetical and depends on the judgement of some outside observer' (Shand, 1990, p. 189). Moreover, 'social cost-benefit analysis imputes values that individuals have not expressed in practice in the market: it produces calculations that are hypothetical and of interest only to economists' (Shand, 1990, p. 189). Therefore costs and benefits can only be properly assessed by the individuals themselves, and thus attempts to derive the social cost and benefit are external assessments which may bear no explicit relation to the aggregate harm or benefit which accrues from a particular distribution of assets.

This subjectivist argument leads to the same conclusion as Coase's theorem. We can agree that externalities exist, but they cannot be calculated as an aggregated notion. Moreover, it is only meaningful to discuss the concept in relation to the subjective desires and preferences of subjective agents. The role of government may therefore be limited to the maintenance of a requisite system of enforcement and redress whereby individuals can seek to define and enforce their property rights. To reiterate, the way to internalise an externality is to ensure reciprocity with regard to the enforcement of property rights. An individual has to have adequate means of redress if their property rights are violated and the violator should be aware they are unlikely to escape sanction. Indeed Schmidtz (1991) suggests that reciprocity is a moral norm which forms the basis of cooperation. According to Ridley (1996), reciprocity works best were we can actively discriminate and build up trust. It is thus where relations are localised and devolved to the extent that we can impose sanctions on others and build up trust through interrelationships. This is eminently possible with housing.

4.5 Redistribution and the *status quo*?

The issue of redistribution is obviously a key difference between the two arguments presented by Oxley and myself. I suggested in my initial argument that the issue of distribution is settled by production, in that if ownership has been derived legitimately there are no other legitimate grounds (other than voluntary transfer) for the redistribution of resources. Oxley picks on two issues with regard to this. Firstly, he questions whether one should accept outcomes merely because they represent a particular set of property rights. He wishes to know what makes the *status quo* acceptable. Secondly, he criticises me for rejecting a redistributionist position and then discussing specific institutional arrangements which presuppose a level of redistribution. I shall deal with the second issue in the next section and concentrate here on the issue of redistribution and the *status quo*.

The key difference between Oxley and myself is that he sees distribution in terms of outcomes, whilst my position is more concerned with process. Oxley adopts the consequentialist position of economic theory and judges policy (and my normative arguments) on the grounds of efficiency and equity criteria. Policy and principles are to be judged according to their instrumental effect. This allows for a more sanguine attitude to be taken with regards to the means of achieving an outcome. The property of some can be legitimately used by the state because of the 'improved' situation which derives from doing so in terms of greater equity or economic efficiency.

However, as I have shown in section 2.5, this is only one perspective on equity. An alternative view is to see equity in terms of the manner in which the state treats its citizens. Or, put another way, it is where the state operates neutrally towards every member of society. This means that instead of outcomes being central we should look at means and processes.

Oxley argues that 'the determination of rewards is a social not an individual process' (p. 107), but this does not mean that once those rewards have been arrived at they can be arbitrarily changed. Nor does it place any limits to the ownership of those rewards. So long as outcomes have been arrived at by non coercive and voluntary means – which means by legitimate means – they can be justified, and this remains the case regardless of the particular distributional effects. The prevailing configuration of property rights are in this sense not, as Oxley puts it, 'correct' (p. 107), but legitimate and any argument seeking to justify a move away from these arrangements would have to suggest why they can be legitimately changed.

This is not the same as arguing though that any form of redistribution is illegitimate. It rather suggests that redistribution is legitimate when it has been actively (and individually) consented to. On these terms redistribution does not violate the rights of individuals. I will return to the issue of redistribution in section 4.6, below.

By adopting an outcome-based position Oxley is led into questioning why I would choose one particular configuration of property rights rather than another. But when one sees the issue of distribution and property rights in terms of a process it becomes clear that one accepts a particular configuration because of how it has been derived. It is when the process is just that matters here and whether that leads to a more or less equitable outcome according to Oxley's view is subsidiary to it.[12]

What I am clearly not accepting though is the current *status quo*. Indeed, Oxley's argument, with its support for enforced redistribution and state provision is more representative of the current configuration of property rights and the mechanisms which control and limit them. I had rather believed that my argument represented a somewhat radical departure from the *status quo*, which I see as dominated by collectivist thinking and by an over-reliance on social notions to the exclusion of individual rights and choice. I am advocating a radical shift away from the *status quo*, while Oxley is considerably more accommodating towards it.

4.6 Philosophical absolutes and pragmatic policy

There is always a difficulty when one tries to relate a normative position to pragmatic policy positions. It is appealing to state one's normative position in clear and perhaps even absolute terms in order to achieve maximum clarity and to adequately juxtapose them with other equally stridently stated positions. However, when one comes to discussing policy proposals which derive out of this normative position, it quickly becomes apparent that the absoluteness of one's position has to be tempered by more pragmatic considerations relating to actual existing institutions, practices and expectations. In this sense, Oxley is quite correct to criticise Chapter 2 for apparently 'expressing a thoroughgoing dislike for redistribution', while 'the actual reform measures proposed involve subsidies' (p. 112). I hope that I have dealt with my views on redistribution in section 4.5, above. Here, however, I wish to discuss the relationship between my apparent moral absolutism and the pragmatism of my position with regard to housing subsidies. In addition I will seek to suggest that, despite Oxley's avowed pragmatism, he too adopts an absolutist position in his use of economic efficiency criteria.

As I suggested in the opening section of my initial chapter, normative statements are prescriptive in that they are concerned with what we ought or should do. These statements can be given law like status, but in any case will be stated as imperatives, for example, 'thou shalt not kill'. However, being a law or a moral imperative does not ensure its adherence. Normative principles are perhaps properly seen as *ideals* which we should seek to attain, but which we might not. However, they form the basis for individual and group behaviour and social norms. Most moral codes are broken – 'Thou shalt not kill' does not prevent murder – but this does not mean it becomes invalid as a law by which we seek to judge behaviour and action. Indeed, the purpose of the law or moral imperative is precisely because we know that acts like murder do indeed occur. In this case the moral law makes murder less likely because of the sanctions which flow from the general acceptance of the prescription.

One does not judge a moral law proscribing killing because of its effectiveness in preventing murder, but because of one's belief in the sanctity of life and the need to ensure a sense of moral order in which that sanctity is respected. Likewise, a normative statement on redistribution should be judged not on the level of its attainment, but on the basis upon which that statement is justified.

The role of normative absolutes then is not merely to control behaviour, but as means of adjudicating on actions. Moral absolutes allow us to judge actions by criteria which are generally accepted and which form part of the structure of social norms within a given society. These norms might change, and thus what are deemed to be moral absolutes might change, but at any one time they form the basis for moral judgements about the acceptability of certain types of behaviour.[13]

I would suggest, in answer to Oxley's criticism, that there is indeed an apparent disjuncture between by absolute position and the policy proposals I discuss in Chapter 2. However, these proposals are to be judged on the basis of *how close they are to attaining these principles relative to any other plausible set of proposals possible from the position we are at now*. Of course, one could state a position somewhat more consistent with my normative premises,[14] but what I am concerned to do is to suggest what is achievable under the current set of institutional arrangements, having taken account of the prevailing set of expectations and inertial factors which impinge upon the policy process. These proposals would take one nearer to my ideal, but would not do so of themselves. As Oxley indeed suggests, my proposals are interim, but one can state that all measures are properly interim. It is unlikely that any policy will be so far reaching and effective that it ends the need for future change. These limitations are by no means to be regretted, if only because they derive from normative prescriptions themselves.[15]

In any case there are only certain methods which one can legitimately use to achieve the ends I seek *and remain consistent with them*. One of my main arguments against redistribution is that it is coercive and militates against voluntary activity. I may wish to see a fundamental transformation of current societal arrangements, but the very principles I espouse rule out the use of coercive measures. As I have stated in Chapter 2 and elsewhere (King, 1998), revolution is by definition coercive and thus illegitimate for the type of libertarianism I espouse.[16] The only legitimate form of change is that which is generated from within as an evolutionary consensual process. What this means in terms of practical politics and policy making is that one must work with current institutions and seek to modify them through dialogue and debate. The 'year zero' approach is not an appealing one, nor would it be anyway consistent with the normative position which I have espoused. Thus there is an apparent compromise between a desired end state and the means of achieving it, but this is by no means untypical and unusual.

I wish now to turn to the avowed pragmatism of Oxley and suggest that he is being more philosophically absolutist than he claims. At times

Oxley comes close to suggesting that 'what works is what's right', which is about as pragmatic as one can be. He suggests that moral absolutes, such as my view that the liberty of individuals should be paramount, can be contested on the basis of empirical evidence (the nature of which we have already considered in section 4.4. on externalities). However, on what basis does Oxley judge whether my normative position is false? Moreover, on what basis does he prefer one outcome over another? He might claim that this is due to empirical evidence, but what test is used to assert that one set of empirical conditions outweighs another? We should return here to the discussion in section 4.4, where it was suggested that Barr's distinction between aims and methods was an arbitrary one. We saw that it was not necessarily possible to separate out methods from aims in that certain aims presupposed particular outcomes, whilst other aims carry with them a perceived illegitimacy of certain other methods. We saw that Oxley appeared to agree with this view, but then continued to use Barr's distinction as the cornerstone of his argument on market failure.

What I believe Oxley, following Barr, is doing is to reify abstract technical measures – in his terms, the methods of economic analysis – into normative prescriptions in themselves. Thus instead of my dictum regarding the overriding interests of individuals, his normative principle could be stated as *the criteria of economic efficiency should override all other concerns*. It is this normative prescription which gives Oxley's argument a sense of moral imperative when he comes to criticise the individualist arguments I give in Chapter 2. He is not then merely countering my argument on pragmatic ground, but is starting from a particular normative position, and, as I have shown in section 4.4 (and as Oxley himself does in Chapter 3), it is deeply problematical.

4.7 Institutional arrangements

Unlike Oxley's criticism of Chapter 2, I do not wish to suggest that the policy prescriptions he outlines in Chapter 3 are inconsistent from his general argument or that it does not flow from his normative presumptions. Indeed there is a high degree of consistency within Chapter 3. But, while this consistency is admirable, it does mean that Oxley's specific policy proposals are open to general criticisms discussed above. For instance, if one accepts the arguments against externalities given above then much of Oxley's discussion for the need for higher levels of investment and for the enforcement of standards loses its legitimacy. I shall therefore concentrate most of my comments in this section on specific points made by my colleague.

However, before doing so, it would be churlish not to recognise where our two positions come together and where agreement is possible. Oxley offers qualified support to my proposal for the reform of housing allowances. He supports my view that it will enhance choice and minimise the effect of the poverty trap. He believes that allowances should be linked to notional, rather than actual costs. Furthermore he is in agreement with the needs for tenure neutrality. More broadly, Oxley is sceptical of the role played by social landlords, arguing that ownership is less important than function and outcomes. Therefore, Oxley's position is by no means a collectivist one, nor is he necessarily adverse to increased diversity and an enhancing of market disciplines in housing. But, having said that, there is a considerable divergence between our positions which, in my view, outweighs the similarities.

One area where we have a fundamental disagreement is over the aims which any housing system ought to be fulfilling. This can be seen in several points in his proposals. Having offered qualified support for my proposal favouring the demand side, he then goes on to discuss why he considers that a specific housing allowance is necessary. He offers the argument of cost differentials which I suggest can be dealt with by a damping mechanism. However, he also appears to suggest that one reason for maintaining specific allowances is 'that the subsidy is designed to promote housing consumption not consumption generally' (p. 115). This is not so much producer capture as 'advisor capture' – 'if we don't have housing subsidies what are we academics for?'. It is tantamount to arguing that subsidies cannot be changed from their initial purpose, whereas one of the main aims of my proposal was precisely to create a change to their purpose. A non-specific subsidy is designed to support household income, part of which ought to be used to fund adequate housing, but that exact proportions are to be left as a matter of choice. My view would be that, so long as subsidies were not excessive, it is not a problem that they support general consumption and not just housing. Housing consumption is no more (or less) vital than other areas of consumption.

This divergence of aims is seen when Oxley states that '*(t)he objective of decent housing* will not be achieved simply by giving people more money' (p. 117, my emphasis). My point here is not to argue with the latter part of Oxley's statement, but rather the highlighted part. In this case he is not arguing against, but across me. It is not particularly my objective to create or provide 'decent housing'. My objective is the furthering of choice and individual decision making. My view is that housing choices are best left to individual households. This means that I have no particular objective with regard to housing, except in the negative sense of reducing the role of the state and centralised decision making. To put the case more abstractly, my objective is to ensure that individuals are seen as ends and not means. Housing is a means to these ends and it is therefore not my intention to suggest any objective with regard to housing.[17]

Thus it is important to realise that our aims are markedly different. This divergence, it seems to me, arises from our different epistemological presumptions about the role of government and the competence of individuals. Indeed, this divergence constantly crops up when comparing our two sets of proposals. For instance, while Oxley is generally supportive of an increase in demand side subsidies, the specific qualifications he places on this proposal would negate much of its impact. He appears to be sceptical about the ability of individuals to take decisions for themselves and thus states that if payments are only to be made to households and not landlords, then a considerable amount of counselling and support would be necessary to promote this sense of responsibility. The clear implication is that that sense of responsibility would have to be learnt on the part of households who are currently not capable of it. However, much of my argument is based on the premise that individuals are already competent and this is shown by how they currently manage to understand the operation of existing benefit and allocations systems. Oxley therefore is taking a much more pessimistic view of benefit recipients than I do.

I am aware that my proposal here will have to be limited to the extent to which certain households, through no fault of their own, are incapable of proper decision making. However, as I stated in section 2.10, we should not allow the exceptions to dismantle the rule. There ought to be a general presumption of competence regardless of tenure.[18] Oxley, I would suggest, appears to hold the tenure based view of competence which I have argued against. I find it interesting that he chooses to mention, with apparent approval, the so-called Delft model of housing allocation later in this section. This is somewhat ironic in that current thinking coming from the Netherlands is towards a choice based system with limited or no eligibility criteria and with a reduction in support to applicants on the grounds that such support is disabling. It appears that there is at least some recognition here of the competence of individuals to determine their own interests. As with payments to individuals, there is an apparent 'epistemological block' which prevents Oxley from taking his arguments to their logical conclusions.

A major contradiction in Oxley's proposals arises out of this 'block'. At one point of his argument he calls for the state to maintain, and even enhance, its regulatory role to ensure decency and quality. Yet at another, he calls for a liberalisation of policy to increase competition between within and between sectors. I wish to explore this contradiction further.

While suggesting that direct state provision is not necessary, he argues that the state has a role in regulation and that this 'should not be limited to a sector called 'social rented housing' (p. 117). He then goes on to discuss enhanced regulation to control standards and mechanisms for subsidies based on outcomes and not ownership. This is an interesting discussion because he argues that 'there is a case for further expanding the competition and increasing the variety of housing, and housing suppliers, from which consumers might choose' (p. 118). He is thus advocating that government subsidy can be used as a means of diversification. This would potentially allow for new forms of landlords and potentially for greater choice.

However, the proposal is seen as fatally flawed as soon as one starts to consider the sorts of mechanisms through which government would operate such a competitive system. Indeed, the only choice open to consumers would be over type of landlord, because one cannot foresee a government managing a competitive subsidy system which offered differential subsidies to landlords. Subsidies would be offered according to a standard pattern and this applies whether it is grants, loans or tax concessions.[19] The issue therefore is that government would control the process and offer a standardised system. Subsidy would only be offered to those landlords prepared to perform their prescribed function by government. Indeed, this would be entirely consistent with Oxley's desired role for the state as a regulator. What Oxley is describing therefore is a liberalisation in name only, with competition being measured purely in institutional terms. This latter issue may benefit tenants, but there is no guarantee as such, as has been shown by the experience of housing associations in Britain since 1989 (Page, 1993; Whitehead *et al.*, 1995). The major limitation of Oxley's system is that it does nothing to break the control of landlords.

Oxley links the issues of quality and quantity to that of household preferences, stating that the central supply side issue is to ensure that quality and quantity is acceptable to meet preferences. This is all very laudable, but he does not explain how, under a state regulated system, these preferences are made manifest. The price mechanism will clearly be of limited use in Oxley's regulated system, but no alternative mechanism is offered. One is left to presume that the government's 'experts' are the ones capable of determining these preferences. But this merely returns us to the argument about how government can possibly be aware of the subjective preference of diverse individuals (see section 4.4). These preferences can be merely assumed and it is therefore likely that there will be the same mismatches under Oxley's model as under current practices.

The final point I wish to consider is Oxley's justification for a diversity of suppliers – which I take to mean a continuation of socially owned landlords – on the basis that this will ensure that broader objectives of dealing with social exclusion and promoting urban regeneration are met. He contends that profit based landlords will be less inclined to get involved with these projects and that this is a justification for a *de facto* limitation of their role. My response here is to question why landlords should be involved in these activities at all. Landlords, of whatever type, ought to concentrate on their contractual obligations to tenants and the efficient management of their stock of dwellings. That, in itself, would be a considerable help in dealing with the broader social issues which Oxley raises. I see no reason, however, for landlords to be involved in areas beyond their expertise and competence, especially as there are agencies much better placed to deal with these issues.

More fundamentally, of course, we need to appreciate the role which social landlords have had in creating both urban blight and social exclusion. Only once this is understood, and remedied, can any role for the state be sensibly countenanced.

4.7 Conclusion

There is always a danger that one overstates one's differences merely for the sake of a good argument and to maintain interest. However, I hope that in this rejoinder I have acknowledged the merits of Oxley's argument as well as the areas of agreement. Inevitably though in a project of this nature, I have concentrated on the areas of disagreement or where I feel Oxley is in error. He has done likewise in Chapter 3 and I would expect him to do so again in the chapter which follows. This should not hide the fact though that there are considerable areas where we agree, and many other issues over which we would share our disagreement.

I wish to conclude by mentioning what seems to me to be the biggest issue which separates us. I believe this rests on where the limits of individual competence are. I wish to suggest that individuals are to be deemed competent unless they prove otherwise, and I am confident that this proof would seldom be required. Oxley, however, is more pessimistic with regard to individual competence and thus falls back on social or collectivist decision making. It is this distinction which makes Oxley the welfare liberal, and me the libertarian. It may appear to be a matter of degree, but the debate so far has shown it to be a fairly fundamental gulf. However, I await my colleague's response with optimism that on this issue – but only this – I might be wrong.

5
Emphasising the Need for Policies

Michael Oxley

5.1 Introduction

This chapter is a response to the rejoinder set out by King in Chapter 4. As such it is not a blow by blow reaction to each point made but rather an analysis of what I consider to be the main criticisms of the stance I have taken in Chapter 3. I respond to some arguments by restating a position, hopefully with added clarity, and to others by extending the analysis to reinforce the propositions that I have advanced.

I begin by questioning again the differences in the objectives which we have for change. My arguments are housing policy specific in that I argue for well-defined housing policy aims. This contrasts with King's desire for more individual freedom but no housing specific objectives. This is a major difference between our positions and I restate the case for clear and measurable housing policy objectives.

I respond to King's suggestion that I have adopted a position based on technical efficiency criteria. I consider the concept of efficiency in the use of resources to be central to the standpoint I am taking and it is important to understand efficiency not as a value free concept but one which relates to the use of resources in relation to preferences. There is not a unique efficiency outcome for an economy or a single most efficient housing system but it is essential to know which arrangements are more efficient than others and also which arrangements are more equitable than others.

I have argued for the activities of the state and the activities of the market being viewed as aspects of a single system of social organisation. They should not therefore be seen as separate and antagonistic resource allocation mechanisms. This is the case generally and for housing in particular. I have thus rejected as misleading and analytically inappropriate the notion of the state 'intervening' in housing markets, or any other market. King has taken issue with this view and I have restated the value of rejecting the spurious state/market dichotomy.

The inability of individuals to deal with housing externalities has been an essential part of my argument. King has not sought to deny the importance of externalities but has argued against the need for significant government action to respond to external cost and benefit situations. I have tried to show why collective action, and not individual action, is essential to processes which promote efficiency in the light of housing externalities.

King has set out a case against my points on the redistributive role for government. I have attempted to re-explain why I consider it legitimate for governments to redistribute resources and why a strong redistributive role for government should be an essential part of a successful housing policy. An effective housing policy will redistribute resources and it is important to acknowledge the connections between housing policy and redistributive measures.

King has reemphasised the centrality, to his position, of individual choice. I have tried to explain that I am not seeking to restrict individual choice where such choice is meaningful, viable and effective. However, I propose that individual decision making will not be capable of bringing about the changes in the supply and consumption of housing that are necessary for the elimination of poor quality housing and its associated costs to society. Choices which result in an efficient and equitable production and allocation of housing have, therefore, to be essentially social and political and not only individual choices.

5.2 An improvement in what?

The fundamental difference between the positions taken by King and Oxley is revealed by examining the following quotation from King in Chapter 4 and contrasting that with the position which I have taken in Chapter 3:

> It is not particularly my objective to create or provide 'decent housing'. My objective is the furthering of choice and individual decision making. My view is that housing choices are best left to individual households. This means that I have no particular objective with regard to housing, except in the negative sense of reducing the role of the state and centralised decision making. (pp. 144–5)

It is my objective to examine and suggest policy changes which will result in more decent housing and improve access to this housing. I do see the case for investigating a set of activity which may reasonably be called 'housing policy' and examining the aims and the instruments of this policy. King is rejecting the concept of a housing policy.

I consider it reasonable to conceive of a society with efficiency and equity objectives related to the overall use of resources within that society and to have housing policies which are consistent with these objectives. There can be much individual decision making and many choices made by individuals within this society but, as I have explained in Chapter 3, an over reliance on these individual decisions is likely to lead to outcomes which are incompatible with general efficiency and equity objectives and specific housing provision objectives. Some housing choices are best left to individual households but some decisions relating to housing are best made through social decision making processes. This is because these social processes can possibly take account of phenomena which the process of individual decision making fails to take into account. These phenomena include the market failures and the distributional issues identified in Chapter 3. It is the failure of a process which is being questioned here. This is not about presumptions regarding the competence of individuals, as King suggests. I am not seeking to demean any individuals by suggesting that they are incompetent and therefore do not possess the necessary personal attributes to make decisions about their housing situation. There will be, however, severe limitations on what, as individuals, many households are able to do about the quality of the housing they occupy and the consequences of their housing conditions for the welfare of others. Households acting as individual decision-making units can do very little about the distribution of income and wealth or positive and negative housing externalities. This does not mean that the alternative that we have to consider is reliance on a centralised state to make decisions, but it does mean that the decisions will have to be made through social processes which seek to recognise factors such as externalities and distribution.

The social decision-making processes which are germane to housing will depend on the form of government that we have and the powers which that government ascribes to a variety of agents. In practical terms this means that one needs to examine the housing functions in modern Britain of, for example, municipalities, regional government, national assemblies, national governments and the European Union. As well as these politically accountable bodies, one would need to ask questions about the powers and function of housing suppliers such as registered social landlords, of banks and building societies, and of land owners and construction firms, to name but a few. Society is not just composed of decision making units which we can call 'individuals' and 'the state'. There are many sorts of decision takers with many objectives and many instruments at their disposal to achieve their objectives. If there is good government of the state, decision-making powers will rest, on specific housing matters, with those best able to make the decisions. Many of the important decisions for households will, with good government, be left to individuals but several will be dependent on other decision makers.

By having a housing policy, a government can set aims related to access to decent housing which can be defined in measurable terms. Usually governments avoid such precision. There is much to be said, however, for, governments having closely defined indicators of decent housing, homelessness, access to housing and the external costs and benefits of poor quality housing. This is not a simple straightforward set of tasks. However, it will ultimately be easier to determine whether there has been, for example, an increase, in the quantity of decent housing, a reduction in homelessness, and a reduction in illness caused by damp housing than to determine whether there is more choice and individual decision making.

5.3 The meaning of efficiency

The concept of economic efficiency is not a narrow technical matter. It is rather a broad concept which relates to the desirability of arrangements which make the best use of limited resources. The Pareto concept of economic efficiency is about the production of goods and services and the consumption of goods and services. Efficiency is maximised where production and consumption activities are such that no one can be made better off without making someone else worse off. In determining well being, the individual is assumed to be the best judge of his or her own welfare. There are thus explicit value judgements involved. There is a normative underpinning to Pareto efficiency. In using the concept of Pareto efficiency, economists are not trying to be value free. Such a position for an activity which seeks to prescribe action to improve welfare would, of course, be untenable. Gains which make some people better off and make no one else worse off are efficiency gains. It is such efficiency gains which can be argued to be compatible with several theories of society.

To argue for an efficient allocation of resources is, for example, to argue that the maximum output of housing and other goods and services should be produced from given resources. If more housing can be produced without reducing the outputs of other commodities then this should be done. The combination of housing production and other production should also take account of consumer preferences. It is not efficient to produce more housing if consumers do not value the housing. This valuation will be a function of preferences. It is a combination of resource constraints and preferences which determine an efficient level of production. There is nothing mechanistic in this concept of efficiency nor is there anything which is contrary to a concern with what people desire. The principal reason for Pareto optimality gathering normative significance is that it is based on value judgments which endorse consumer sovereignty. The coincidence of Pareto efficiency and perfectly competitive markets would not be of importance if individual preferences were to not to be of paramount significance. Market processes tend to be supported on the grounds that they promote efficient allocations of resources which are responsive to consumer preferences. The arguments for state activity to counteract market failure, which have been set out in Chapter 3, are not augments for ignoring individual choice or rejecting the preferences of individuals. They are rather arguments which rest on propositions that, in given circumstances, market processes are not able to produce outcomes which do fully respect individual preferences.

This does, of course, beg many questions about how preferences are to be known in the absence of market transactions and how resources and commodities are to be valued in the absence of appropriate market prices. Because these are difficult questions to answer, it does not mean that one has to pretend that the market failure does not exist and revert to a reliance on markets despite their inadequacies. Thankfully, many economists have sought to address these questions and provide answers.[1] The answers are, unsurprisingly, varied and often controversial. Their acceptability varies with one's ideological position as well as what one views as practical. For these reasons, the vast literature on valuations in the absence of suitable prices, the derivation of social choice from individual preferences and the reconciliation of conflicting preferences will continue to grow as long as there is a desire to address, rather than assume away, market failure. The goal, of course, of that effort is to promote efficiency.

Efficiency is not a simple value free concept, nor does the application of the concept lead to a plan for achieving a unique position. Differences between alternative efficient combinations of resources will have to be judged by equity rather than by efficiency criteria. Whilst economists sometimes try to keep the normative essence of efficiency subliminal, they are usually completely open about the normative nature of equity and economists firmly ensconced in the positivist school use this as a reason for justifying drawing the boundary on their enquiry at this point. They believe that it is up to other disciplines to decide on the criteria for an equitable distribution of resources. I will return to some personal views on equity in section 5.6.

To argue for an efficient allocation of resources is to argue for avoiding producing items which are not wanted and for producing items which are wanted, using methods which avoid waste. It is to argue for using productive resources rather than have them lying idle. An efficient housing system would produce dwellings which people wanted and it would not contribute to the production of items which were not desired, such as ill health. If a change to the housing system does not produce more housing which people want, and less of what they do not want, the change is not an efficient change. I am in favour of a more efficient housing system. While acknowledging the many difficulties in determining whether a given change is efficient, I do not believe that changes which depend only on individual, as opposed to collective action are likely to bring about all the possible efficiency gains in any society.

5.4 The spuriousness of the market/state dichotomy

In Chapter 3 I argued that the division between markets and the state amounted to a false dichotomy, that markets worked on the basis of property rights which were endorsed by the state and that the notion of government interference in markets was misleading. King has responded by claiming that the division is not just useful but essential. He states that;

> It arises because of the antithetical nature of markets and government action, whereby markets facilitate (however imperfectly) individual choice, whilst governments deal with imperative conditions where choice is deemed inappropriate. The separation between markets and government is therefore a key political distinction based on the perceived competence of individuals. (p. 131)

I disagree very strongly with the idea of the separation of markets and the idea that government is concerned with conditions where choice is suspended. The view that governments do certain things and markets do other different things and that markets are separate from, and inherently superior to, governments is entirely false and leads to inappropriate pro-market prescriptions. It is as wrong as the views that the state is always superior and that collective ownership of the means of production is always better than private ownership. Each of these views leads to equally false prescriptions.

The false nature of the state/market division can be reaffirmed by restating the importance of property rights to the operation of markets. It has been argued that the ownership of property provides the right to services that the property is capable of yielding. Private ownership usually allows for the exclusion of the enjoyment of the rights by others. Private property rights also typically include the right to sell the title to the property and to let to others the right to enjoy the property. 'Market prices are, therefore, the prices of property rights' (Burrows, 1979, p. 47). For markets to operate, private property rights are essential. Property rights can, however, be associated with several forms of ownership, including communal and state ownership. Whatever the form of ownership 'property rights are an instrument of society and derive their significance from the fact that they help a man form those expectations which he can reasonably hold in his dealings with others' (Demsetz, 1967, p. 347). It is ultimately the state with its political and legal institutions which governs the definition and the exchange of property rights. Indeed, this is one of the principal functions of the state: 'The definition and allocation of property rights represent a primary preoccupation, some might argue the *raison d'être*, of states' (Bowles, 1984, p. 187). Without private property rights defined and enforced through the apparatus of the state there will be no markets.

Property rights in housing, as in all commodities, change over time as governments adapt them to changing circumstances and new policy objectives. The relationship of governments to property rights and thus markets is therefore a symbiotic relationship. The nature of the relationship is defined by, and helps to define, the sort of society that exists. The relationships regarding housing determine the sort of housing system which prevails. The stance which the state adopts with respect to housing can be termed 'minimalist', 'control', 'subsidy', or 'ownership' (Oxley, 1995). These amount to different roles which are not necessarily mutually exclusive. The terms do not describe watertight boxes but are rather labels for approximate and interrelated categories.

If the state adopts a minimalist position its role will be limited to protecting, guaranteeing and underwriting private property rights in housing. Contracts between owners will allow dwellings to be bought and sold, and contracts between landlord and tenant will facilitate private renting. The state will not become involved in the detail of these contracts. The state does become involved only if private property rights are violated in the sense of, for example, one individual trying to take housing from another by the use of force. Models of freely competitive housing markets assume explicitly or implicitly there is a minimalist role for the state. Minimalist here does not, however, mean insignificant. It means that state activity is restricted to the minimum property right related functions. This is an essential and extremely important role if markets are to function. At the other end of a spectrum from the minimalist position one might imagine the state adopting an 'ownership' role where all property rights in housing rest with the state. The range of roles which lie between the minimalist and ownership positions are many and complex, and the precise nature of the role will determine how the market works and what decisions are left to individuals.

The state, as opposed to taking a 'minimalist' or ownership position might adopt a 'control' or 'subsidy' role. Often the two will be mixed in that subsidies will be conditional on controls being accepted. The control or subsidy role may be exercised in relation to housing which is 'owned' individually or by the state. The control role might take the form of control over location, design and construction, rents, security of tenure, allocation of dwellings or the profits from renting. Control over location, design and construction is typically to promote certain positive, and reduce certain negative, physical externalities and is usually dealt with through planning and building controls. Rent controls and security of tenure legislation tend to go together. The declared aim of restricting the otherwise private contacts between landlord and tenant is usually to prevent exploitation of tenants by altering the balance of power in their favour. Such controls have been widely used in Europe in the twentieth century. Whilst controls on the allocation and profits of housing are theoretically possible it is difficult to find examples, outside of wartime, of governments telling private and unsubsidised owners of housing to whom they should sell or let their housing, or of governments imposing specific limits on profits from rental or sale, other than through general taxation measures. Once, however, subsidy is used as a lever, the exercise of the control function becomes widespread. States throughout Europe have subsidised the production and continuing supply of housing on certain conditions whilst leaving 'ownership' with individuals. The full ownership role is used only in very limited circumstances, for governments have found that they can exercise much influence through a combination of controls and subsidies. When one recognises the differing nature of these roles, one may come to appreciate the lack of meaning which one can attach to the term 'the level of government involvement' (King, p. 130) in housing. The level of government involvement might be measured by government expenditure on housing or the cost of housing subsidies but all of these are extremely difficult to quantify in practice (Haffner and Oxley, 1999). They can, anyway, provide only a very imperfect, and potentially misleading, indicator of the influence of governments on housing provision. Governments can do much without spending large sums of money.

In each of the minimalist, control, subsidy and ownership positions the state has a major part to play. It is not possible to say that it is bigger or smaller, or more or less significant in any of these roles. It is rather different and the processes of the production, distribution and pricing of housing are different. There is no inevitable outcome which can be generalised regarding the welfare of households in any of these stances. Nor can one state that the power of the choices which households exercise are inevitably better in any of these stances. They will, however, be different.

King seems to want the state to assume only a minimalist role in relation to housing on the grounds that this maximises individual choice and he implies that other roles deny the competence of individuals to make decisions for themselves. It is rather the case that the minimalist position can result in decent housing being denied to many households who have inadequate resources, and action by the state can empower and not restrict the ability of individuals to make choices. This is not, of course, an inevitable outcome. The provision of social housing according to some models of allocation can restrict choice and contribute to reductions in well being. The outcomes depend on the specifics of the allocation system.

I am not advocating the widespread provision of social housing nor am I advocating an ownership role for governments in relation to housing. I am, however, strongly rejecting the minimalist position. I am also rejecting the notion that the state has a small and insignificant role in the minimalist position. Its role in this, and in all the stances identified, is strong and important in determining the provision of housing.

King suggests that I am proposing a decision-making process 'captured by an elite' (p. 134) and also that I am proposing a situation in which 'decisions are made by some sort of social entity and presumably grounded in some form of consensus' (pp. 126–7). In fact I am arguing neither for an elite taking decisions nor necessarily for consensus. I am arguing only for a decision making process which takes account of matters which individuals do not and cannot influence when they act individually. This process might be called collective decision making or social decision making or political decision making. I have expressed a preference for political processes which involve some form of democracy. I have not gone further and specified the form of democracy and the nature of the constitution which governs the state and the activities of governments. This would take us into additional well-worn debates on political systems. In fact the nature of the political system is, of course, crucial to the nature of the housing system one prefers. Democratic processes need to be robust enough to avoid capture by any elite. They also need to involve information and debate.

A major worry about current political debate with respect to housing in the UK is not the danger of decisions being captured by an elite but there being too little political discussion and too little information about the consequences of poor quality housing. There is a need for much more informed political discussion about the connections between housing and poverty, health, education and crime. There is a need for academics to provide more detailed, closely argued analyses, backed up by empirical evidence and presented in a form which will have an impact on political decision making.

The political debate also needs to separate the cases for governments regulating, subsidising and providing housing. I have tried to argue the case for strong government activity which involves regulation and subsidy but I have not argued strongly for government provision of housing. Rather, I have set out in Chapter 3 a limited case for some form of public provision. It is certainly not correct to claim that the case for government activity can, as King suggests I propose, 'be seen as a rationale for the provision of social housing' (p. 136). The case for social housing is a different case than the case for regulation and subsidy.

5.5 Housing, externalities and individuals

I argued in Chapter 3 that the prevalence of externalities related to housing creates conditions where social rather than individual decision making is required to take account of positive and negative externalities. I do not suggest (as King implies, see p. 136) that externalities provide a case for the provision of social housing. I do suggest that externalities are important for individual and social welfare and that individual action will not be able to address the problems created by housing externalities. King in his response does not question the existence of housing externalities but does doubt whether governmental action will be better than individual action in responding to external effects. In support of these doubts he quotes the Coase theorem and the inability of governments to calculate the degree of harm caused by externalities.

The Coase theorem suggests that bargaining between affected parties can produce a satisfactory solution but only (as the quotations used by King on p. 137 acknowledge) if bargaining is costless and bargaining is possible. The bargaining can involve payments of compensation between the affected parties and these payments will reflect the positive and negative values which the initiator and the recipient of the externality place on the activity. The Coase theorem has been, over the years, the subject of much discussion by economists and there are many weaknesses that have been identified in both the essence and the practicality of the theorem.[2] I will not consider all of the many shortcomings of the bargaining approach proposed by Coase but simply highlight some of the factors which make bargaining generally inapplicable to housing externalities.

In practice, transaction costs are likely to be large and the effected parties will find it not only costly but impractical to negotiate. If my neighbour builds an extension to his house which blocks my view I may be able to strike a bargain with him which either allows him to build and me receive compensation or me to get my continued access to a view and him to receive compensation. But how we bargain will depend on the distribution of property rights. If my neighbour does not have a right to build but I have a right to a view, my hand will be greatly strengthened in the bargaining process. If he has the right to build, will he frequently threaten to construct a new extension in order to blackmail me into more compensation payments? If he is rich and I am poor, I might easily be persuaded to take a small sum of money while he gets a very large gain from the new construction. How bargaining works clearly depends on the initial distribution of property rights and the distribution of income between the affected parties. A claim of the Coase approach is that it takes account of the two way nature of the externality process. In fact as Ng argues:

> One of the basic difficulties of the bargaining solution is that no matter how we assign property rights or what liability rule we adopt,

> it tends to be 'one-sided' and fails to tackle the two-sided nature of the externality problem adequately. The payment of compensation only makes the payer take into account the cost he imposes on others, failing to make the receiver and prospective receivers of compensation take account of the cost they impose on the payer.
>
> (1983, p. 184)

The bargaining solution will be costly and impractical when large numbers of people are involved, as will often be the case with housing externalities. If a new housing development restricts the views of a large number of existing residents, the costs of the residents organising themselves into an effective bargaining group may be very large indeed. It has been argued that, 'bargaining will never proceed if large numbers of individuals are involved' and, 'It is not necessarily the case that negotiation will produce a Pareto optimum if both parties do not have access to all the available knowledge' (Cullis and Jones, 1998, pp. 34–5). Residents will be better able to bargain with the developer if they know the profits that are probable from the development. The developer might have strong incentives to conceal the relevant predictions.

There may be several sets of externalities involved in a given situation and many sets of parties to the externalities. The housing development might, besides having negative effects on existing residents, positively effect motorists who will be able to travel a shorter distance because of a new road which is a necessary condition for the development. Can the motorists be identified as a bargaining group and how are their benefits to be bargained relative to the residents' costs and the developers' benefits? For situations of more than one externality the Coase theorem has been restated as 'the elimination of each externality is independent of the assignment of property rights so long as there is separate liability for each externality, bargaining on one externality is independent of bargaining on all others and the zero transactions cost assumption holds' (Mueller, 1989, p. 33). The probability of these conditions holding is small. After reviewing the issues Cullis and Jones (1998) conclude, 'The list of transactions problems . . . casts some doubt on the proposition that the market can adequately resolve the problem of externalities' (p. 36).

The bargaining solution assumes a relatively simple situation with two parties, the initiator of the external effect and the recipient bargaining with each other. The reality of the housing externalities I have identified in Chapter 3 is much more complex than this. Take, for example, the proposition that poor quality housing has adverse effects on health. This is a proposition for which convincing empirical evidence with respect to specific illnesses has been amassed (see, for example, Conway, 1999). However, the answer to the question 'who has caused the adverse effect?' is not straightforward and neither is the answer to the question 'who are the affected persons?'. In the case of an old damp house which is contributing to the resident's respiratory problems, if the house is rented, we may argue that is an issue for the landlord and the tenant to work out. If it is owner occupied, what does the bargaining solution suggest then? Is the owner to bargain with himself or herself as the occupier?

Poor housing does not usually come in the form of individual isolated dwellings. In a neighbourhood of run down housing the adverse effects might reasonably be argued to be collectively produced. There may be a multiplicity of owners. The housing has deteriorated over the years. There has not been a purposeful act which has led to the production of 'harmful housing'. The built environment is moulded by a complexity of agents over time and pinning the responsibility or the blame on specific agents may not be meaningful or useful. Those who will benefit from an improvement to the neighbourhood will not just be existing residents but also future generations. Who is to bargain for them?

Even if we argue that the value of a 'better quality' neighbourhood will be reflected in the market values of the improved properties, existing owners acting individually may have little or no incentive to improve. This proposition can be supported by the 'prisoner's dilemma' (Harrison, 1977, pp. 71–2; Robinson, 1979, pp. 101–3). This refers to the problem of making decisions under conditions of uncertainty caused by a lack of information about the decisions of those who can affect the outcome of the intended action. It describes a situation where coordinated informed decisions are better than uncoordinated uninformed decisions. It has been argued that:

> it is possible that a landlord (or owner) will be deterred from improving his own property because of the fear that his returns will be jeopardised by the external costs imposed on his property by unimproved adjoining ones. Because each landlord is faced with uncertainty about his neighbour's activities, no one will be willing to risk investing in maintenance and repair work. However, if they all *did* invest, both they and society in general would probably be better off.
>
> (Robinson, 1979, p. 101)

If it was just a question of two landlords collaborating with each other, a mutually beneficial solution might be found through cooperation, or one landlord might purchase other run down properties and thus 'internalise' the externalities and provide a solution. However, when the numbers of properties are large such outcomes are unlikely. It has been suggested that, 'Thus we may conclude that atomistic behaviour is likely to prevail and to lead to an inefficient outcome' (Robinson, 1979, p. 103). In a city with a large volume of poor quality housing in a multiplicity of ownerships, it may require much more than improvement to individual properties to raise the quality of housing. Demolition and the redesign of housing layouts may be necessary. Changes in road layouts may be required. A change in the physical environment which creates new housing in conjunction with improved social infrastructure might be the only feasible way that a run down environment may be transformed into an area of good quality housing. It is most unlikely that individual property owners will communicate, collaborate and change the built environment in such a way.

The most serious housing externalities involving health, education and crime are complex. The parties that have 'caused' external costs are not well defined. Those who would need to cooperate to improve the quality of the housing stock are the many owners of complex bundles of property rights. The beneficiaries of improved housing are also many but they will not all easily be identified. If improved housing conditions do have positive effects on health education and crime, it is not just the inhabitants of specific dwellings or the residents of a given neighbourhood but the members of a much wider society who will benefit. There is some similarity between the correct application of externalities to housing and the application of the concept to environmental pollution in that adverse effects are typically collectively produced and collectively received. Tackling pollution is recognised to require action which is initiated by governments and imposed on large numbers of decision makers. Improving the quality of the housing stock, likewise, involves many decision makers. It certainly is not correct to claim that, 'In cases of externalities involving housing, property rights are likely to be unambiguous and the numbers involved not large' (King, p. 138).

It does not, of course, follow that because individual decision making fails to deal with housing externalities, state activity can inevitably and easily find a solution. Activity by the state involves costs, requires information and needs to be weighed against the probable benefits. The type of state activity also needs to be considered carefully.

There is a long list of actions which economists have proposed as potential remedies for adverse external costs and for the promotion of positive externalities. It includes laws which carefully define the property rights of effected parties; the merging of affected parties into a single decision making body; the use of regulations; taxes on those who initiate external costs and subsidies for those who promote external benefits. These options are variously suggested as means to be used as alternatives to the bargaining solution or as actions which will assist a bargaining solution. The relevance of each of the options to housing depends on the specific circumstances that are considered.

The right to develop housing is limited by laws which define the boundaries to what owners may do with their physical property. Thus one does not typically have a right to build a house in a green field or to construct a large extension to one's property. Rights to a view across green fields or to freedom from the sight of an obtrusive extension to a neighbour's house could be, but are not always, defined in law. The right of a builder or a landlord to supply unsafe housing can be limited by laws, and environmental health legislation can provide occupants with some rights to healthy housing. However, making, overnight, all housing of an unacceptable standard illegal would do nothing to increase the supply of decent housing.

When landlord and tenant become one under owner occupation it might be argued that some of the external effects of poor quality housing become internalised but, again, the reality of the poor quality will remain without further action. The merger solution may have some significance for firms who are parties to each other's polluting outputs (Burrows, 1979, pp. 80–96) but its usefulness in housing will be severely limited.

The use of regulations, combined with related laws is, in practice, a common way of dealing with many housing externalities. The use of planning and building control regulations can be used to limit negative and to encourage positive externalities associated with the construction and improvement of housing. While regulations are unlikely to be capable on their own of promoting the transformation of problem estates or the development of new higher quality dwellings, regulations which set minimum acceptable standards are essential to a housing policy which seeks to promote decent housing.

The notion of taxes on the perpetrators of unacceptable housing is difficult to perceive. Who would be liable for the taxes? In the sense of fines on those who contravened minimum standards legislation, one can see some realism, but as a more general proposition, they would be a lot more difficult to apply than in the case of an industrialist who is to pay a tax once output exceeds some pollution inducing level. The difficulty here is that the tax solution is usually advocated in as a means on balancing the social costs and the social benefits on a variable level of production. The aim is to achieve equality between the marginal social cost and the marginal social benefit of an activity. At the optimal production level, the cost to society of an additional unit of output will be equal to the benefit to society from the output. The concept may, in this sense, be of some value in trying to find the optimum density for residential development on a given estate but of little help in finding an acceptable level of slum housing in a country.

Subsidies are intended to encourage desirable activities. If the extra desirable activity has a value which is greater than the cost of the subsidy, the subsidy can be argued to be justified on efficiency grounds. Subsidies which lead to improvements in the housing stock which bring benefits to society, and subsidies which promote the building of housing which has social benefits that are greater than the private benefits to be received by the developer, can therefore be argued for on efficiency grounds. There is, without doubt, a significant empirical problem here. The valuation on the benefit to society will not easily be determined. This does not mean that it should be ignored or assumed to be zero. It does mean that there should be a major research effort directed at defining and measuring the wide benefits to society of an improvement in the quality of the housing stock. The efficiency case for housing subsidies is dependent on a demonstration of the social benefits of decent housing. If all the benefits of decent housing were to be reflected in the capital values and the rents of such housing there would be a much diminished case for subsidy. It is because a market system does not reflect these benefits that a case for subsidisation can be made.

The prevalence of significant externalities which cannot be simply internalised by redefining property rights, or by bargaining between affected parties, is central to the argument for a positive housing policy. It is not, however, central to any case for state provision of housing. The case for council housing or of any form of state ownership of housing cannot be made on externality grounds, nor have I sought to make such a case. It is certainly not the case that, 'This can be seen as a rationale for the provision of social housing' (King, p. 136). It is part of the rationale for appropriate housing policy instruments not for a particular form of ownership. Poor quality housing is not tenure specific. It is, of course, to be found in all tenures and negative external effects will require a remedy whether they relate to social or to private housing.

5.6 The inevitability of redistribution

The redistributive role of government and the conditions in which it is acceptable for government to redistribute appears to be a major point of disagreement between my position and that of King as expressed in Chapter 4. This difference is fundamental to the housing policy actions which we might advocate that governments should take. We both acknowledge that the distribution of rewards is linked to the distribution of property rights. I not only believe that it is acceptable for governments to change property rights and the distributions of income and wealth in society, but suggest that such redistributive actions are an essential and inevitable function of governments. I suggest, furthermore, that housing policy goals cannot be achieved without redistributions of resources in society.

King suggests that the prevailing configuration of property rights is legitimate if it has been arrived at by non-coercive means. He also suggests that 'redistribution is legitimate when it has been actively (and individually) consented to. On these terms redistribution does not violate the rights of individuals' (King, p. 140). I wholly maintain the position I argued in Chapter 3 which is that, if adhered to, these principles will support the *status quo* regarding the prevailing configuration of property rights.

If one is to argue about the legitimacy of the process by which property rights have been configured and distributions determined, one may have to unravel the semantics of 'coercion' and also question the relevance of the point in history at which the coercion occurred. Is inheritance of property acquired by force in a previous generation legitimately acquired? What degree of coercion does a monopolist exploit in achieving income and wealth? If consent of the type advocated by King were deemed to be a necessary condition for legitimate redistribution, governments could not equitably collect taxes unless all consented voluntarily to pay. Some degree of coercion is essential to the existence of a state, to the collection of taxes and to the functioning of government. King does in fact accept that 'the state cannot operate without a degree of redistribution through the tax system' (p. 135). A voluntary, non-coercive tax system is an oxymoron.

It is the legitimacy of the actions of government within the constitution of the state that has to be assured. As long as redistributive acts are constitutional they might be judged to be legitimate. Whether they are wise or politically sound, whether they enhance or deplete the national income and whether or not they assist in promoting specific policy objectives are different questions to be judged by different criteria.

I have argued in favour of redistribution as a means to an end and not an end in itself. The end is an improved supply of decent housing. Government induced redistributions can either put more resources in the hands of housing consumers or of housing suppliers. The case for more resources in the hands of consumers in the form of a housing allowance is supported by King and by me. However, I see such a measure as achieving much less than King, largely because of the supply side response to the increased demand which it will produce. Increasing the demand for decent housing and turning the need for decent housing into effective demand for such housing is a merit-worthy and essential part of an effective housing policy. As a redistributive act it will promote the goal of an improved quality of occupied housing if certain supply side conditions are met. Redistribution generally is thus an inevitable and essential aspect of the government of a state and redistribution in the form of personal housing subsides is a desirable but not a sufficient condition for achieving housing policy aims.

5.7 Preferences, choices and housing conditions

King suggests at several points that I am questioning the competence of individuals to make decisions in their own interest. This is not what I am doing. I am rather questioning the ability of individuals to make decisions which are in their own and in society's best interests. I am not suggesting replacing the decisions of individuals by 'an elite who take decisions based on some assumption that they are more capable or have more or better information' (King, p. 134). It is not the inadequacy of individuals but the inadequacy of processes which rely only on individual decisions which I am arguing against. I am not pretending that social decision making is easy but neither am I suggesting that such decisions work against individuals. Social decision making should take account of individual preferences. Indeed, much of the economics literature on collective decision making analyses the difficulties in doing this and suggests rules which harmonise individual and public interests. Some of the relevant literature is summarised in Cullis and Jones (1998).[3] It is claimed that, 'Collective decision making rules provide, or seek to provide, a mechanism for aggregating the social welfare functions of individuals. If such a process were successful then we would be in a position to make a *social choice*' (Cullis and Jones, 1998, p. 71). Much of the literature is about voting systems and the links between economic and political decisions. The search for appropriate rules is a continuing process. There is no perfect political system just as there are no perfect markets in practice.

Housing decisions are not made only by governments or by individuals. They are made by a variety of institutions, firms and public bodies. We might think of macro-housing, intermediate-housing and micro-housing decisions. The macro-housing decisions are made by governments and they are about, for example, the aims of policy, the types of policy instruments to be used, the value of subsidies and the forms of regulation to be used. Intermediate decisions are those taken by private and public sector institutions such as banks and building societies, setting interest rates, and planning authorities, deciding on residential development applications. Micro-housing decisions are made by individual households and individual suppliers of housing. These are decisions for households about, for example, where to live and for suppliers about, for example, where to build and to whom dwellings should be sold or let. King seems to be concerned mainly with the micro decisions made by households. In focusing on individual choice he is in line with neo-classical economists who viewed such choices as promoting individual freedom and supporting the allocation process of the market place.

Decisions about housing externalities and redistribution, according to my analysis, are necessarily macro-housing decisions. This is not incompatible with decisions about where to live being taken at the micro level by individual households as long as the institutional arrangements established at the macro level do not inhibit this process. This inhibition will be the case if state-sponsored landlords allocate housing without reference to household preferences. I am not suggesting that the state should do this. Arguing that some decisions cannot practically, or are not best taken, at the micro level does not mean that all decisions are eliminated at the micro level.

The allocation of dwellings is best done on the basis of individual preferences for those dwellings. In a market based system, if individual preferences are backed up by the ability to pay, demand and relative prices will determine who gets what. If the dwellings are supplied by the state or an agency of the state it does not follow that preferences should be ignored. Allocation will, however, most probably not be simply on the basis of ability to pay. Thus strength of preferences has to be determined through some other mechanism. The Delft system, to which I referred in Chapter 3, does attempt to allocate Dutch housing on the basis of consumer preferences. That is a merit of the system and it is why it is currently of interest in the UK.

Social decision making does not seek to abrogate to the state micro housing decisions which can be taken by individuals. It does, however, respond to the limitations of individual choices and the circumstances in which preferences cannot be expressed through a market system. Individuals can only, in the market place, express preferences for that which is on offer and that which they can afford. An improved housing stock which has less external cost and more external benefit attached to it is not contrary to individual preferences but individuals cannot express a preference for this through the market place. They could, possibly, express such preferences through the ballot box. Such choices are not, however, usually explicitly on offer in the polling booth. Along with whether or not we want more or less defence, health services, roads, environmental pollution, and a very long list of other items which are not directly subject to market processes, we have to rely on political processes which imperfectly reflect individual preferences to determine the strength of the desire for fewer adverse housing externalities.

Even when we consider the more simple choice of where we shall live, our preferences as expressed through the market place are confined to what is on offer. If consumers buy more beans and fewer peas, the production and delivery to the shops is likely to swiftly reflect this change in preferences. Increased purchases of flats rather than semi-detached properties may eventually have some effect on the relative supplies of these two housing types, but in a city with very few flats it would take a long and determined purchasing campaign and a matching and arduous production effort to change the composition of the housing stock. The power of the individual purchaser is inevitably more constrained in the housing market by what is available than in many other markets. The power of individuals to change the housing stock, to improve its quality and to configure the built environment according to consumer choice, is limited by the practicalities of production.

We should not leap from recognising the imperfect nature of individual decision making to a position where we advocate the supremacy of macro or intermediate decision making. We should, however, recognise the importance of the decisions made by private and public institutions and of governments and attempt to influence decision making processes so that they do promote social welfare objectives. This should be compatible, if the processes are appropriate, with respecting, not overriding individual preferences.

5.8 Production and allocation

King has suggested that differing views on the 'limits of individual competence' is 'the biggest issue which separates us' (pp. 147–8). He has suggested that 'individuals are to be deemed competent unless they prove otherwise' while I am 'more pessimistic with regard to individual decision making' (p. 148). I have in fact tried to suggest that while individuals are competent to make some of the housing decisions which directly affect them, they are unable, as individual decision makers, to make decisions which appropriately take account of the wide impacts on society of the quality of housing.

The quality of housing which households experience is essentially the outcome of production and allocation processes. If a society relies on housing markets to drive these processes, the essential influence which the individual exercises is through the demand for housing expressed in purchasing and renting decisions. Assuming that the individual is competent to make personal choices and to decide which dwelling to buy or rent, and putting to one side the very important limits which income and wealth impose on the outcomes of this competence, the power of the individual to influence the overall housing production and allocation processes is very limited indeed. The impact of complementary social decision making on these processes should be designed to enhance social well being.

Housing production processes can be highly individual in those relatively rare circumstances where self building is undertaken. When firms are producing for consumers, individual preferences can, to a limited extent, be expressed through the market. Governments tend to want to exercise strong influence over the housing production process when the outcome is perceived to be too few houses being built, too few houses of an acceptable quality available to consumers, or insufficient houses of the right type in the right locations.

When too few houses are being built, as in a recession, or after a war, governments either try to get firms to produce more, by giving them incentives, or they engage in housing production directly or through local authorities or housing associations (or some other sort of state sponsored producer, depending on the institutional arrangements in the country). In the UK, the government took a major interest in production as a response to the post Second World War housing shortage and used local authorities as the principal means to get houses built. The ability of individuals to express a demand, and for firms to respond to the demand, was clearly limited. The competence of individuals to influence the production process was clearly in doubt. The subsequent allocation of the dwellings tended also to deny significant degrees of individual choice. Only now is serious consideration being given by government to the possibility of more choice-based allocation systems. The removal of individual inputs to the production process does not mean that the removal of the individual from the allocation process must follow.

When the issue is the quality of the existing housing stock, governments tend to subsidise improvements or regulate to promote improvement. Individuals do not fail to improve housing because they lack competence but rather because they lack the resources or the incentives to improve. Governments can take action to address these issues without assuming all the responsibility for deciding what improvements take place, when and how. Public action can facilitate housing improvements without engulfing and predetermining the outcomes of the whole process.

As an example of government seeking to influence the location and type of new housing we might consider the current desire in the UK to have more housing built on previously developed 'brownfield' sites and less on rural 'greenfield' sites. The reasons for government's objective of 60 per cent of future residential development at brownfield locations and its decisions to take action to achieve this outcome is not linked to any beliefs about the competence of individuals. It is rather tied to assumptions about the environmental benefits of more urban and less rural development and a recognition of the fact that market processes do not take sufficient account of the environmental factors. Once developed, additional houses at urban locations will not be sold or rented if individuals do not decide to live in the dwellings. Government action can help to promote a process of change which has positive benefits for individual households and for society as a whole. Market based activity is much less likely to promote some forms of beneficial change.

Changes in the production of dwellings are less responsive to consumer preferences than changes in the allocation of completed houses. It is the ability and feasibility of individual determination with respect to production, more than to specific housing allocation decisions, that is in question.

6 Conclusions

Peter King and Michael Oxley

6.1 What we set out to do

Unlike many housing texts, we have set out to enunciate principles, to give our opinions and to prescribe action. We have done this from contrasting perspectives which involve differing beliefs and differing priorities. We have placed our arguments in paradigms provided by, in one case, political philosophy and in the other by economics. We have tried to provoke thought and to question the rationale for housing policies. This has involved dealing with abstract concepts as well as with practical proposals for the reform of housing policy and practice.

By engaging in a debate with each other, the contrasts of our differing viewpoints have been exposed and the arguments for alternative policy approaches examined rigorously. Our views have not changed as a result of our deliberations. These conclusions do not, therefore, represent an agreed position on how housing policy should be changed. Instead they summarise our agreements and disagreements and illustrate the relevance of our debate to current policy discussion.

6.2 Who decides?

Our title suggests we are interested with decision making about choices concerning housing provision. These are fundamental decisions about housing and its relationship to well being. The choices of residential location, what type of house to live in, and how dwellings will be provided are crucial to this well being. We have examined the extent to which choices related to housing provision should be choices made by individuals and to what degree political processes should determine housing outcomes. Individual choice has been seen to be made through market processes and by voluntary actions which include charitable giving and negotiation with others. Government action has been examined as policy choices involving the supply, subsidisation and regulation of housing. The relationships between individuals, markets and governments have thus been at the centre of our debate and our analyses are not confined solely to housing but have implications for additional areas of public policy where we could each have applied similar principles.

6.3 Agreement

The debate has taken place within parameters which became increasingly explicit as we progressed. We both favour a role for the state which is limited to achieving specific ends. We agree that there is no case for the state being a significant provider of housing. Neither of us favour state bureaucracy and the potential restraints of extensive direct public provision. We both see policy as ideally improving the welfare of individual households. It is also apparent that we both see housing policy as linked to other areas of public policy and recognise the need for analyses which connect with all aspects of social and economic policy. We both deplore the tenure orientated nature of housing policy in the UK and would prefer a more tenure neutral approach which leaves the choice of renting or owning to household preferences.

The need for fresh thinking and for reform based on a reappraisal of the role of the state in relation to housing is fundamental to the stances we take. We are agreed that housing issues are too often considered in a piecemeal fashion and policy decisions are frequently driven by justifications based on immediacy. The broader theme relating to the long-term purpose of policy is usually put to one side for future deliberation. We consider the broad objectives of policy and reforms which could be instituted now and which are compatible with our objectives. On some specific points, despite taking different routes, we arrive at similar destinations. This relates, for example, to our support for an emphasis on support for households in the form of a reformed housing allowance system. The idea of demand side support which is tenure neutral is attractive to both of us. This is partly because we both favour a significant element of individual choice over personal housing decisions such as where to live, what sort of house to live in and how much to spend on housing.

From different points of view, we both doubt the value of categorising housing as a merit good. For King, the problem with treating housing as a merit good is that it rests on a deferential view of human competence. For Oxley, the problem is that merit good arguments suspend the notion of consumer sovereignty in a fashion which is not relevant to the case for social promotion of the consumption of good quality housing.

While espousing very different views on redistribution, the goal of equality is rejected by both authors. Neither of us concludes that the objective of equality can be defined or achieved in a meaningful fashion and the desirability of equality as an aim is subjected to critical appraisal.

Therefore, there are significant areas of agreement, but this debate could not have been sustained if there were not also many areas of dispute and disagreement. This dispute is important because it both highlights the complexity of decision making processes in housing and shows the extent of possibilities for policy making itself.

6.4 Disagreement

There is a significant difference in the ways in which we have viewed the purpose of policy. King has argued that the aim of policy should be to further individual choice and that there should be no particular housing objective other than a reduction in the role of the state and that there should be less centralised decision making. He thus rejects objectives related to achieving explicit housing outcomes. Oxley, however, has argued in favour of explicit housing objectives such as improving the quality of the housing stock and reducing homelessness. There is thus a difference between a view which favours the government disengaging from processes which try to influence the production and consumption of housing and one which seeks to clarify specific objectives related to these phenomena. King argues that he wants a less centralised, less invasive and less controlling form of housing policy whilst Oxley argues that achieving King's aim would mean that there was no longer a significant set of government actions which could usefully be described as 'housing policy'.

King's support for an individualistic approach is founded in his belief that there is no social or common interest as such, only an aggregation of individual interest. It is, in King's analysis, the individual that is put first and it is the individual which is the essential entity for making decisions and for experiencing well being. Oxley, in contrast, has argued for social decision making through political processes which are designed to promote social welfare. Whilst King has argued that the liberty of the individual should override all other concerns, Oxley has stated the case for an approach which promotes social welfare and seeks efficiency and equity in resource allocation generally and in housing provision in particular.

King has examined an essentially antipathetic relationship between markets and governments with markets constituting a means for individuals to signal their self determined wants and to express personal choice. There is a plea for the desirability of individuals, through their choices, also taking responsibility for the outcomes of the decisions which are made. Markets are seen as vehicles for choice and self-expression. It is argued that it is not for the state to shield individuals from the consequences of their actions. It is, furthermore, suggested that an inevitable consequence of government action is government failure. King poses a dichotomy between the role of the individual as a decision maker and the role of the state as a regulator and provider of goods and services. In contrast, Oxley suggests that there is a symbiotic and interdependent relationship between governments and markets with governments providing an essential property right protection and enforcement role which enables markets to function. Governments are additionally seen, in this light, to have the power to modify market outcomes for the benefit of a social interest. While markets can respond to effective demand they do not take any notice of socially determined housing needs. Thus the existence of housing need without effective demand is central to Oxley's case for housing policies. Markets have an important part to play in the housing provision process in Oxley's analysis but they are seen as a means, with the assistance of subsidy and regulation, to promote social welfare and not just promote individual satisfaction.

The role of government should be limited to facilitating individual choice and removing restrictive and centralising barriers to choice and freedom in King's view. The role of government in relation to housing is more extensive and has more dimensions in Oxley's vision of a state which engages in empowering, but also in regulating, activities. Governments take, in this view, a significant interest in the housing provision process and the details of its outcomes.

We have given much attention to the concept of the competence of individuals. King has proposed that a general assumption in favour of the competence of individuals to make housing decisions, which are in their interest and promote their well being, should govern public policy towards housing. This is central to his individualistic approach to housing provision. Whilst acknowledging that there may be specific exceptions to the competent individual he suggests that these exceptions should not be a guide to policy making. Oxley, while not doubting the competence of most individuals to make informed choices about where and how they live, has been much more cautious about the value of a general presumption of competence. He suggests that the exceptions to individual competence may be significant and that public policy should acknowledge the inability, due to lack of resources and the inadequacies of processes, of individuals to always make housing decisions which advance social welfare. He stresses the need for policy actions which recognise the inability of some individuals to obtain decent housing because of their lack of personal and financial resources. He questions the value of the competence proposition not by demeaning the attributes of individuals but by doubting the capabilities of the processes by which individuals may express choice.

The case made by Oxley for active participation by government in the housing provision process relies heavily on the concept of market failure. Thus, the inability of markets to promote efficient production and consumption of housing, because of the inherent weaknesses of markets to respond to such considerations as the external costs of poor quality housing and of homelessness, forms an important part of the case for governments acting to promote the consumption of good quality housing. King doubts the ability of governments to deal with such phenomena given the information and implementation requirements. He makes a case for collaborative agreements between affected parties as a means to respond to externalities. Oxley has stressed the need for governments to regulate, tax and subsidise to ensure the provision of decent housing in the light of significant housing related market failures.

A major difference of perspectives is apparent regarding the redistributive role of the state. The need to redistribute resources to achieve housing policy goals is essential according to Oxley's analysis of housing problems. Governments need, according to this view, to increase the relative volume of resources at the disposal of those who are unable to compete successfully in the market for good quality housing. King, however, argues that governments have no right to take from individuals, as part of a redistributive process, that which is legitimately theirs *without their consent*. The principle of consent is applied to limit the applicability of state inspired redistributions. Governments are urged to let rewards be determined by processes of production and not by processes designed to appropriate to the state resources which have been attributed to individuals. King argues that it is not legitimate to redistribute income according to a notion of justice which conflicts with a pattern of rewards arrived at by the process of production. Oxley argues that there is no convincing reason in principle for not redistributing incomes and wealth, which are seen as socially and not individually determined, and that without redistribution there cannot be effective housing policies.

King suggests that any redistribution should not occur so much through the state as through voluntary and charitable activities. In fact, he argues that his ideal is a voluntary system based on charitable organisations and mutual aid. Oxley rejects any reliance on what he sees as the vagaries and uncertainties of charitable activities, arguing that the provision of resources to ensure the supply and consumption of decent housing is too important to be left to chance.

While both authors have a predilection for demand rather than supply subsidies, King has much more faith in the effectiveness of consumer oriented housing assistance, which he sees as part of a package of measures to promote individual choice and responsibility. Oxley sees the effectiveness of these measures as inhibited by supply side inefficiencies and inelasticities and predicts that part of the proceeds of consumer subsidies will be absorbed by enhanced returns to suppliers without, necessarily, a corresponding increase in the provision of accommodation. There is therefore, according to his view, a need for supply orientated measures to promote sufficient investment in good quality housing. In this context he makes a case for a range of supply side policy instruments, including regulations, to promote improvements in the quality of the housing stock.

While neither author favours large scale provision of state owned housing, Oxley does see a case for a limited supply of social housing provided by a variety of landlords. Although not wishing to see the demise of housing associations, King does want them to return to their mutual and charitable roots, and to seek donations and establish trusts to help their work. He believes their role should, within this framework, be localised. The management and control of associations should be within the local community. In this context, with strong partnerships with local authorities, the Housing Corporation would cease to have financing and regulatory roles and thus become redundant. Oxley sees the role of existing housing organisations as being moderated by competition from a variety of suppliers, with various forms of ownership, and governed by compliance with specified social purposes.

6.5 Relevance

In the UK we currently face the superficial incompatibility of empty social dwellings, which no one wishes to inhabit, and a continuing case, put by organisations such as Shelter, for more social housing development. The resolution of these issues is related to reconnecting the implications of housing needs, individual preferences and housing demand which have featured at several points in our debate.

We hope that our debate will encourage housing policy makers and practitioners to rise above the mundane nature of much of the discussion about housing issues and to shift their thinking from parochialism to fundamental questioning regarding the purpose of public policy towards housing. We hope that the limits of individual decision making, and of governments' powers and responsibilities, will be considered with respect to what should be the respective roles of all the parties to the housing provision process. The questioning of purpose should be accompanied by a questioning of the *means* to achieve ends. The appropriate thought processes might be provoked by considering the extent to which there is agreement or disagreement with the views on individual competence and social welfare which have been expressed in this debate.

The challenge should penetrate as far as a consideration of whether there is any case for something called a 'housing policy', which has distinctive aims that give it an identity as a separate entity. We have at different points in our debate questioned the very existence of housing policy and suggested, if there is to be a housing policy, markedly contrasting objectives for such a policy. Others will have other aims in mind. The important point is that the purpose of policy should be clearly articulated and should govern subsequent action.

Just as the purpose of housing policy has to be reconsidered, so does the purpose of social housing. We have both argued that the provision of a distinctive tenure form is not essential to our aims. Neither of us has, however, gone as far as to suggest the abolition of council housing or of housing associations. We have instead suggested changes in the way social housing organisations operate and have questioned whether other forms of housing might provide housing which is at least as capable of meeting perceived objectives.

The way that social housing organisations operate, the ethos of housing providers, and the expectations which government has of these organisations are changing markedly. The extent to which these organisations are agents of government policy or more independent bodies responding to needs and demands is in question. If they are to be more market orientated, and more responsive to individual preferences, can they also fulfil a redistributive function and should they perform such a function? The allocative processes which associations use, and the function of rents as indicators of preferences and as a means to guide allocation, have been debated here. It is possible, according to one perspective, for both local authorities and housing associations to be more responsive to individual preferences and meet social objectives related to providing decent housing for those unable to compete fully in the open market. The way that social housing providers are to respond to the interests of tenants, local communities and government should be clarified in relation to a reappraisal of what the functions and motivations of the organisations should be.

Contrasting views have been expressed here regarding the relationship of housing organisations to the social exclusion agenda. Social landlords can be viewed as contributing to both problems and solutions. Whether the legitimate remit of housing providers extends as far as the wide involvement with the debated causes of poverty and social exclusion has been questioned. As registered social landlords take on wider roles, the issue of how to regulate diversity has arisen. This can only be properly addressed by questioning the relationship of social housing both to tenants and to the broad institutional arrangements within which they operate. We have argued for positions which require a critical examination of the framework that governs the activities of these organisations.

Both of our analyses raise the question of whether social landlords are trying to do too much. Is everything they are trying to do legitimately part of their territory and do they have the personnel with the necessary skills to do all that is expected of them? We have variously identified problems of poverty, personal trauma, and inabilities to cope with social systems as reasons for individuals lacking access to adequate housing. Which of the problems faced by homeless people, and those who are poorly housed, are best identified as housing problems and which should, more usefully, be viewed as issues which require assistance that is not essentially housing in nature should be considered in relation to the functions of both housing policy and social housing providers.

As government struggles with the reform of housing benefit there are some detailed suggestions by King on what changes should be made and his exposition has brought forth the proposition that ultimately housing benefit be abolished and replaced by a notional element to cover housing costs within income support payments. However, Oxley has warned against expecting too much from such demand side assistance.

Faced with projections of several million new households, the British government has reconsidered the issues of where new dwellings should be constructed. Arguments for urban regeneration and more urban living have been advanced. There are social objectives related to environmental, transportation and quality of life arguments that have entered the discussion that favour an urban renaissance. But here, very clearly, the relationships between the choices and preferences of households will have to be compatible with the visions of planners and politicians if the renewal of cities is to be successfully achieved.

With new constitutional arrangements for Scotland, Wales and Ireland and regional assemblies in England we now face in the UK a situation where many new tiers of government, as well as Westminster and local authorities, will have a voice in the construction of housing policies and a hand in their implementation. The European Union, whilst having no direct competence in housing matters, is concerned with very many related issues such as planning, building regulations, employment and social exclusion. With this complexity of political decisions affecting housing provision it is important that the role of competent individuals and socially responsible governments is appraised to redefine the boundaries of those decisions which should and can be made by the participants in the housing decision-making process.

Notes

1 Housing: Who Decides?

1 Some might argue, e.g. Letwin (1992) that there was no contradiction within the Thatcherite policy of individual choice and the strong state, in that, the former could only be achieved through the latter. We would suggest here that this is to assume that responsibility and choice are the same thing. One can be (made) responsible without having an choices. Likewise, one can question, at least in the short term, the effectiveness of the coercion explicit within the Blair government's New Deal for the young unemployed.

2 See Gamble *et al.* (1999) for a comprehensive discussion of the continued influence of Marxism in the social sciences.

3 See Barry (1986) and Ryan (1993) for a full discussion of the distinctions between liberals and libertarians.

4 Indeed in the USA the designation of liberal is usually reserved to those on the left who in Britain would be referred to as social democrats or even socialists. See Boaz (1997) and Hayek (1960) who consider the use of the term in the USA.

2 Individuals and Competence

1 I discuss this issue in much greater detail in King (1998a). See also Chapter 3 of *Housing, Individuals and the State* (1998b).

2 The distinction between justification – why we need to do what we are doing – and explanation – how we came to be doing it – is an important one. I am not claiming these principles explain state provision, but merely that they are used to justify the continuation of that provision.

3 There is also the issue of whether households are capable of determining what is in their best interests. I discuss this in section 2.7.

4 See King (1998b) for a fuller discussion on these issues.

5 I leave aside the issue of whether one would ever want to eradicate all unintended consequences. Both Hayek's and Popper's social theories see unintended consequences as an explanation for social change. They can thus be said to be necessary.

6 I imply no sinister intent here. I am not proposing entryism, but merely suggesting that libertarians engage in current debates and within current institutional arrangements rather than waiting in pure and splendid isolation for 'the big push' or for the inevitable development of a revolutionary consciousness.

7 I am aware that Boelhouwer and van Heijden describe a further stage in the development of policy which sees a return to a concern over shortages of housing. However, in Britain this has not been manifested in policy, merely

in academic and professional commentary. I would therefore see no reason to qualify my argument.

8 I discuss this issue more fully, offering a detailed critique of arguments for the supply side in *Housing, Individuals and the State.*

9 See Chapter 8 of *Housing, Individuals and the State.*

10 See Chapters 2 and 5 of *Housing, Individuals and the State* for a more detailed discussion of the effect of exogenous factors on housing markets and policies.

11 See Chapter 5 of *Housing, Individuals and the State* where I argue that personal subsidies based on entitlements are less amenable to central control because government finds it harder to control the numbers eligible for benefit.

12 I am aware that the issue of tenure neutrality goes wider than just the benefit system. Nonetheless the neutralisation of benefits is a key requirement for a more rational housing system. For a wider discussion of tenure neutrality see Chapter 6 of *Housing, Individuals and the State.*

13 Not to do so would, of course, create perverse incentive effects by placing the notional allowance at too high a level and thus allow claimants to afford dwellings out of the reach of working households on low incomes. See Chapter 22 of Hayek (1960) for a discussion on this point.

14 See, for instance, Barry (1975) when he castigates Nozick (1974) for apparently 'proposing to starve or humiliate ten per cent or so of (our) fellow citizens' (p. 331). Nozick, of course, proposes no such thing, but merely concerns himself with the implications of the basic Kantian assumption that individuals are ends and not means because of the rights they are imbued with as humans. I find all of Nozick's work full of an optimism about human capability and potential missing in much of the political philosophy of the left.

4 Limiting the Role of Government

1 Although neither of us would claim to be typical or representative of our respective disciplines.

2 My aim, of course, is not to misrepresent my colleague's views. This summary though is not necessarily one which Oxley would agree with, nor would he concur with the relative importance I have given to the various parts of his argument. Fortunately he has a further opportunity to put me right!

3 Whether governments are likewise social constructs, and what effect this has for the relationship between markets and the state, is not discussed. One wonders whether this is because this is essentially a normative issue.

4 I also ought to state that Oxley offers no argument for suggesting I do represent this position.

5 The issue of how we arrive at this position *from where we are now* is another matter, and one which is disputed between us. I attempt to deal with this in section 4.6.

6 See Mises (1981) for a thoroughgoing methodological individualist critique of government planning.

7 There is no space here to fully debate the nature of the state and who it acts for, except to say that it is considerably more complex than Oxley's presumption of government as the agent of the state, which in turn acts on behalf of society.

8 This though is why the issue of what the state is so important. Oxley's assumption that society = state = government is shown to be particularly problematical here. I shall return to this in section 4.4 on social decision making.

9 I shall have more to say on the nature of knowledge and centralised decision making when I discuss externalities in section 4.4.

10 I discuss this issue of technical arguments as justifications for normative aims in some detail in Chapter 4 of *Housing, Individuals and the State* (King, 1998b).

11 I ignore here, as Oxley does, the very real difficulties in determining what constitutes a sufficient improvement or reduction (or indeed an improvement at all), as well as issues of who and how one measures such a shift (objectively; subjectively; collectively; individually; on a utilitarian or a Kantian/Rawlisan basis?). However, later in this section I do discuss whether externalities themselves are ever measurable.

12 Although it is not a matter of indifference, in that social norms of fairness are likely to voluntarily moderate behaviour (Elster, 1989).

13 I am aware that the situation is somewhat more complex than this, in that there are certain metastatements which determine the very acceptability of certain sets of discourse which may become, or seek to become, moral absolutes. In this sense 'thou shalt not kill' is one of these metastatements, whilst my arguments against redistribution are of the lesser form. Having said this, the very issue of whether there are moral absolutes or whether they are historical and culturally relative is a key debate in social and political theory (see Rorty, 1989 and the response by Geras, 1995; also Nussbaum, 1999).

14 As I do in *Housing, Individuals and the State*, Chapter 8.

15 One can ensure that the trains run on time, but not through the use of extermination and concentration camps.

16 I have chosen to call my position *conservative libertarianism* as a result. The ordering of the words is important here. My libertarianism is tempered by a philosophical conservatism which seeks to justify change as necessary rather than as an end in itself. What I am not espousing is a modified conservatism.

17 That is, except those of my own family, of course.

18 However, if social housing tenants are seen to be less competent it is incumbent on those who argue this to explain how it has come about – is social housing the symptom or the cure; were these individuals incompetent before or only after their tenancy commenced?

19 But if differential subsidies were to be offered, and made open to all landlords, this would merely encourage landlords to shift to a position where they could avail themselves of the most generous subsidy conditions and levels. Of course, if the subsidies were restricted to certain tenures or types of landlord this would not represent the neutrality which both Oxley and myself are calling for.

5 Emphasising the Need for Policies

1 For a summary of the key contributions see Cullis and Jones (1998), particularly Chapter 4 entitled 'Collective decision making: searching for the public interest' (pp. 71–91).
2 For a summary of the major criticisms see Ng (1992, pp. 182–5) and Cullis and Jones (1998, pp. 31–6).
3 Op. cit.

Bibliography

Anand, P. (1993): *Foundations of Rational Choice under Risk*, Oxford, Oxford University Press.

Armstrong, H. (1998): 'We Need Housing Which Goes on Working', *Housing Today*, Vol. 83, 14 May 1998, p. 13.

Barr, N. (1998): *The Economics of the Welfare State*, 3rd edn, Oxford, Oxford University Press.

Barry, B. (1975): 'Review of *Anarchy, State and Utopia*', *Political Theory*, vol. 3, no. 3., pp. 331–6.

Barry, N. (1986): *On Classical Liberalism and Libertarianism*, Basingstoke, Macmillan.

Barry, N. (1996): *Classical Liberalism in the Age of Post-Communism*, Cheltenham, Edward Elgar.

Bell, D. (1993): *Communitarianism and its Critics*, Oxford, Clarendon Press.

Bengtsson, B. (1995): 'Politics and Housing Markets: Four Normative Arguments', *Scandinavian Housing and Planning Research*, Vol. 12, pp. 123–40.

Berlin, I. (1969): *Four Essays on Liberty*, Oxford, Oxford University Press.

Bevan, M., Kemp, P. and Rhodes, D. (1995): *Private Landlords and Housing Benefit*, York, Centre for Housing Policy.

Blair, T. (1998): *The Third Way: New Politics for the New Century*, London, Fabian Society.

Boaz, D. (1997): *Libertarianism: a Primer*, New York, The Free Press.

Bobbio, N. (1996): *Left and Right*, Cambridge, Polity.

Boelhouwer, P. and van der Heijden, H. (1992): *Housing Systems in Europe, Part 1: a Comparative Study of Housing Policy*, Delft, Delft University Press.

Bourdreaux, D. (1994): 'The Coase Theorem', in Boettke, P. (ed.): *The Elgar Companion to Austrian Economics*, Cheltenham, Edward Elgar, pp. 179–86.

Bowles, R. (1984): 'Property in the Legal System', in Whynes, D. (ed.): *What is Political Economy?: Eight Perspectives*, Oxford, Basil Blackwell, pp. 187–208.

Bradshaw, J. and Millar, J. (1991): *Lone Parents in the UK*, London, HMSO.

Bramley, G., Bartlett, W. and Lambert, C. (1995): *Planning, the Market and Private Housebuilding*, London, UCL Press.

Brown, T. (ed.) (1999): *Stakeholder Housing: a Third Way*, London, Pluto.

Brown, T. and Passmore, J. (1998): *Housing and Anti-Poverty Strategies: a Good Practice Guide*, Coventry, Chartered Institute of Housing/Joseph Rowntree Foundation.

Burrows, P. (1979): *The Economic Theory of Pollution Control*, Oxford, Martin Robertson.

Coase, R. (1974): 'The Problem of Social Cost', in Staaf, R. and Tannian, F. (ed.): *Externalities: Dimesnions of Political Economy*, New York, Dunellen, pp. 119–62.

Coleman, A. (1985): *Utopia on Trial: Vision and Reality in Planned Housing*, London, Hilary Shipman.

Conway, D. (1995): *Classical Liberalism: the Unvanquished Ideal*, Basingstoke, Macmillan.

Conway, J. (1999): 'Health and Housing', in Brown, T., pp. 54–66.
Cullis, J. and Jones, P. (1998): *Public Finance and Public Choice*, 2nd edn, Oxford, Oxford University Press.
Daunton, M. (1987): *A Property Owning Democracy?*, London, Faber.
Demsetz, H. (1967): 'Towards a Theory of Property Rights', *American Economic Review*, Vol. 57, pp. 347–59.
Department of the Environment (1977): *Housing Policy: a Consultative Document*, Cmnd. 57, London, HMSO.
Department of the Environment, Transport and the Regions (1998): *A New Financial Framework for local Authority Housing: Resource Accounting in the Housing Revenue Account*, London, DETR.
Department of Social Security (1997): *Social Security Support for Housing Costs*, Welfare Reform Focus File 5, London, DSS.
Department of Social Security (1998): *New Ambitions for our Country: a New Contract for Welfare*, Cm 3805, London, The Stationery Office.
Doyal, L. and Gough, I. (1991): *A Theory of Human Need*, Basingstoke, Macmillan.
Elster, J. (1983): *Sour Grapes: Studies in the Subversion of Rationality*, Cambridge, Cambridge University Press.
Elster, J. (ed.) (1986): *Rational Choice*, Oxford, Blackwell.
Elster, J. (1989): *The Cement of Society: a Study of Social Order*, Cambridge, Cambridge University Press.
Elster, J. (1993): *Political Psychology*, Cambridge, Cambridge University Press.
Etzioni, A. (1993): *The Spirit of Community: Rights, Responsibilities and the Communitarian Agenda*, London, Fontana.
Etzioni, A. (1997): *The New Golden Rule: Community and Morality in a Democratic Society*, London, Profile Books.
Field, F. (1996): *Stakeholder Welfare*, London, Institute of Economic Affairs.
Friedman, D. (1989): *The Machinery of Freedom: Guide to a Radical Capitalism*, 2nd edn, La Salle, Ill, Open Court.
Friedman, D. (1996): *Hidden Order: the Economics of Everyday Life*, New York, HarperBusiness.
Gamble, A. (1988): *The Free Economy and the Strong State: the Politics of Thatcherism*, Basingstoke, Macmillan.
Gamble, A., Marsh, D. and Tant, T. (ed.) (1999): *Marxism and Social Science*, Basingstoke, Macmillan.
Geras, N. (1995): *Solidarity in the Conversation of Humankind: the Ungroundable Liberalism of Richard Rorty*, London, Verso.
Giddens, A. (1998): *The Third Way: the Renewal of Social Democracy*, Cambridge, Polity.
Glennerster, H. and Hills, J. (eds) (1998): *The State of Welfare: the Economics of Social Spending*, Oxford, Oxford University Press.
Graham, G. (1988): *Contemporary Social Philosophy*, Oxford, Blackwell.
Gray, J. (1995a): *Isaiah Berlin*, London, Fontana.
Gray, J. (1995b): *Enlightenment's Wake: Politics and Culture at the Close of the Modern Age*, London, Routledge.
Gray, J. (1997): *Endgames: Questions in Late Modern Political Thought*, Cambridge, Polity.

Green, D. (1996): *Community Without Politics: a Market Approach to Welfare Reform*, London, Institute of Economic Affairs.
Griffin, J. (1986): *Well-Being: Its Meaning, Measurement and Moral Importance*, Oxford, Clarendon.
Haffner, M. and Oxley, M. (1999): 'Housing Subsidies: Definitions and Comparisons', *Housing Studies*, Vol. 14, no. 2, pp. 145–62.
Hargreaves-Heap, S. and Hollis, M. (1984): 'Bread and Circumstances: The Need for Political Economy', in Whynes, D. (ed.): *What is Political Economy: Eight Perspectives*, Oxford, Blackwell, pp. 7–30.
Harrison, A. (1977): *Economics and Land Use Planning*, London, Croom Helm.
Hayek, F. (1948): *Individualism and the Economic Order*, Chicago, Chicago University Press.
Hayek, F. (1960): *The Constitution of Liberty*, London, Routledge.
Hayek, F. (1967): *Studies in Philosophy, Politics and Economics*, London, Routledge.
Hayek, F. (1978): *New Studies in Philosophy, Politics, Economics and the History of Ideas*, London, Routledge.
Hayek, F. (1982): *Law, Legislation and Liberty*, London, Routledge.
Hayek, F. (1988): *The Fatal Conceit: the Errors of Socialism*, London, Routledge.
Hills, J. (1991): *Unravelling Housing Finance: Subsidies, Benefits and Taxation*, Oxford, Clarendon.
Hills, J. (1995): *Joseph Rowntree Foundation Inquiry into Income and Wealth*, Vol. 2, York, Joseph Rowntree Foundation.
Hills, J. (1997): *The Future of Welfare: a Guide to the Debate*, rev. edn, York, Joseph Rowntree Foundation.
Howenstine, E. (1986): *Housing Vouchers: a Comparative International Analysis*, New Brunswick, NJ, Center for Urban Policy Research.
Infantino, L. (1998): *Individualism in Modern Thought: From Adam Smith to Hayek*, London, Routledge.
Jenkins, S. (1995): *Accountable to None: the Tory Nationalisation of Britain*, London, Hamish Hamilton.
Joseph Rowntree Foundation (1995): *Inquiry into Income and Wealth*, Vol. 1, York, Joseph Rowntree Foundation.
Kemeny, J. (1992): *Housing and Social Theory*, London, Routledge.
Kemp, P. (1997): *A Comparative Study of Housing Allowances*, London, The Stationery Office.
Kemp, P. (1998): *Housing Benefit: Time for Reform*, York, Joseph Rowntree Foundation.
Kennett, P. (1998): 'Differentiated Citizenship and Household Experience', in Marsh, A. and Mullins, D. (eds), pp. 30–56.
King, P. (1996): *The Limits of Housing Policy: a Philosophical Investigation*, London, Middlesex University Press.
King, P. (1998a): 'Needs and Choice in Housing: an Individualist Approach', *Scandinavian Housing and Planning Research*, Vol. 15, pp. 5–17.
King, P. (1998b): *Housing, Individuals and the State: the Morality of Government Intervention*, London, Routledge.
Konukiewitz, M. (1985): 'Taming the Housing Market', in Lane, J.-E. (ed.), pp. 181–98.
Kuellberg, J. (1997): 'From Waiting Lists to Adverts: the Allocation of Social Rented Dwellings in the Netherlands', *Housing Studies*, Vol. 12, no. 3, pp. 181–98.

Lane, J.-E. (ed.) (1985): *State and Market: the Politics of the Public and Private*, London, Sage.

Leicestershire Health Authority (1999): *Annual Report of the Director of Public Health*, Leicester, Leicestershire Health Authority.

Letwin, W. (1983a): 'The Case Against Equality', in Letwin, W. (ed.), pp. 1–70.

Letwin, W. (ed.) (1983b): *Against Equality: Readings on Economic and Social Policy*, London, Macmillan.

Letwin, S. (1992): *The Anatomy of Thatcherism*, London, Harper Collins.

Levinas, E. (1969): *Totality and Infinity*, Pittsburgh, Duquesne University Press.

Levine, D. (1995): *Wealth and Freedom: an Introduction to Political Economy*, Cambridge, Cambridge University Press.

Lukes, S. (1973): *Individualism*, Oxford, Blackwell.

Macfarlane, A. (1978): *The Origins of English Individualism: the Family, Property and Social Transition*, Oxford, Blackwell.

Maclennan, D. and More, A. (1997): 'The Future of Social Housing: Key Economic Questions', *Housing Studies*, Vol. 12, no. 4, pp. 531–47.

Malpass, P. (1999): 'Housing Policy: Does it have a Future?', *Policy and Politics*, Vol. 27, no. 2, pp. 217–28.

Marsh, A. and Mullins, D. (ed.) (1998): *Housing and Public Policy: Citizenship, Choice and Control*, Buckingham, Open University Press.

Miller, D. (1976): *Social Justice*, Oxford, Oxford University Press.

Mises, L. (1981): *Socialism: an Economic and Sociological Analysis*, Indianapolis, Liberty Fund.

Mises, L. (1996): *Human Action: a Treatise on Economics*, 4th rev'd edn, San Francisco, Fox and Wilkes.

Mueller, D. (1989): *Public Choice II*, Cambridge, Cambridge University Press.

Murray, C. (1984): *Losing Ground: American Social Policy, 1950–1980*, New York, Basic Books.

Murray, C. (1996): *Charles Murray and the Underclass: the Developing Debate*, London, Institute of Economic Affairs.

Narveson, J. (1988): *The Libertarian Idea*, Philadelphia, Temple University Press.

Newman, O. (1973): *Defensible Space*, London, Architectural Press.

Ng, K.-W. (1992): *Welfare Economics: Introduction and Development of Basic Concepts*, London, Macmillan.

Nozick, R. (1974): *Anarchy, State and Utopia*, Oxford, Blackwell.

Nussbaum, M. (1999): *Sex and Social Justice*, Oxford, Oxford University Press.

Oxley, M. (1975): 'Economic Theory and Urban Planning', *Environment and Planning A*, Vol. 7, no. 5, pp. 497–508.

Oxley, M. (1987): 'Housing Allowances in Western Europe', in van Vliet, W. (ed.), pp. 165–78.

Oxley, M. (1995): 'Private and Social Rented Housing in Europe: Distinctions, Comparisons and Resource Allocation, *Scandinavian Housing and Planning Research*, Vol. 12, pp. 59–72.

Oxley, M. (1998a): 'Demand-Side Subsidies', in van Vliet (ed.), pp. 107–8.

Oxley, M. (1998b): 'Supply-Side Subsidies', in van Vliet (ed.), pp. 569–70.

Oxley, M. (1999a): 'Institutional Structure of Social Housing Finance in the UK: Recent Developments', *Urban Studies*, Vol. 36, no. 4, pp. 673–82.

Oxley, M. (1999b): 'Housing and Europe', in Brown, T. (ed.), pp. 94–105.

Oxley, M. and Smith, J. (1996): *Housing Policy and Rented Housing in Europe*, London, Spons.

Page, D. (1993): *Building for Communities*, York, Joseph Rowntree Foundation.
Page, D. (1994): *Developing Communities*, York, Joseph Rowntree Foundation.
Paraja Eastway, M. and san Martin, I. (1999): 'General Trends in Financing Social Housing in Spain', *Urban Studies*, Vol. 36, no. 4, pp. 699–714.
Percy-Smith, J. (ed.) (1996): *Needs Assessment in Public Policy*, Buckingham, Open University Press.
Pigou, A. (1932): *The Economics of Welfare*, 4th edn, London, Macmillan.
Plant, R. (1991): *Modern Political Thought*, Oxford, Blackwell.
Popper, K. (1989): *Conjectures and Refutations: the Growth of Scientific Knowledge*, 5th rev. edn, London, Routledge.
Power, A. (1987): *Property Before People: the Management of Twentieth Century Council Housing*, Hemel Hempstead, Allen and Unwin.
Power, A. (1993): *From Hovels to Highrise: State Housing in Europe Since 1850*, London, Routledge.
Power, A. and Tunstall, R. (1997): *Dangerous Disorder: Riots and Violent Disturbances in 13 Areas in Britain in 1991–92*, York, Joseph Rowntree Foundation.
Power, S. and Whitty, G. (1995): *No Place to Learn*, London, Shelter.
Priemus, H. and Dieleman, F. (1999): 'Social Housing Finance in the European Union: Developments and Prospects', *Urban Studies*, Vol. 36, no. 4, pp. 623–31.
Rawls, J. (1971): *A Theory of Justice*, Oxford, Oxford University Press.
Ridley, M. (1996): *The Origins of Virtue*, London, Viking.
Robinson, R. (1979): *Housing Economics and Public Policy*, London, Macmillan.
Rorty, R. (1989): *Contingency, Irony and Solidarity*, Cambridge, Cambridge University Press.
Rothbard, M. (1970): *Man, Economy and State*, Los Angeles, Nash.
Rothbard, M. (1978): *For a New Liberty: the Libertarian Manifesto*, rev. edn, New York, Collier.
Rothstein, B. (1998): *Just Institutions Matter: the Moral and Political Logic of the Universal Welfare State*, Cambridge, Cambridge University Press.
Ryan, A. (1993): 'Liberalism', in Goodin, R. and Pettit, P. (eds): *A Companion to Contemporary Political Philosophy*, Oxford, Blackwell, pp. 291–312.
Sacks, J. (1997): *The Politics of Hope*, London, Jonathan Cape.
Samuelson, P. (1954): 'The Pure Theory of Public Expenditure', *Review of Economics and Statistics*, Vol. 36, pp. 387–9.
Saunders, P. (1990): *A Nation of Home Owners*, London, Unwin Hyman.
Schmidtz, D. (1991): *The Limits of Government: an Essay on the Public Goods Argument*, Boulder, Westview Press.
Selbourne, D. (1994): *The Principle of Duty: an Essay on the Foundations of the Civic Order*, London, Sinclair-Stevenson.
Sen, A. (1992): *Inequality Re-examined*, Oxford, Oxford University Press.
Shand, A. (1990): *Free Market Morality: the Political Economy of the Austrian School*, London, Routledge.
Smith, A. (1976): *An Inquiry into the Nature and Causes of the Wealth of Nations*, 2 vols, Indianapolis, Liberty Fund.
Sparkes, A. (1991): *Talking Philosophy: a Wordbook*, London, Routledge.
Stephens, M. (1999): 'The Fiscal Role of the European Union: the Case of Housing and the European Structural Funds', *Urban Studies*, Vol. 36, no. 4, pp. 715–35.
Turner, J. (1976): *Housing by People: Towards Autonomy in Building Environments*, London, Marion Boyars.

van Parijs, P. (1995): *Real Freedom for All: What (if Anything) Can Justify Capitalism?*, Oxford, Oxford University Press.

van Vliet, W. (ed.) (1987): *Housing Markets and Policies under Fiscal Austerity*, Westport, Greenwood.

van Vliet, W. (ed.) (1998): *Encyclopedia of Housing*, Thousand Oaks, Ca, Sage.

Ward, A. (1983): 'The Idea of Equality Reconsidered', in Letwin, W. (ed.), pp. 199–206.

Whelan, R. (1998): *Octavia Hill and the Social Housing Debate*, London, Institute of Economic Affairs.

Whitehead, C. *et al.* (1995): *Rents and Risks: Investing in Housing Associations*, York, Joseph Rowntree Foundation.

Wilcox, S. (1997): *Housing Finance Review 1997/98*, York, Joseph Rowntree Foundation.

Williams, B. (1962): 'The Idea of Equality', in Laslett, P. and Runciman, W. (eds): *Philosophy, Politics and Society*, Oxford, Oxford University Press.

Williams, P. (ed.) (1997): *Directions in Housing Policy: Towards Sustainable Housing Policies for the UK*, London, Paul Chapman Publishing.

Winch, D. (1971): *Analytical Welfare Economics*, Harmondsworth, Penguin.

Wolf, Jr, C. (1987): 'Market and Non-Market Failures: Comparison and Assessment', *Journal of Public Policy*, Vol. 7, no. 1, pp. 43–70.

Index